THE UNFOLDING STORY OF A
Dreamer

Barry Borneman

Published by Barry Borneman
Contact details: bornemanb53@gmail.com

First published August 2025
Second reprint September 2025
Third reprint December 2025

Copyright © 2025 by Barry Borneman

All rights reserved. No part of this book may be reproduced or transmitted by any person or entity in any form or by any means, electronic or mechanical, including photocopying, recording, scanning or by or on any information storage and retrieval system or otherwise, without the express prior written permission of Barry Borneman, except for brief quotations for critique/review as permitted by fair use / fair dealing and similar copyright legislation.

The author and publisher have taken care in the preparation of this book, but make no expressed or implied warranty of any kind and assume no responsibility for errors or omissions. No liability is assumed for incidental or consequential damages in connection with or arising out of the use of information contained herein.

Cover design by Communique Graphics
Internal design and typesetting by Communique Graphics
Printed and bound by IngramSpark

 A catalogue record for this book is available from the National Library of Australia

ISBN, print ed. 978-1-7642006-0-8

Barry and I have been friends for over 50 years. It's been one of only a handful of relationships I have that deepens and never changes over time or distance. His journey always challenged and excited me. This book is a true reflection of a real bloke in love with Jesus and following the wind of the Spirit. This story is raw and real, transparent and spiritual in the true sense of the word. It's Barry's life, 'a letter known and read by many'. Enjoy!

Jeff Hulls, friend and pastor

What word can I use to commend Barry Borneman's book? Engaging? Readable? Encouraging? Informative? Relevant? Captivating? Entertaining? Genial? Inspiring? The choice is impossible. They all apply. And perhaps I could add one more. It is authentic. I have had the privilege of knowing Barry and Marg for many years and I can vouch for the integrity of this story. Their deeds match their words. Theirs is a tale worth telling and most certainly worth reading. Of the many aspects on which I could comment further, the ongoing record of the work of the Holy Spirit in the lives of these faithful followers of Christ is convincing and convicting. It is powerful without being presumptuous, natural and yet supranatural. Don't be surprised if, once you have picked up this book, you don't want to put it down.

Dr Barry Chant, author and teacher,
Founding President of Tabor College

In all my years of knowing Barry, I observed that *status quo* was not really in his vocabulary. Barry always has an idea or more! These *dreams* were no idle *daydreams* but they had a spiritual quality about them. This delightful book gives a glimpse of why this was so. Barry talks, walks and dreams from proximity to God. These accounts in his biopic will encourage the reader to similarly trust God when He speaks to us through His Word and yes, also through dreams. It will be a life worth living.

Simon Wan, Singapore,
Former Director of Wycliffe Alliance Asia-Pacific

Barry's memoir takes us on an unpredictable ride. Just when the reader is settled in one place, the Lord whisks Barry and Marg off to another location, with different roles and experiences. The reader feels the tension between the *Man of the Soil* (from Barry's farming upbringing) and the *Dreamer* who hears the whispers of the Holy Spirit propelling him into new directions in time, space and vocation with remarkable consequences for communities and people around him. Read how the Holy Spirit can expand the kingdom through a life devoted to hearing and acting on His promptings. An inspiring and challenging ride for us all.

Wendy Bytheway, author and teacher

The Unfolding Story of a Dreamer is a compelling read. Barry Borneman is a wonderfully gifted story teller. He shares so honestly and vulnerably the ways in which Jesus has led him since coming to faith in Christ in his teens. Barry is down-to-earth in the way he writes and has a great sense of humour. He has no airs and graces. If you're weary in well-doing *The Unfolding Story of a Dreamer* will encourage you to keep following the Lord with the whole of your life. I highly recommend it.

Paul Arnott, author, journalist
and former executive director of CMA's Q4

In *The Unfolding Story of a Dreamer*, we witness what happens when the Giver of Dreams meets a man caught between heaven's call and earth's demands. This is a raw, Spirit-drenched journey of surrender, identity, and grace – not a map, but a companion for any soul bold enough to dream with God. Story after story of how God disrupts and leads a man, his wife, family and an organisation into the spaces between heaven and earth. You will read with laughter and tears and come away inspired to love Jesus and others to the ends of the earth.

Kim Hood, Intercultural Training Australia

The Unfolding Story of a Dreamer functions on two levels. On one level it describes his upbringing, how he became a follower of Christ and subsequent work supporting Bible translation through literacy, training, leadership positions to eventually being invited to be the Director of Wycliffe Australia. On the other level, the most significant for me, he shares how God meets him in intimate ways, and how the Holy Spirit providentially ordered certain events in his life so as to bring healing, guidance and blessing to others. It is my prayer that through the reading of this book God will bless others as he has done me.

Dr Colin G Kruse, Emeritus Scholar, Melbourne School of Theology

I've known Barry Borneman as a friend for over two decades. He is beautifully unique, brilliant yet down-to-earth. His career was spent in a conservative evangelical context, and yet few are more led by the Holy Spirit. He breaks every mould and convention, but does so without attitude; a general who retains a boyish enthusiasm. Barry won't fit into any box, because neither will God. And as such, he – in his book *Dreamer* – reveals his journey into the heart of God, and in doing so, reveals the heart of God himself, the *giver of dreams*. This book will be good for your soul. But a user warning: It could change your life.

David Stephenson, Director of YWAM, Newcastle

Barry listens to God, and the experiences that come from that inner dialogue are inspiring, encouraging and humbling. May you find a way to listen more intently to God's direction as a result of reading this book.

Jason Potter, Author, Educator and National Director of OAC

CONTENTS

Chapter   Page

	Prologue	ix
	Acknowledgements	xi
1	The Wind At My Back	1
2	Salvation Comes	7
3	Joe And The Dreamer	9
4	Meeting The Giver Of Dreams	13
5	God, Sex And Sport	19
6	Nothing Ventured, Nothing Gained	25
7	Unhinged And Free	33
8	Experiencing Heaven	37
9	Is She 'The One'?	41
10	The Soil Beckons	47
11	An Unexpected Road	53
12	An Unlikely Pair	57
13	Our First Home	65
14	Hospitality Expands The Heart	73
15	A Day Of Reckoning	79
16	Hidden Dreams Of A Hitman	87
17	Entrenched In The Soil	97
18	Dreaming Of Cricket	101
19	Unto Us A Child Is Born	105
20	An Oasis	107
21	Elimination	111
22	Illumination	117
23	No Salary!	121
24	New Soil	127
25	A Red Account And The Classroom	131
26	New Life And New Direction	137
27	Further Up And Further In	143

CONTENTS

28	Back To The Books	151
29	Coming In From The Cold	155
30	Is The Devil Real?	161
31	Stranded Again	167
32	Embracing Limitations	171
33	The Parable Of The Good Samaritan	177
34	Labelled	185
35	Bottom Camp	189
36	'This Sit-Down Money Is Going To Kill Us!'	195
37	White Man Always Pushing	197
38	Morrow's Farm – More Than A Place To Stay	203
39	The Legacy Of Pastor Bill And Madge Rosas	209
40	One Country, Two Worlds	215
41	Teach Me To Read	219
42	Come Holy Spirit	223
43	The Great Australian Dream	227
44	Compelled	233
45	Leave Me Alone God	237
46	Betrayal	241
47	Thoughts Fulfilled	251
48	Judgement In The Public Square	255
49	There Is No Precedent	261
50	Twelve Remarkable Days	269
51	I Don't Need God!	277
52	The Just Shall Live By Faith	281
53	Being Yourself	285
54	The Bond Of Friendship	291
55	Living With Imagination	295
56	Nominations Closing	303
57	Dream On	309
58	Giving What I Have In Jesus' Name	313

PROLOGUE

In 2009 I was driving along the New England Highway in the Darling Downs region of South-East Queensland. As was my custom I played no music, listened to no podcast, but allowed my own thoughts to fill the space. I found myself contemplating the down-to-earth writings of Toowoomba born novelist Steele Rudd (1868-1935). His series of stories of a pioneer family were published in 1899 as *On Our Selection*. Later it was depicted in a radio series called *Dad and Dave from Snake Gully*. From an early age, my ear was bent towards the family wireless eagerly anticipating the daily episode of *Dad and Dave*. I was attracted to the down-to-earth humour and intrigue it generated from everyday rural life.

On impulse, I pulled the car into a roadside stop, took out my computer, placed it on a bench table, sat down, looked down at the keys and began to write. The first words tumbled out: *The Wind at My Back*. That was to be the title. I was both the subject and the projected audience. The story itself would end at a significant event in my life that occurred in May 2007. How I would describe getting there I did not yet know.

What I did know was that I meandered through life like the great inland rivers of Australia. There was a starting point and an ending point but everything in between was rarely predictable or straight forward. What I did recognise was that from time to time I found the wind at my back propelling me in a particular direction. It was this wind that defined me and determined my future.

As I wrote in the following months and then years, I struggled with the idea of my private writing becoming public property. Some people have described me as a man of action, a leader, pursuing a particular vision. But in reality I don't see myself like that. I have lived my life mostly in my head, in dialogue with myself and my God. This is the place I prefer to dwell. Away from people, away from the action, and alone with my own thoughts and dreams. I don't think I am unique in this. We all live to some degree with a hidden dialogue in our minds. This is the hidden part of me that in writing, I was choosing to make public.

The lens through which I would describe my unfolding journey became clear to me as I wrote my father's demand to 'Get your head out of the clouds and stop bloody dreaming'. My story became about the Dreamer and his tension with the external and internal man of the soil. So, *The Wind at My Back* became *The Unfolding Story of a Dreamer*.

The other lens focuses the spotlight on Jesus and his disruptive influence on my life. When the Spirit came I was compelled towards an intimate relationship with *The Giver of Dreams*. He challenged who I thought I was, and who I thought I should be. This is a personal story of how I navigate that challenge. It is not a prescription, or a theological treatise, but simply a story that involves myself and my God in the nitty gritty of everyday life and everyday decisions.

Barry Borneman
July 2025

ACKNOWLEDGEMENTS

My first word of appreciation goes to Margaret Clarke, my wife of almost 50 years. Marg and I are quite different except in one regard. We both have met Jesus and he has permission to disrupt our lives. It means that we are both capable of embracing the road less travelled. Marg also edited the text and reminded me of facts when, in telling a story I took more liberty than I should have

Thanks also to my former colleague and friend Rod Niejalke with whom I first shared my desire to write. Rod encouraged me to embrace my country roots for storytelling. 'Show, don't tell what happened,' he said. This forced me to place myself in situations as if they were happening all over again.

The text would not flow as fluently if it was not for the editing undertaken by Wendy Bytheway. She became an advocate for the reader, suggesting additional content for the curious reader. The addition of *Marg recalls* was her suggestion. Thanks Wendy.

Thanks also to my small men's group that has been intentional in talking about faith and following Jesus. For me, it was an accidental group I joined in 2023. The group happened to have new friends who had experience as authors and publishers. So I asked them to be my accountability group to remove the final stumbling blocks to getting the job done and overcoming my continuing insecurity about making public what up until now has been my private sojourn. Thanks for your encouragement.

Finally, thanks to Ivan Smith from Communique Graphics for doing the layout, painting the book cover and also enlivening my stories with his cartoons and humour.

1

The Wind At My Back

Location: Katherine
Date: Saturday 5 May 2007
Event: Release of the first full Bible in an Australian Indigenous language

All day long four-wheel-drives, buses and trucks covered in red dust wound their way down the gravel track into Morrow's Farm, ten kilometres west of the township of Katherine in the Northern Territory of Australia. Some had travelled for two days from remote communities more than a thousand kilometres away and others from Aboriginal communities[1] nearby.

A special occasion drew them, but no registrations were asked for and no directions given. Each vehicle found its home by the same tree, or the same portion of the river bank, or next to the same machinery shed as they had year after year for the annual Katherine Christian Convention which was always held on the first weekend in May. Swags were laid out, tents set up and wood gathered. Camp fires and the smell of freshly cooked damper soon spread out along the banks of the Katherine River and across the paddock behind the Morrow's farm house. The chatter of those gathered around the camps merged with the sounds of nature. It was heaven on earth.

---

1. I use the term 'Aboriginal' here because this is the term my Aboriginal friends in northern Australia used. The term 'Indigenous' was rarely heard. 'First Nations' was introduced more recently but at the time of writing still had little traction in remote communities. I will use all three at different times without prejudice.

Later in the day cleaner cars and buses more acquainted with bitumen roads came down the same gravel track and parked in an orderly fashion next to each other. These were mainly white people from Darwin, the Northern Territory's capital three and a half hours to the north, who got out of their vehicles, stretched their stiff bodies, and immediately broke into conversation with those around them.

Some drifted off towards the campfires to exchange greetings, some stopping for a longer stay around the fire. The Anglican Archbishop of Melbourne was one of these. As the former Bishop of the Northern Territory, Philip Freier was among friends. He was not the only dignitary who knew of the occasion. Queen Elizabeth II was on her throne in England, and she penned a letter of congratulations, courtesy of the Governor-General of Australia. The Prime Minister through the NT Chief Minister's representative was present. An ABC TV news team arrived to capture the moment. Another videographer and friend from Wycliffe Bible Translators was rustling up interviews.

The cause of the celebration was a quarter of a century in the making and involved countless Kriol speakers and numerous supporting organisations. It was a weekend of celebrating the dedication of the Kriol Holi Baibul. What was historic about this occasion was that the Kriol Bible was the first full Bible to be translated and published into an Australian Aboriginal language. It was not only important to Kriol speakers and to the Christian church. It was a significant event in the history of interactions between the first Australians and the nation birthed out of the First Fleet's arrival at Sydney Cove in 1788.

I sat alone lost in my thoughts as I took in the ambience of white and black easily mingling together and at peace with one another. I was surprised that the Kriol translators had asked me to give the first message from the Kriol Bible after it was dedicated. There were people more deserving of that honour than me. I had protested, but to no avail.

I should not have been surprised if for a moment I stopped and viewed the world from the perspective of the translation team. We were friends. We had been colleagues in the Kriol translation team for fifteen years. My wife's and my role in literacy, training and encouraging the use of the translated Kriol Scriptures meant our connections ran deep.

All these thoughts had been overridden by the fact that eight years earlier we left the Northern Territory for Brisbane to support Bible translation work in the Pacific. My mind had been clouded by a western mindset that talked about moving on and leaving the past behind. Aboriginal colleagues viewed the world differently. Once relationships are formed there is no moving on or leaving behind. You are always connected through your shared lives and stories no matter where you are in the world and no matter how much time has passed. The translation team had asked me because in their minds I had never left. We were forever connected. I should not have been surprised.

My eyes began to tear up in gratitude. My mind saw myself again as a free-spirited, bare-footed, unchurched teenager rounding up the cows from the back paddock for milking, totally oblivious to what the future might bring. The teenager had no grid that could imagine this occasion or the sense of honour that I felt. There was nothing straightforward about my journey in life. It was more often propelled in different directions by an unseen wind at my back than following a carefully planned course of action. Yet it brought me here to an occasion that I could have only dreamed about.

I hardly noticed Gumbuli ambling towards me. He wanted my attention. I stood up and greeted him. The Rev Michael Gumbuli Wurramara was the first fully ordained Aboriginal Anglican Minister in the Northern Territory. When Gumbuli spoke, you listened. He was the minister at Ngukurr where the translation work had begun. He himself had an excellent command of English but he knew that Kriol was the language spoken at home and around the campfire. It was the language of the people. He was the one who insisted that the full Bible be translated for his people. He was confident the Aboriginal translators could finish the work with us whitefellas supporting them. And that is just what happened.

The broad smile on his face disarmed any concern that I might have had. His eyes twinkled with a mischievousness that comes from those who are secure in themselves. Gumbuli got straight to the point. In an authoritative but gentle voice he spoke as a father would to his son, or an elder to the next generation. 'Today we are celebrating Kriol. I would like you to give your message in Kriol.'

I understood his request. The twinkle in his eye was matched by a grin of my own. I nodded in affirmation. There was no need for further conversation. Gumbuli knew exactly what he was asking. Today we would break sociolinguistic convention. Normally in such a large crowd, split evenly between white and Aboriginal, a public address would be in English. If Gumbuli was speaking he would speak in English. But for tonight he was asking this white man to speak in Kriol. Today the hidden camp language of Aboriginal people would prevail in the public square. The dominant all-encompassing English language of society, of education, of economics, of politics would take a back seat. Today Aboriginal Kriol, a modern Aboriginal language based on stockman's English but developed by Aboriginal communities for their own use, would be celebrated as a legitimate language equal to English. Even more, the Bible in the Kriol language that had just been dedicated was as much the word of God as any English translation.

As Gumbuli, the supreme statesman, wandered away satisfied with how the day's events were unfolding, another wave of emotion swept over me. I fought to control it. A conversation with the Giver of Dreams would wait for another time. A community band was tuning up and the service was not long from starting. I went back over my message and adjusted my English into a Kriol turn of phrase. I was grateful that I was more a storyteller than a preacher, and that Kriol was a great language for telling stories.

2

Salvation Comes

> Location: Family dairy farm, Leitchville
> Date: 1956
> Event: An accident

The old Vauxhall engine purred into life one more time. If it was a horse, it would have already been put out to pasture, but necessity brought gratitude. For the driver it shortened the hour walk from the farm to the sale yards to five minutes. For the family it meant the two oldest boys at seven and six years of age could be driven the three miles to school, even if they had to walk home. For the mother it meant she could make a weekly visit to the post office for mail and essentials from the local store.

Perhaps because of its age and utility the old Vauxhall never departed without fanfare. It was the custom for the two oldest boys to wait for the motor to start, give the car a push from behind as if they added a cylinder that set it in motion, then run down the driveway in pursuit as it gathered speed. Tradition had been set. Today though was different. The two oldest boys were at school. No fanfare was expected as the driver started the engine, engaged the gears and slowly moved forward along the dirt driveway. As he eased through the gears his thoughts remained unbroken. He was oblivious to a far different story unfolding behind him.

His two youngest boys, one maybe three years old and the other four, had seen their older brothers' routine and stepped in to fill the void in their absence. As the youngest one pushed the car, some part of his clothing got entangled in the shiny back bumper bar of the Vauxhall. Instead of running behind a departing vehicle he was now pulled along at an increasing speed. His soft skin gave him no protection from the hardened dirt and gravel driveway. His legs and thighs first bore the brunt of the pain but then it moved to his stomach as he slumped down and was dragged along the ground. From intense pain he erupted into a scream that was crowded out by the noise of the engine.

The four-year-old took the short cut across the paddock running as fast as his legs would carry him, screaming at his father to stop. As the Vauxhall turned onto the road the release came. The boy's clothing broke loose. He fell to the ground, still and bloodied. He looked down the road and saw the car slowly pulling to a halt somewhere in the distance. He was alive. He knew that from the pain. His immediate instinct was to crawl back towards the house, but every movement brought a shot of sharp, excruciating pain. The screams turned to tears.

It was then he saw the most beautiful of sights: his mother running down the driveway. She called his name as she ran, frantic at what she might find. She did not pause as she picked up the ball of flesh in her arms and carried him back to the house. Cradled in her arms the boy knew he was safe. The pain was still there, but the fear was gone. Salvation had come.

So it proved as she sterilised the tap water, poured it into a small enamel green bowl, added Dettol antiseptic, dipped in cotton wool and slowly dabbed away at the tender skin to remove the dirt and grime. Then came the balm of antiseptic cream that took away the heat in the skin. While the pain persisted, the tears dried up.

This incident remained my earliest memory. Traumatic as it was, it was not the pain that I remembered. That was outshone by a memory of my mother's swift action and the relief of being wrapped up in her arms where fear and abandonment were vanquished and replaced by hope and healing. I knew what it was to be saved.

3

Joe And The Dreamer

Location: Family dairy farm, Leitchville
Date: Any given day 1968-70
Event: Father and son

My father's urgent demand pierced my solitude,

'Jesus Christ! Get your head out of the clouds and stop your bloody dreaming. Get over here and give a hand.'

The words reverberated and jolted me back into the present. Confronted by a young calf careering towards the gate I sprang into action and slammed the gate shut into the head of the calf, stunning it briefly. The calf halted its run for the paddock and recoiled back in the corner of the yard with the other *poddies* being readied for market. Whatever those dreams were, they were crowded out by the flow of blood through my veins that demanded an immediate physical response and re-entry into the world of action. My dreams would be rekindled another day when I again faded out of the factual world and entered a world of stories that spoke of infinite possibilities and a different reality.

Constantly, Joe needed to remind me that I should stop being a bloody dreamer as it was the real world that needed my attention. There were very good reasons why Joe's feet were firmly planted in the soil and in the here and now. The time and circumstances that he grew up in were dominated by the need to survive.

He was four-years-old when his mother, at the young age of 21 and expecting her third child, died 250 kilometres away from their small rural town, in the big city of Melbourne. Her death was attributed to causes unknown just a year after Joe's sister had been born. With no mother to care for him, and his father away seeking itinerant work, Joe's maternal grandparents and aunts raised him and his sister on the family farm.

Joe had been named Alan at birth but at an early age it was 'Joey' or 'Joe' that he answered to. In his old age, when asked why he was called Joe, he replied solemnly that it was after the young orphaned joey who had no pouch to come home to. He added that one of his regrets in life was that he knew so little about his mother. Her parents had managed their pain in silence. The silence left a void in Joe as a child where the word 'mother' was for others to use but not for him. Times were tough. The Great Depression was at its worst, and the concept of *teenager* had not yet been invented. Life was what you made it.

Joe attended school when the three R's, Reading, 'Riting and 'Rithmetic, dominated the curriculum. The headmaster expressed all the authority that his title conveyed, backed up by the cane wheeled freely to keep his charges in line. He did not restrict himself to the standard curriculum nor the comfort of mediocrity. With a stern disposition, he drove his students as far as they could go in the eight years of schooling that was available to them. Young Alan excelled in mathematics and took to history with relish.

Alan's school days ended as World War II began and Joe went straight to work putting his hands and sharp mind to any available work. His father, a distant figure, became even more inaccessible when he enlisted in the army to fight in the Middle East and later in Papua New Guinea.

At sixteen, Joe took the long train ride to the *Big Smoke* and lived with a relation in Richmond learning how to service small motors. However, the smell of the bush that had given him comfort in his younger years, never left him. Home beckoned.

A pretty young lass named Phyllis from school remained in the back of his mind. She happened to be at the Leitchville Station when he alighted from the train! They never agreed as to why Phyllis was there. Phyllis said she was just doing her business picking up the mail for the post office where she worked, while Joe figured that she was there to meet him!

When the war was over, but goods were still in short supply, they married in the church, dressed in their best. They celebrated their wedding with an afternoon tea in the backyard of the bride's parents' humble home. After a honeymoon in Daylesford they moved back into the same cottage where Phyllis had been raised and which Joe's grandfather had built. Joe went to work driving milk trucks for the local dairy factory.

Joe's maternal grandfather, who had taken his grandson and granddaughter back into his home at a time when the toil of life was beginning to bare its teeth, was an upright man with a generous heart. He helped Joe broker a loan with the local bank manager to buy a dairy farm not far from his own. He saw a lot of potential in his grandson, an unspoken reminder of his own daughter whose life was cut short.

The newly married couple now had an old mud brick home, a rundown farm and one of Joe's greatest values – independence. The first years were tough with long hours of work and just enough money to get by on. Rabbit stew was often on the menu and Joe and Phyllis both took on additional work when it was available. They needed the extra cash to help make ends meet. Four boys were added to their family in quick succession: Graeme, Russell, Maxwell and Barry. The following year a new concrete dairy stood as testament to a community that gave of itself for one of its own.

The constant cow milking and responsibilities of feeding a family, demanded Joe and Phyllis plant their feet firmly in the soil they worked. Milk prices of the 1950s promised a better future and better times did come. When the last of the four boys started school, Joe thought about replacing the old mud brick house with a new grand design. This was a time to dream. Throughout the following year at the end of the day's work he designed and redesigned his ultimate house. He built a classic four-bedroom, cement brick, whitewashed farmhouse to stand the test of time.

Now they had a home and family, but one familial term was missing. As a child Joe had no one to call Mum or Dad. Perhaps he felt awkward introducing these words that had an unfamiliar ring to him, to his children. So it was that for his sons, Dad was substituted with Joe, and Mum substituted with Phyllis. Emotionally it was easier that way. For me he was Joe by name but Father by deed. Joe was the provider, protector, taskmaster, and a no-nonsense disciplinarian. Joe would never be my best friend but I knew, with absolute certainty, he wanted my best.

Without the word *Dad* in my vocabulary, I found another familial term that served its purpose. He became *my old man*. It was an advance on *Joe* as it carried a hint of affection and a sense of belonging. He was not any old man but my old man! I was the son of Joe and Phyllis, the son of my old man and my mother. If I had been *Heather*, the daughter they hoped for, perhaps it would have been different. Joe may have become *Dad* and I'm sure that Phyllis would have become *Mum*.

There was another special old man in my world: *The Old Man Up Top*. I learnt this from Joe. Joe was not a man of religion but this did not exclude him from God. The Old Man Up Top was there for everyone. To Joe, God was a benevolent father figure who brought some order to the world. We were taught,

You don't steal

You pay your debts

You don't eye off someone else's woman

You remain content in the circumstances you find yourself in.

I later found the key to accessing The Old Man Up Top and it changed everything. I found that The Old Man Up Top was not a set of social laws but was both a Father and a Dreamer just like me. He had a grand story to tell that went from the beginning to the end of time, and it somehow included me.

4

Meeting The Giver Of Dreams

Location: Belgrave Heights
Date: Easter 1970
Event: Keswick Christian Convention

The invitation from my school friend Graeme to an Easter camp was unexpected. Five years earlier we had sat together in our first class at Cohuna High School. We introduced ourselves and became firm friends. Both farm boys, we enjoyed our sport and took our studies reasonably seriously. We deviated on one point. He came from a church going family. I didn't.

'What sort of camp is it?' I asked.

'It's in the Dandenong Ranges out of Melbourne. I go every year. We camp in a tent and have a great time. My friend added the clincher, 'There are plenty of girls there.' This final comment closed the deal. If I could go, I would.

Although I had just turned seventeen, I was hesitant to make my own plans. When I mentioned it to Phyllis she liked the idea because she trusted my friend. He came from a respected family who didn't smoke, drink or swear. My mother was proud of the fact that drink had never touched her lips. Any influence for moderation on her youngest son was a healthy one as far as she was concerned. She approved but didn't know how much at risk I really was.

Four months previously I was chosen by my school principal to attend a camp run by the Australian Navy. It was at Jervis Bay in New South

Wales, requiring a three-hour bus trip to Melbourne, an overnight stay at the YMCA Hostel, then a twelve-hour train trip to Sydney before bussing another three hours out to Jervis Bay. Phyllis approved of this trip. Perhaps it reignited in her a memory of her boyfriend Joe, who at the time was just a little older than I was, when he had passed all the academic tests to be accepted into the Royal Australian Air Force at the end of the War Years. All was well until they tested his eyesight and found he was colour blind. Any new adventures this opportunity offered him were cut down before they began.

I was one of fifty young men recommended by schools around Australia for our leadership potential. The camp was meant to build character and assess if any of the students would be suitable officer material. Instead, this time away told me more about my character flaws. Overnighting in Melbourne I found a late-night porn movie theatre, queued with bigger and older men, and shelled out the little pocket money I had to join them. Given opportunity my sense of right living failed miserably.

Once at the Naval College the prankster in me found other like-minded compatriots. The fire alarm ringing out in the middle of the night and the accompanying sirens of the incoming fire brigades were our doing. No amount of intimidation from the drill master unearthed the culprits. A smelly dead stingray found lying on the beach, mysteriously found its way into the bed of a private school boy. When he snuggled up against its cold flesh instead of bedsheets, shock took over. A piercing scream broke the dormitory silence and he was reduced to a blabbering mess. He stammered, 'My father was almost killed by a stingray.' Nothing seemed to console him. This prank was not quite as cute as I had thought but it did nothing to prick my conscience. No apology or self-disclosure was required. It was just good clean mischief. What seared my conscience occurred on the return train trip from Sydney to Melbourne on the Southern Aurora. I knew that at sixteen, I was under-age for procuring and drinking alcohol. It did not stop me. I managed to buy and smuggle half a dozen beers onto the train and I became totally drunk. When I saw the same poor fellow who found himself sharing his bed with a stingray, I threatened to punch his face in for no reason that I could think of. Alcohol affected my judgement badly. Again, given an opportunity my sense of right living failed miserably.

My bus from Melbourne to home did not leave until the afternoon so I went to the home of one of my new friends. His parents were already at work. We opened the fridge and instead of taking out the bacon and eggs we found two cans of beer and downed one each for breakfast.

I returned to the farm and life returned to normal but this episode unsettled me. Why did I get drunk at the first opportunity? Why was I so careless? Why did my inclination towards adventure lead to base behaviour and not the pursuit of higher ideals?

Joe had shown me firsthand the destructive effect of alcohol just two years earlier. He took me to the hut of a returned soldier. A foul stench greeted us as I followed Joe inside. The returned soldier was barely conscious, as he lay unmoving on a filthy mattress. Cheap wine and methylated spirit bottles were strewn across the dirt floor. Days of drinking had not quelled the memories of war that haunted him. Joe helped him to his feet and bundled him into the car.

'Grab the sheets and blankets,' he ordered as he pulled the filthy mattress from the wire framed bed and dragged it to the fire pit. 'Throw it all in here', he said as he set the mattress alight. The old soldiers' shame would not remain for others to see. Joe brought him home, cleaned him up and gave him a change of clothes. The sight and smell of that day never left me. He was my grandfather.

As I grew beyond the need for my father's approval I chose to do what I should not do and I seemed powerless to stop it. Simply put, the *good me* was not in control of me. My next trip away from the farm was to the Easter Belgrave Heights Christian Convention. This camp was to produce a different outcome.

The smell of rain and the fresh air of the Dandenong Ranges were intoxicating. It was such a contrast to where I lived on the flat flood plains bordering the expanse of the Murray River, downstream from Echuca. The air smelled of something new, something refreshing. Nevertheless, the turmoil hidden inside me still threatened an appearance. A group of teenage girls seated across the back wooden bleachers of the auditorium demanded my attention and they got it! They were not girls to be known but simply objects for the hunt. As I introduced myself and took my seat next to my intended prey, my crude advances were rightfully rejected.

The preacher talked passionately about Jesus, his death and resurrection and what it meant for us today. There was an invitation to come to the front of the auditorium to show a desire to follow Jesus. I stayed fixed to my seat. While I escaped responding to the invitation, I could not escape the sight and sound of two thousand ordinary people lifting their voices in worship to God. As the auditorium filled with song, I found myself attracted to what it was, or who it was, who stirred such a response.

Late that night as I lay in my sleeping bag on a stretcher in a canvas army tent, I discussed the existence or otherwise, of God with my two school friends. After they shared all they knew and silence settled in I was left to my own thoughts and dreams. In the stillness of the evening, I felt a stirring and an invitation to take a risk. It was the simplest of thoughts that entered my mind. *Why not talk to God about God? Why not talk to The Old Man up Top?* A simple thought, but it seemed an exceptionally bold thing to do. What does one say to God when specifically talking to him for the first time? *Hello God, I'm Barry. I would like to introduce myself.* This was not what I said. Instead, I pondered the question for quite a while. The thought came to my mind, *God if you are real, then I'm interested.* It was not a hypothetical question but the sort of curiosity question one might ask a stunningly beautiful girl. *If you are real, and you are what you seem to be, gorgeous and interested in me, then I am interested in you.*

For a moment I hesitated. Was it a prayer or just a thought? I had no experience, no tradition to call on, and no mentor to lead me. At seventeen years of age, I had rarely graced the doors of a church. What would happen next? I had no idea. I settled on that simple enquiry and said, 'God if you are real then I am interested.' Yes, it was a prayer.

I had hardly finished my line of enquiry when something or someone began to draw near and take hold of me. It was not a new raw energy but more like a calming sedative that settled my mind and my body. I found myself entering into a deep sleep like I had seldom experienced before. There were no dreams that I remember, no spoken words, just a deep, deep, peaceful sleep. When I awoke next morning, I felt wonderfully refreshed. I did not dwell on what happened the night before or mention it to my friends, but I knew something was different. The Old Man Up Top was no longer just a thought or a concept. Somehow God and I had spent some time together. I could not understand nor explain it, but it was real and I treasured that good night's sleep.

There was a sharper edge to everything around me. The trees were now greener, the smell of the air even more invigorating, and each person I saw, unique. Then there was a linguistic miracle. I had stopped swearing!

Joe had modelled swearing to me well. I had not gained his proficiency but I was clearly his disciple. Swearing was only to be used when full expression was required, but definitely not in the presence of a woman. The pinnacle of the craft came with the emphatic insertion of *Jesus Christ* between everyday common expletives. It was the same Jesus I had talked to the previous night. I knew little about him, but knew enough that he was no longer a swear word. The frustration, the anger or competitiveness that had fuelled my tongue was dissipating and this new friend Jesus, had everything to do with it.

I concluded that God had somehow entered my mind and my emotions as I slept and operated on my inner person. I did not and could not understand it but I accepted it in its simplicity. I knew almost nothing of him, but the little I now knew was enough for me to not want to give up on him easily. Something or someone touched the Dreamer in me and prised open a doorway leading to a place of bigger and brighter dreams. He was inviting me to explore it with him.

5

God, Sex And Sport

Locations: Cohuna (Year 12), Bendigo
Date: 1970-71
Event: Changing priorities

As I travelled back to the soil that had bred me, I wondered what would change. Was this experience a temporary event that would fade, or was it more enduring? Would the hurly burly of life at home, farm, school and sports arena knock this inner calmness out of me? I hoped it wouldn't.

A week later I found myself getting the milking cows in from my favourite back paddock. It took longer than the front paddock leaving me more time to day-dream. The cows, by force of habit and instinct, took the well-worn track to the shed. Similarly, by force of habit, my eyes remained alert for any black, brown or tiger snake crossing the same path as my bare feet. But the watchfulness for snakes could not replace a new song that constantly filled my thoughts. It was as if the giver of dreams had planted it permanently in my mind.

I had heard the song when I witnessed the 2000 ordinary people in the Dandenong Ranges singing praise to their Maker. A combination of the beat and the words attracted me. I welcomed it as my song given to me by The Old Man Up Top.

> Surely goodness and mercy shall follow me,
> All the days, all the days of my life X2
> And I shall dwell in the house of the Lord forever

> *And I shall feast at the table spread for me*
> *Surely goodness and mercy shall follow me,*
> *All the days, all the days of my life*[2]

Without opening a Bible, I conscripted the final verse of Psalm 23 as my personal theme song. The cows now had it as company as I sang it at the top of my voice. I sang it as God's promise for me. His goodness and mercy will follow me in everyday life. Then there was the promise for the Dreamer of an even bigger party with The Old Man Up Top in the afterlife. Wow! I didn't know it at the time, but it was my first theology lesson. It painted a picture that was for the long haul, not a temporary infatuation.

My friends gave me a *Good News for Modern Man* New Testament. I kept it among my books at school and read it at every opportunity during my free periods. As I read the Gospels of Matthew, Mark, Luke and John I was amazed by what Jesus said and by what he did. I was overawed by him. The more I read the more interested I became.

I began to see God at work in the ordinary events of life. When I read in the newspaper of a man lost at sea who cried out to God for help, I knew it was The Old Man Up Top who saved him. When I read the Scripture verse in *The Sun* newspaper it spoke directly to me. In the privacy of my mind I became a Jesus follower though I didn't yet know that term. Privately I harboured a pearl of great price. The big question that occupied me was what does this *Jesus thing* practically mean for real life? What was I meant to do?

I am unsure how that conversation started. I continued to sleep well so perhaps God communicated in my sleep as well as by what I was reading. His answer was to hone in on my attitude towards women and sex. It was bold and totally practical for a seventeen-year-old. Jesus wanted me to commit myself to finding a woman who would be the only woman for me as long as we both shall live. I would stay a virgin until I found and married that woman. It was totally counter-cultural to the flippant conversations that bounced off the walls of the local sports clubs that were a second home for me.

---

2. These are the last two verses of hymn *Surely Goodness and Mercy* written in 1958 as a collaboration between two well-known gospel music writers John W. Peterson and Alfred B. Smith.

However, the idea of faithfulness to one's wife was not a new idea. The black swans that frequent the Gunbower Creek not far from our farm paired up for life as too did the wedge-tailed eagles that soared in our skies. I had heard the Ten Commandments in our religious education lessons at school and the injunction, 'Thou shall not commit adultery'. I knew it from Joe as the husband of one wife. Joe had told me in a brutal allegory that only a man of the soil can muster. 'Any dog can find a stray bitch on heat', was his summary comment on adultery. He had little sympathy for those who broke their promise and left one for another. I took his advice to heart. I knew the ideal but I also knew that as a young man I was unlikely to keep it.

Now God was telling me that faithfulness and loyalty expressed through sexual purity were important to him. I needed to take heed now and not at some future time. My relationship with my future bride was somehow linked to my relationship with him. The transformation this brought was immediate. It did not take away my attraction to the opposite sex, but it took away the inclination to view them as objects for my own gratification. This was so profound that I surmised that perhaps this was all I needed to do for God. If this was to be the case then it was enough.

Other changes kept surprising me. I could no longer watch on when a fight broke out in the school yard. I used my position as a prefect to step in and break up the fight in a way that both combatants could keep their dignity. Amongst my fellow students I became known as the peacemaker.

Whenever a boxing troupe came to town for the local Agricultural Show, an entry ticket to the fight tent where spectators could witness local legend Billy Trigg taking on a touring boxer, was an essential purchase. Australian boxers were among my sporting heroes. As a teenager I religiously listened to Friday night boxing from Festival Hall following my boxing heroes Tony Mundine, Lionel Rose, and Johnny Famechon. Boxing was a well-loved sport in our household. It was therefore with great anticipation we gathered in our lounge to watch a replay on our black and white TV of the lauded *fight of the century*. World Heavy Weight Champion Joe Frazier faced off against Muhammed Ali at Madison Square. I was not expecting what was to come. It was a brutal fight as the speed of Muhammed Ali and his stinging left and right combinations were worn down by the power of

Frazier and his thuggish left hook. My eyes became transfixed on every savage blow to the head. It jolted me. I felt sick in my stomach. It was no longer a sport.

I silently slid out of the lounge and went to my bedroom unable to explain myself. I lay in bed in silence traumatised by the violence. I knew deep inside, this reaction had everything to do with Jesus. He had experienced brutality on the cross so he was sensitive to it as well.

These changes were private secrets between God and me. They were not something I talked about with other people, but I reflected on them. I was a better citizen because of it and a more respectful son. My improved behaviour pointed to a better future in terms of academic study and employment options. The clashes between Joe and his youngest son were now rare. Joe never argued with good reason and sensible decisions. Our next major clash was of my own making.

Twenty months had passed since I first went to Belgrave Heights and started on this *God journey*. This time the Convention was held between Christmas and New Year. I geared myself up to learn as much as I could. The previous Easter I had bought my first Christian book, *Victorious Christian Living: a study of the book of Joshua* by Alan Redpath. I devoured that book. I was ready to cross the Jordan.

I am not sure how the question arose but it was a pertinent question because sport was a well-established rhythm in my life. What did God think about me playing sport on Sundays? Was I putting sport ahead of obeying God and keeping the Sabbath? For my church-going friends it did not seem a big issue. Their church and family sub culture had already drawn their line in the sand. I decided to take up the challenge. If following God meant giving up sport on Sundays then I was good for that. Maybe the sporting god needed to be slayed.

I arrived home and leapt out of one fishbowl and into another where sport, honour and loyalty ruled supreme. I announced that I was unsure about playing sport on Sunday. Joe's retort was quick and to the point. 'If that is the case, pick up your bags and leave home now.' He had reason to raise the stakes.

Joe was president of our local cricket club. My older brother was vice captain. I was both a bowler and batter and the youngest member of the team. We hadn't won a premiership in years. Joe had instilled discipline in the team and expectations were building as our performances improved. Our matches were played each Saturday over summer. However, the grand final was played over a long weekend, Saturday, Sunday, and Monday. If we made the grand final Joe would have to face the embarrassment of his son's decision. If we lost the premiership, it would be a sour point for years to come. One could imagine the conversation at the local pub:

> *We did without a bowler and middle order batsman because Joe's youngest son wouldn't play on Sundays. We bloody well lost our best chance for a premiership in years because of him. You would think Joe could breed them better than that!*

I would be sullying my father's reputation, not my own. He came from a pioneering family who were part of the fabric of the district. It would always be home for him. But I was moving away to study and take up a career as a school teacher. I understood why he was annoyed with me. He had reason to be but I wasn't about to let his declaration determine what I would do. Joe had brought me up better than to be persuaded by a little intimidation.

It was the man of the soil versus the Dreamer, and the battle swords were drawn. I paused and went to my bedroom as if nothing had happened though the adrenalin was pumping through my body. I had painted myself into a corner but my natural inclination whenever confronted was not to back down. I took courage and returned to the kitchen table. Joe looked at me but said nothing. Indeed, not another word was said on the topic between us. Joe had made his feelings felt. He was giving me time to see sense. I hoped that God had an answer because I didn't.

My more senior cricketing mates took a soft approach. Around the bar with beers in hand and a lemon squash in mine, we discussed the issue. They accepted that my spiritual relationship with God was real. They did not denigrate it. What was up for discussion was whether God would allow me to play on the Sunday. They concluded that I could because Brian Booth, a stylish middle order batsman for Australia was a lay preacher and he played test cricket on a Sunday. To back up their argument they added that the Reverend David Shepherd opened the batting for England. If it was okay for a reverend to play on a Sunday it was okay for me.

The stakes were still high even though we were in a truce period. Joe had stated his position and my cricket team mates theirs. I now just needed to draw my own conclusion. It was while on a long walk that the answer came with such clarity that I wondered how I had missed it.

'When you are in your father's house living under his roof which he built, and eating food which your mother cooked, then you do exactly what they ask. This is called honouring your parents and it is what I expect of you.' The reasoning was compelling. I also concluded that I owed some loyalty to my team mates and it did not need to be put in opposition to God. I would not play regularly on a Sunday but I could play a final.

The conversation with Joe was brief. One Saturday morning as Joe relaxed at the kitchen table examining the racing form guide, I said without introduction, 'Don't worry. I will be playing on Sunday if we make the finals. While I am under your roof I will do as you say.'

Joe looked at me, gave an approving nod of his head and nothing more was said. The Dreamer had seen sense this time. We made the grand final and won. It was a cause of great celebration in the town and the premiership year entered into local folklore.

My faith journey, which had been personal and private was now more public. With no theological training and barely acquainted with church, the Dreamer was given a new nickname by his older brother and sporting mates. I was affectionately called, 'Reverend'.

/ 6

Nothing Ventured, Nothing Gained

Location:	Bendigo
Date:	1971-72
Event:	Teachers College Christian Fellowship

When high school finished it was time to either find a job or begin tertiary studies. I was enquiring about a clerk position with the Reserve Bank in Melbourne when I received a late call up to Bendigo Teachers College. I enjoyed economics but education was my preferred vocation. The decision was easy. I would become a primary school teacher.

As soon as our morning milking was finished, we washed, dressed in our country best and Joe and I began the two-hour drive to Bendigo. We travelled in relative silence. Casual conversation between us was never easy but nor was travelling in silence difficult. We both enjoyed our own company and our own thoughts, even in the company of each other. Phyllis would be happily milking the cows tonight, proud that her son was stepping into a profession that she herself may have chosen given different circumstances. Joe was fulfilling his unstated desire as a father. All his actions and his discipline was for one purpose: he wanted to see his son independent and able to forge his own destiny. It was a sentiment we both shared. No last words of instructions or warnings were given. It was up to me from here on.

The door of the small miners cottage in Bendigo swung open and a beaming older lady was there to greet us. 'So good to see you, Alan. I have a cuppa tea ready for you.' The warmth of the welcome was tangible. Joe responded with a softness that I seldom saw. We walked down the passageway that divided the house in two and made our way to the kitchen at the back. A table set for a king was laid out with the best of country cooking. This was a celebration! In Joe's loss as a child, I could imagine his aunt as the best substitute for the mother he never had. He was not Joey to her, an orphaned child. He was and always would be Alan. My father, Joe, for all his forthrightness was essentially a mystery. Alan was perhaps the real *him*. I now felt privileged to experience the warmth and intimacy that had surrounded him in his darkest times. The same Aunty who embraced Alan as a child, welcomed me unreservedly, the love of my grandmother living on through her older sister. A week later Joe returned to help me in my search for more permanent accommodation closer to the Bendigo Teacher's College which was on the other side of town.

It had been a long tiring day for both Joe and myself as we knocked on the door of homes of strangers. Each address we had been given offering to take a boarder proved to be in vain. There was no room in the inn! We were desperate by the time we came to 29 Carpenter Street. Mrs Harms met us at the door. She was a warm, matter-of-fact lady with no pretences. After our introductions she took a surprising interest in our surname. 'Was Borneman German?' she asked.

Joe answered, 'Yes it is. The second *n* was dropped soon after our forebears arrived in Australia.' Mrs Harms enquired further, 'Are you Lutheran?'

'No,' came Joe's reply.

I had never heard of Lutheran before but the strong sense of welcome overcame any uncertainty.

Mrs Harms' face filled with life as she said, 'Just this morning our student boarder told us he was taking up an offer at Melbourne University. He is moving back to Melbourne. That means you are welcome to stay with us.'

It proved to be a wonderful oasis for a young impulsive country boy transitioning out of farm life to the provincial city. Rent was $10 per week from Monday to Friday with breakfast and evening meals. Weekends were spent back home on the farm at Leitchville.

Viola Harms was married to the Rev Theo Harms, a fourth-generation Lutheran pastor. They had five children, full of life and love, ranging from five years through to sixteen. It was not long before the back lawn developed a firmly worn dirt strip from hours of backyard cricket, and a nine-hole golf course spread out down the drive way, around the garden and between the fruit trees. Viola loved the noise of 'the boys' consuming hours in the backyard, while Theo worried for his vegetable patch and fruit trees being peppered by flying balls.

I came as a stranger needing a roof over my head and some food on the table and two years later left as a member of the family. The Harms family gave the Dreamer a safe place to grow and ponder this God thing and also to observe the everyday life of a Christian family. Meals were always around the table together and started with a prayer and ended with devotions. A relationship with God was assumed even if not always spoken about, and Christian literature was available as easily as the local newspaper. I lapped up back copies of the monthly Lutheran Magazine in the solitude of my downstairs room. I was convinced that The Old Man Up Top was looking out for me and had contrived to bring this about.

Three weeks after starting College a notice on the information board caught my eye. It read;

> *All invited: Christian Student Fellowship*
> *Wednesday 7:30pm. Student Lounge.*

I was intrigued. I had not yet met any other Christian in my short time at the College, but nor had I made an enquiry of anyone. My faith was still private. Over the following days the invitation weighed on my mind. Should I go and find out who the other students were at the College who wore the tag, *Christian*? Before I needed to make that decision another announcement caught my attention. The running of the annual cross-country race was to start in 30 minutes. I had missed any earlier notice completely! A group of 20 young men warming up in their athletic outfits confirmed the race was about to start. I thought, *I'll be in that. I have shorts and a T-shirt in my locker.* I didn't let the lack of running shoes deter me.

It was the Dreamer inflicting his belief that all things were possible even if the practical evidence was stacked against him. Within minutes the race was on. The field separated, and I surprisingly found myself in the lead bunch except for a third-year student who scooted away and was not seen again until he crossed the finishing line. Exuberance however, can only get one so far and when I moved off the dirt and onto the bitumen road, the bare soles of my feet told me this was another good idea badly thought through. Once again, the reality of the people of the soil caught up with the infatuations of the Dreamer. But determination can bring victory in stupidity. Winston Churchill's war cry, 'Never, never, never give up', instilled in me as a child, was the heroic response in adversity. I held on to third spot. I made it onto the dais. I could hardly walk on my blistered and bloody feet for the next week, but inwardly I was satisfied, indeed very satisfied. Nothing ventured, nothing gained! I had thrown caution to the wind and suffered as a consequence but in doing so I had given the Dreamer a chance to achieve something extraordinary.

A week later I found myself gingerly walking up the driveway to the college. It was not feet that were holding me back but uncertainty. I was still wrestling with the question, 'Did I really want to associate with students who called themselves Christians?'

I had already made myself known to the cricket team. That was straight forward. This was completely different. I stayed in the shadows keen for no-one to see me. A car unexpectedly came up the driveway. I scooted behind a tree until it passed. The abandonment to reason and love of running that thrust me into the cross-country race was totally absent. But deep down I felt a compulsion to keep going. This was a race that I knew I needed to enter.

It was a very apprehensive and unsure rookie who found the student lounge and joined nine other students. They were sitting in a circle on bean bags and cushions singing folk songs to the strum of a guitar and the beat of a bongo drum.

The welcome was warm and the atmosphere easy going. They were gentle people, not loud or rude and more women than men. I could not identify a footballer or cricketer among them. The singing of Christian ballads was followed by a Bible reading. Two or three talked about what it meant and how it applied to their lives. I listened amazed at their knowledge. I said nothing. The leader drew the meeting to a close saying, 'We will finish off with a time of prayer. This time we will pray around the circle in turn.'

I froze. I could not pray out loud. I had only ever prayed in my head. I had nowhere to hide. The level of intimidation built as each prayed in turn. The girl on my left said her 'Amen'. It was my turn. Silence reigned. Words resembling a prayer formed in my mind but nothing came out. Eventually my embarrassment was relieved by the young lady to my right. So it played out for the rest of the year. I wondered if this was how it would always be for me.

Despite my own feelings of inadequacy, I still felt accepted and that I belonged. I was attracted by the individual and collective faith of these people. From that first night I made sure the monthly meeting was firmly fixed in my diary. Nothing could keep me away. My new friends' faith and confidence in God encouraged and challenged me. I inadvertently heard that the bongo player prayed in a heavenly language. He was the Christian whom I admired the most.

Towards the end of the year I gave God a simple request, 'Jesus could you show me if there is more to this Christian life? If there is not, I'm okay with that. I am just asking. But if there is more, could you turn up in the next four months so I am not left wondering.'

That was the deal. It wasn't an ultimatum. I was seeking clarity about what I could expect and how I should live as a follower of Jesus.

Sunday evening saw me make my way to *The Way In Coffee Shop* just down the street from the famous Bendigo Central Fountain. It was a place young people came to drink coffee, eat raisin toast, and ask questions about Jesus. Large posters in psychedelic pinks and greens hung on the walls declaring boldly that *God is Love* and *Jesus is the Way*. Jeff, the bongo player, ran the place. Jeff raised his voice above the murmur of the crowd and gave an invitation. 'Before we close tonight, if anyone would like prayer, come to the back of the shop and I will pray for you.'

A female student I knew from Teachers College walked to the back. A second followed. Others finished their conversations and slowly ambled out of the shop. I remained in a corner, alone, observing and pondering,

'Should I ask for prayer? Why do I need to have someone pray for me? Praying in my head worked for me before, so why change now?' On the other hand, I had asked God if there was more to know about how to live this Christian life. Perhaps this was the time. I decided to take the risk. Nothing ventured, nothing gained. This was a race worth running.

I made my way to the back of the shop. Jeff was still praying for someone else. Not being sure what to do, I got down on my knees while I waited for my turn. As I prayed silently I felt a gradual growing connection with Jesus while at the same time a disconnection between my mind and my body.

A few minutes later Jeff came, and taking one look at me he declared, 'You have come for the Baptism in the Holy Spirit.' I wasn't sure what I had come for.

He placed his hand on my head and prayed quietly, 'Come Holy Spirit and fill Barry up.'

As Jeff prayed I felt a gentle stillness move through my body from the top of my head and into every cell of my body. It relaxed me right through. That peace and stillness aroused an insatiable desire to worship God. For the first time I found myself praying aloud quietly. It was not a conscious effort. I could not contain the words. 'Jesus you are everything. Jesus you are Lord. I worship you Jesus,' I whispered.

A deep joy began to bubble up within me. I found it hard to contain as the presence of God came in wave after wave. I could hear myself thanking God. I was fully present in my mind and spirit, but lost an awareness of my body. Words turned to song. Songs in English turned to songs in a heavenly language. It was as if a small part of heaven had come to earth.

It only seemed like minutes before I returned to time and space as I knew it. I could hear Jeff laughing as I gained awareness and sat up from the floor where I laid. He said, 'Welcome back Barry. You have been off with God for over an hour.' Then he added with a grin, 'And singing in perfect harmony'. This was impossible. I could not hit a tune any time of day. As for *heavenly tongues* it was not what I had imagined. I was fully aware of each word I articulated in praise of God from deep in my spirit.

Jeff closed the shop much later than he had planned. I ran home forgoing the footpath for the tram tracks down the middle of Carpenter Street, leaping, clicking my heels, punching the air, and praising God. I was exhilarated. I was free. The Holy Spirit had taken me to another realm as if I were joining with the angels to sing hosanna to the King. For that hour the world of the soil had completely faded away. This could not be explained to a person set in the soil. For the Dreamer it did not need any explanation. Nor was it something I could, nor felt that I should, explain to others. It was between God and me.

The results were immediate. The Bible became my favourite book to read. Now I could talk to God with my mind and my voice. He had answered my questioning prayer of four months earlier. God wanted more for my life than being faithful to one woman though I didn't know what. Life was an adventure to be uncovered. I devoured whatever books I could find on the Holy Spirit and the strange gift of *speaking in tongues*.

It was then that I came across a thick scholarly book that gave its whole thesis to refuting what I had experienced. The writer argued that speaking in tongues all ceased with the apostles. His logical conclusion was that if the Holy Spirit no longer acted in this way, then any such occurrences today were a counterfeit from Satan. Wow!

This tossed everything on its head. I had no doubt he was a Christian so to draw such conclusions confused me. For the first time I became unsure about what I had experienced. The internal discussion would not have been so bad if it remained academic but my deep joy was replaced by doubt which led to a darker mood. Before the darker mood could bring despair, I ran as fast as I could to the only place I knew where to go.

It was dinner time when I knocked on the door. Jeff opened it. Standing on the doorstep, I blurted out, 'Jeff, can speaking in tongues be from the Devil?' Jeff finished chewing what was in his mouth and asked, 'Do you love Jesus more?'

I replied with a resounding, 'Yes!'

'Are the Scriptures more alive to you now?'

Again, I replied with a resounding, 'Yes!'

'Are you more able to love and forgive others?'

'Yes!'

Jeff then drew his logical conclusion. 'Then what are you worried about?'

'Absolutely nothing,' I replied.

Jeff returned to his meal and I ran home shouting and leaping and praising God. Joy, freedom and an overwhelming sense of privilege of knowing Jesus replaced my dark mood immediately. It was the darkest hour of the first two years of romance between the Spirit and the Dreamer. It was an experience the Dreamer would never forget and never wanted to go back to. That dark world without God simply sucked all the dreams away. The Giver of Dreams spoke of a different future: one full of hope, adventures, and companionship. The journey was just beginning.

7

Unhinged And Free

Location:	Bend go
Date:	1972
Event:	Baptism and deep joy

The Giver of Dreams was now my constant companion. It was as if Jesus was saying to me the same words he had spoken to his disciples two thousand years earlier, 'I no longer call you slaves, because a master does not confide in his slaves, but I call you friends' (John 15:15).

I never expected that my taking an interest in God would lead to a personal relationship. I expected help with moral choices and help in times of trouble but not access to a God friend who confided in me. But for the Dreamer it was not a difficult concept to embrace. The story of a King hiding his royalty and taking on the nature of a common man to become best friends with a pauper was the grandest of tales. It was a story made in heaven and now lived out in the present on earth.

The sense of joy continued to invade my life. A bright outlook on life was not foreign to me. My mother said that I was born laughing. Why that was so is hard to know. However, the gift of laughter as rich as it is, was not the same as this deep, deep joy. God expanded my world and wanted my worship.

As I read the Bible an inevitable question came to mind. 'Why not get baptised? It is the one thing Jesus asked his followers to do.' I understood *the why*. I didn't have the answer to *the how* and *the who* might do it. I was not regularly going to church. I asked Jeff. The conversation moved quicker than either of us expected.

'I'm thinking of getting baptised Jeff.'

'Well you will want to do it someday simply because it is an act of obedience to Jesus' command.'

'Well, why not now? Can you give me a reason why I can't get baptised now?'

'I guess I can't,' Jeff cautiously replied.

The Dreamer boldly declared, 'Then let's do it! You can baptise me.'

The who was answered for me, and now for *the how*.

'It will have to be the bath,' Jeff offered.

On went the hot and cold water and the tub slowly filled. Without any ceremony I stepped into the tub, sat down, and waited for Jeff to do his thing. Jeff held one hand on my head and the other one under my back. He said the prescribed words, 'I baptise you in the name of the Father, the Son, and the Holy Spirit,' and tipped me backwards under the water. As I lay waiting for my head to be lifted up, Jeff splashed more water over me. I came up out of the water baptised and to a laughing Jeff.

'The water was not deep enough. I just baptised you with immersion and sprinkling,' Jeff laughed. 'At least we have both bases covered.'

The humour and slight absurdity of this situation did not escape me and drying off brought more laughter than solemn reflection. I was relieved. The deed was done. I had obeyed Jesus. My habit of welcoming spontaneous opportunities with a nothing-ventured, nothing-gained attitude gave me a rare water baptism story. I was nineteen years of age and totally free. Any lingering teenage insecurity vanished. I had one Lord and Master.

The sun glistened off the waters of Lake Eppalock welcoming the students for the annual Christian Fellowship Camp. The Bible teacher from the Australian Fellowship of Evangelical Students (AFES) was painstaking in his approach as he exegeted word by word, phrase by phrase some verses from James chapter 1. We read and re-read,

> *Count it all joy, my brethren, when you meet various trials, for you know the testing of your faith produces steadfastness. And let steadfastness have its full effect, that you may be complete, lacking nothing.* James 1:2,3 RSV

The simple phrase reverberated in my mind. 'CONSIDER IT ALL JOY my brethren when you encounter various trials.' I could not think of anything more radical: *Instead of anger, try joy. Instead of frustration, try joy. Instead of self-pity, try joy.*

God was asking me to live an upside-down life where the ideals of the Dreamer were not for the imaginary perfect world but were best found in the muck of the soil. He had led the way himself. The Bible describes the ridiculous paradox with the words, *for the joy set before him he endured the cross.*

My mind raced from scenario to scenario. So, what if the love of your life decided you were not the love of her life. Would you choose joy? What if you were told not to come home again and were disinherited? Would you choose joy? What if all your friends disowned Jesus and you were the only one left believing? Would you choose joy? To each challenge I answered 'Yes'. The Dreamer embraced this radical way of thinking. The man of the soil was still to prove it.

By the end of the weekend it was personal. This was what Jesus wanted of me. The mark of my life as a follower of Jesus was now fourfold. I had already agreed:

- to follow Jesus because he first chose me.
- to marry and be faithful to one woman.
- to believe His goodness and mercy would follow me all the days of my life.

I now added,

- to consider it deep joy when I encounter trouble.

8

Experiencing Heaven

Location: Bendigo
Date: 1972
Event: Church

Pulling into the carpark I could hear the music. It was louder and more exuberant than what I expected but perfectly in keeping with a good old-fashioned revival meeting. Curiosity drew me but also anticipation. There were not a lot of places where I could sing and dance and get lost in my own thoughts of God. The boisterous singing and exuberant worship did not disappoint me. But I sensed this was not the main game. All was preparation for the revivalist preacher to do his thing.

An older man, small in stature with a withered leg came on stage. He talked about miracles he had seen and performed. He referred to the gifts of the Holy Spirit and how they were reviving the modern church just as they had in the apostles' time. He warmed to his task. Walking far and wide across the stage and down the aisle, he spoke with authority as he looked out across the audience, 'There is someone here with a pain under your rib cage. Jesus wants to heal it.' A man stood up, as did a second one.

'That was a double-yolked egg,' I thought.

He continued, 'If you are burdened down with depression Jesus wants to set you free.' More people stood.

Fascinating, I thought. *What a great show!*

I became an expectant onlooker wondering whom he might call out next.

As the line for prayer lengthened, I was safe in the knowledge that at 19 years of age I was in perfect physical condition. The thought had barely gone from my mind when the preacher added one final invitation. He looked across the room and said, 'There is a person in the room with a small boil on the inside of their right leg. Could that person come out for prayer. Jesus will heal it.' A little boil inside my right leg had been annoying me for a few weeks. It was nothing of importance and nothing that eating a little less chocolate and drinking more water would not remedy.

I protested to God, 'This boil is of no consequence. Whether you heal it or not does not matter to me. I don't need to go forward for prayer for this. So what are you up to?'

The question invited an answer. God said, 'I haven't brought you here to be an onlooker. I want your attention. Now go out for prayer.'

I stood, self-consciously shuffled past the people sitting next to me and moved to the end of the line of people waiting to be prayed for. I had time to collect my thoughts as the music continued in the background.

While I wait, I might as well worship God, I thought to myself.

Worship was my safe place. I raised my hands in worship. My legs turned to jelly. My feet gave way beneath me and I fell backward. Lying flat on the floor was the safest place to be. The Dreamer entered a world inhabited by a loving God. It was a place of peace and joy. Eventually the world of the soil returned. I opened my eyes to find no-one in line for prayer and the preacher man long gone. I felt for my boil, and was comforted by the fact it was still there.

I bounded into the revival meeting the next night. I knew the routine and was ready to enjoy the music, worship and spectacle. I determined to join the prayer line and tell the revivalist preacher that he was right about a person having a boil inside his right leg. As the night drew to a close, I stood at the prayer line end. The prayer for each person was taking longer than I anticipated. With time to spare I lifted my hands in worship to God. It was not a good idea if I wanted to speak to the preacher. My legs buckled like they did the night before. I left this world, and entered a space somewhere between heaven and earth, worshipping Jesus. While it only seemed like minutes when I returned to the here and now, the preacher had again long gone. I decided the preacher didn't need to know.

The revival meetings lured me back on the final night. Only this time I determined not to engage in worship and leave early. I had a party to attend later that evening. My friend and I found a seat at the back. The room was packed. I was an observer this time, or so I thought. The preacher broke his pattern and did not talk about miracles and healing. He talked about half-heartedness and putting God second in our lives.

'If that is you,' he said, 'then repent. Let's not wait until the end of the meeting to act. Show your repentance by coming down the front now.'

I was snookered. The very night I came to observe and not engage, he called me out.

Quick action was needed. I whispered to my friend, 'That's me. I will just go down to the front, sort it out with God, and then we can be on our way.'

I walked quickly down to the front and told God I was sorry for my half-heartedness. I raised my arms to thank him. It was a mistake if I wanted to leave early. An overwhelming sense of wanting to worship Jesus enveloped me. This time the Spirit totally immobilised me. I lost all sense of sound and touch around me. I was in another world where I could almost feel and touch God's presence. I didn't want to leave. It was home. When I came back to the here and now, the meeting had long finished. There were only a few people remaining, packing up the chairs in the church. I tried to stand up but I couldn't. I was helped to my feet but I couldn't walk. I told my foot to move and slowly one foot followed the other. My speech was slow and slurred. I was still in a haze. I knew the feeling. I was drunk. Eventually, I swayed to the car and struggled to get my seat belt on. My friend drove me back to my house. I was in no state to go to a party. I stumbled inside and onto my bed. I enjoyed the rest of the night with God somewhere in the twilight zone.

I didn't wake up with a hangover. I woke up with a deep appreciation of my cosmic father, The Old Man Up Top who loved me dearly and wanted to be a lot closer to me than I could have ever imagined. The line between heaven and earth had just become less fixed. I didn't go looking for it, it just came. The Spirit of the living God could transport me to another sense of existence if he so chose, but he could equally invade my everyday life about every day decisions. The man of dreams and the man of the soil would somehow coexist. The more I knew and experienced God the more he remained a mystery. Perhaps this was how it would always be. The Dreamer hoped so. He didn't always need answers.

I am not sure when the boil went. I told God he didn't need to heal it but it disappeared. I might have drunk a little more water and eaten a little less chocolate, or he may have decided to just remove the aggravation anyway. It didn't matter.

The College Christian Fellowship group remained my real church. It drew on elements of the Jesus Movement that came out of the US in the late 60s. Christian rock musicians Larry Norman, Barry McGuire and Keith Green were our staple diet. Meetings were informal and everyone could participate. Our ages ranged from 18 to 21. Our leaders came from within. It did not consider itself a church, but it was my church. My comfortable relationship with Christian Fellowship however, was about to change drastically.

For over a year I was a silent listener just sitting in the company of these mature Christians. With my new freedom and commitment, I now inadvertently demonstrated my Christian credentials to those around me. With few options available I was asked to lead the group in my final year at College.

The position came with the uncomfortable title of President of Christian Fellowship and as an automatic delegate to the annual AFES conference. I had no more knowledge of this organisation than I did of church. I agreed to take the position. For me it was a case of someone has to do it rather than it being a measure of Christian maturity. The consequence was that it forced my faith and label as a Christian into the public arena. I could no longer hide away in my own God world with my dreams. God had things for me to do.

9

Is She 'The One'?

Location: Bendigo
Date: 1972-74
Event: Margaret Clarke

Margaret Clarke felt God had directed her to Bendigo Teachers College. Prior to completing her high school matriculation year she had won a scholarship and position to study at the Australian National University in Canberra. She had turned it down. Another offer came from Melbourne University to do a Bachelor of Arts with a view to it leading into Social Work. She turned it down also. In their place she chose the far less prestigious option of Bendigo Teachers College.

She was a country girl born in the Mallee but raised on a mixed wheat/sheep/cattle farm in the flat country west of Euroa. Her parents both became followers of Jesus when she was a babe in arms. She admired their faith and it became her own at an early age. Faith impacted most decisions she made in her life, including what career to choose and where to study.

Margaret, or Marg as she preferred to be called, took her seat in the college auditorium with friends she had already made from the girls hostel. The principal and senior lecturers sat in a row across the platform. Marg listened intently to the principal's welcoming speech. He then introduced the heads of departments. Next the president of the Student Union introduced himself and his executive team. Some general information about campus life and services followed.

The president of Christian Fellowship (CF) was now at the microphone. Marg's ears pricked up. He was a tall final year student with a definite rural accent. Others may have stopped listening but she tuned in all the more intently. She thought she had briefly seen him stand when the Student Union Executive was introduced.

'G'day, my name is Barry. I'm here on behalf of the Christian Fellowship. We are a small group that meets once a month. If any of you first year students are interested in coming, then consider yourself invited to our *Get to know you BBQ*. The time and address are on the student notice board. See you there.'

Marg knew right away that she'd be at that BBQ as did several of her new friends.

I arrived at the BBQ ten minutes after the stated starting time. That was not unusual for the Dreamer. Time was a guide rather than a prescription. I walked into the lounge room expecting a few familiar faces. Instead, it was full of people I didn't know and buzzing with conversation. A whole bunch of first year students had shown up! They outnumbered the rest of us.

■ **Marg recalls**

> *I sat in a corner of the room enjoying conversation with new friends. Out of the corner of my eye I saw him walk through the door, pause and look around. I caught his eye momentarily. What couldn't escape my attention was his relaxed demeanor and the clothes he was wearing. A large blue felt hat on his head was matched by scruffy blue moccasins on his feet. In between was a red body shirt and bell-bottomed trousers. From his hand swirled a walking stick serving no practical purpose. I couldn't help thinking, 'If the clothes are an indicator of anything, he doesn't lack personality or he just doesn't care what anyone thinks.'*

It was my first gig as president of CF and I had no program worked out for the evening. The number of new faces squeezed into that lounge demanded something. Fifteen minutes later I called the group to attention.

The first yearers were the last to stop chatting. The introductions were brief. I gave my name, welcomed everyone, mentioned that CF met on the first Wednesday of each month and opened up for questions.

- **Marg Recalls**

   I was surprised that such get togethers were only held on a monthly basis. Most of my new friends from the girls hostels were from small country churches like myself. We were all looking for fellowship opportunities that would come from being at College, accentuated all the more by not yet having found a local church to join in.

My first decision as president of Christian Fellowship was forced by the dark-haired girl who had caught my eye when I walked into the room.

'Why once a month? Could it be fortnightly?' she asked.

She immediately intrigued me. She had a quick smile, and spoke easily for, and with those around her. Her pleasantness did not hide the fact that she seemed to be someone you could not easily contradict. I had no reason why it couldn't be fortnightly. Fortnightly it would be.

At the end of the evening I overheard Marg speaking with her friends, 'We can't all fit in the car to get back to the hostel. Two of us will need to find another ride.'

It was enough for me to offer, 'If you need a ride I can give you one.' 'Thanks,' she replied with the cutest smile. The only problem was that I did not have or own a car! It was the Dreamer at his impulsive and creative best. I quickly found my only hope. Jim was a third year student who drove a ute. 'Any chance we can give those two girls over there a ride back to College?' 'Sure. Not a problem,' he replied. As the two girls squeezed into the front seat between Jim and myself, I could not help but wonder for a brief moment if she might be *the one*. Marg gave no indication then, or for the months following, that I had reason to think it might be the case. She was just being her normal social self.

CF was now a football team in number. I moved into the captain's role of welcoming and encouraging each person who came. But I was no coach. Others who knew much more about the Bible and the Christian walk became our guest speakers. Our group culture developed, wedged between the unorthodoxy of the Jesus Revolution, the experiences of the Charismatic Movement and the more conservative AFES. We studied the Bible and we shared communion together with dry biscuits and soft drink. We baptised a new believer in the Kennington Reservoir late one night where the sign read *No Swimming* but did not read *No Baptising*. We caught up with each other informally during the week, talking freely about Jesus. We became a community within the student community. Inevitably at the centre of it was Marg Clarke.

I had been surprised at the end of the previous year when the student body resoundingly voted me in to the Student Union Executive as treasurer. When one of the students asked to nominate me I agreed but did not lift one finger in support of my case. It seemed I was the laid-back alternative. Being treasurer was not without benefits. When I gave my end of term Treasurer's Report I challenged the Executive, 'I write a lot of cheques for alcohol for student events. It seems the students who don't drink get very few benefits from their Union fees. Why don't we also provide small subsidies for other official students activities that are not drinking parties?' When I wrote a $100 cheque for the CF annual camp at Lake Eppalock I did so with some satisfaction.

The other benefit of being treasurer came on Wednesday afternoons. Margaret Clarke often ambled past with a friend on their way to the Common Room. Marg would poke her head in through the doorway and greet me, have some small talk, and go on her way. It was just an ordinary conversation, with nothing obvious to suggest it should lead anywhere. However, it occurred frequently enough to suggest it was not coincidental. Deep down I began to wonder again if she might be the one. On the surface it was an unlikely match. Apart from shared faith we were very different people.

I was a better student than most, but gave little interest to grades. High grades were welcomed but not required. Assignments were measured by how quickly I could complete them while meeting the required standard. Margaret Clarke was an A-grade student, interested in learning, studious and responsible, the sort of student lecturers love. She always did the subject justice. Giving a minimum of effort was not an option.

I spent more time on the table tennis and billiard tables, and in the cricket nets than studying in the library. I won the cross-country cup two years in a row after my first year heroics in bare feet. My Saturdays were taken up playing in the AFL Bendigo Football League. My life could be defined by the sport I played.

Sport was something Margaret Clarke could do without. There were too many other things to do in life, chief amongst them was looking out for people around her and following Jesus.

When the year ended, I moved away from Bendigo to teach, but we shared enough common friends to continue to be in touch. Every relationship I stumbled into after that had the unstated shadow of Margaret Clarke hanging over it. I was uncharacteristically cautious when it came to her. Perhaps there was a fear of rejection from the one who actually mattered.

THEY BREED THEM TOUGH IN KORWEINGUBOORA!

10

The Soil Beckons

Location: Daylesford, Korweinguboora
Date: 1974
Event: School Teaching and Discipleship

My three years at Teachers College ended and the real world of daily work awaited. I stalled the inevitable, filling the summer break with cricket and the carefree life. A week before the start of the school year I rang the Education Department to find out where my appointment was. The lady informed me, 'You are teaching Grade 3-6 at Korweinguboora Primary School in a temporary position. It was listed in last month's Teacher's Gazette.' Somehow I had missed it or I hadn't looked.

I got off the phone with a sense of excitement. I had no idea where Korweinguboora was. I searched The Victorian Road Atlas index quickly.

'This is great,' I said to Phyllis, who had been listening in on my conversation. 'It's not far from Daylesford and less than an hour's drive from Bendigo. I can still play cricket and football in Bendigo. Perfect!'

Four days later I drove into Daylesford in my white 1963 Valiant. Memories from my early years came flooding back. Daylesford was where we had our first family holiday. We stayed in a large wooden-clad guesthouse that we shared with others. It had a sand pit with brightly-coloured toy buckets and spades. It was magic for a five-year-old. We drank spring water from the fountains at nearby Hepburn Springs. That was not magical. I spat it out in disgust. We ran free on the Daylesford Botanical Gardens hilltop until my older brother got momentarily lost. It must have been sweet memories that had drawn Joe and Phyllis back as well. They had spent their honeymoon in Daylesford.

Driving along the road towards Hepburn Springs, I noticed an old sign in front of a large drab weatherboard house. *Guest House – Boarders Welcome* it read. It was the only invitation I needed. The negotiation was quick and successful, room unseen. I paid a very moderate amount for a week's accommodation including breakfast. Cash only, no invoice required.

The lady in charge looked to be a little younger than myself, around 17 years old. She showed me down a creaking wooden corridor overlaid by a worn carpet strip. I opened the door. The room was plain but adequate. It included a single bed, a small desk in one corner and a wooden free-standing wardrobe and a set of drawers adjacent to the door. I deposited my suitcase on the floor and my Olivetti typewriter on the desk. I went outside looking for a sandpit, or where one might have previously existed. I couldn't find one.

Next morning I went to the dining room for breakfast at 7:10am. Three older battered-looking men were already seated in what I discovered were their usual places. They looked me over like any long termer would do. We greeted each other with a nod and 'G'day mate.' Nothing more was said. I felt at home but I intuitively knew it was not the expected place for a 20-year-old school teacher.

The young lady who had shown me my room was already in the kitchen. Fried eggs and bacon were cooking in far too much oil. 'One or two eggs?' she asked with a smile.

'Two please,' I replied cordially.

Without any fuss or heaviness, she brought a plate of bacon, two eggs and half a fried tomato to my table. It was then that I noticed her school uniform. She was sure proof that girls mature more quickly than boys. I also noticed her brooding father in the hallway. There was no warm welcome from him.

Korweinguboora statistically had no population in 1974. It was a one-horse town serving the nearby timber cutting families. Spread over several kilometres along the Ballan Road, it consisted of a primary school, a local store, a country fire brigade shed, a football oval and netball courts.

I had already written my name on the chalkboard when fourteen lively and expectant students streamed into the classroom. The day before, I had arranged the classroom with the Grade three students seated in the far aisle near the window and the Grade six students in the desks closest to the door. The students took their seats relatively quietly but it was obvious I was in their territory and not them in mine. I introduced myself pointing to the board. 'My name is Barry Borneman, and you will call me Mr Borneman.'

A few giggles broke out at my name. Then followed more laughter. I knew students had difficulties with my surname but that didn't seem to be the cause. I followed the direction of their eyes fixed on an object behind me. I turned around and saw the grade six girl. She held the classroom broom high above her head pretending that she was going to hit the new teacher over the head. I had been warned. 'They breed them tough in Korweinguboora.'

The classroom management techniques espoused at Teacher's College were left wanting. The only model I instinctively had available was from Joe. I looked straight into the sparkling eyes of my protagonist, ignored her cheeky grin and blasted her just as Joe had done to the Dreamer, only without the accompanying swearing. It worked. She looked shocked, and retreated to her desk but was not cowed. Joy was her name, putting a new meaning to the Bible text I'd taken as my life verse, *'Consider it all joy when you encounter various trials'*. Joy became a favourite student. She was highly intelligent, loud and full of fun.

At the end of each day I arrived back at my boarding room, sat before my Olivetti typewriter and recalled the highlights of the day and distinctive contribution of each student. It was exhausting. It was also wonderfully fulfilling as both the Dreamer and the man of the soil found equal expression.

Life became more predictable and better habits formed. I was now on a $10,600 annual salary, eight times more than my student bursary. I was budgeting my time and money and learning what it was to become a responsible person. My impetuosity was dampened but not extinguished. My classroom became the Dreamer's paradise full of imagination and adventure.

'Hey class, if you finish all the maths and reading by lunchtime we can go adventuring.'

'Where are we going Mr Borneman?' Joy asked.

'You tell me Joy. You know Korweinguboora better than I do.'

'I know just the place,' Joy replied. 'There is a great natural spring a kilometre from here. You go across the paddock opposite the school, down a track and there it is. Beautifully hidden away among the bamboo.'

The class immediately put their heads down to work and a quiet hush came over the room. At lunch time Joy led the class across the paddock and to our secluded hideaway from school. It was spectacular. The tall bamboo created a natural play area for drama and storytelling.

As each day passed the Dreamer became more adventuresome.

'Are you really going to take us to see the Harlem Globe Trotters?' Joy asked with her eyes wide. 'It would be amazing if we could do that.' She was speaking on behalf of the grade five and six students.

'Well I can't see why not,' I replied. 'Six of you can fit in my car. Two on the bench seat in the front and four in the back. I will need to check with your parents first so don't get your hopes up just yet.'

The parents were already well prepared by their children when I came to ask. They offered no resistance. They were as equally excited by the opportunity. With just their verbal agreement we were ready to roll. I filled the parents in on the plans.

'We will leave immediately after school finishes on Friday. That will give us good time to get something to eat before we arrive at the Kooyong Tennis Centre to buy our tickets. You can expect your children back home about 1 am.'

The trip went without a hitch. The Harlem Globe Trotters were quite a spectacle despite playing on uneven boards laid out on the famous Kooyong Centre Court.

One excursion gave impetus for the next one. Twenty years later Joy would tell me it was the happiest time of her life.

It had been another full day at school when I headed for my room and passed the landlord coming down the stairs. As I squeezed by I could smell his breath tainted with alcohol. That did not worry me, but what did worry me was a tuft of hair that I fleetingly saw caught in the button on the sleeve of his sports jacket. His arm firmly held the elbow of a lady whom I had not seen before. In those few moments not a word was said between the landlord and I, nor a glance shared. Somehow I felt a button pressed in me. I could not stand by and ignore it.

By the time he had bundled the lady into the front seat of his car and driven in the direction of Ballarat I had already started my car. The adrenalin was pumping but I needed to check my assumptions.

I pulled up at the pub and rushed inside where I knew the landlord's daughter and her older brother would be playing pool.

'Is your Mum visiting your father today?' I blurted out.

She immediately replied, 'Yes she is.'

'Is there any chance he might have hit her?' I asked. The answer was in her face.

'She is in the car with him,' I added.

'He will be taking her back to her house in Ballarat.'

'Should I follow them?' I asked.

'Please do,' she said with an urgent tone in her voice.

I jumped into my car and sped down the road towards Ballarat. I was calm and calculated on the one hand, but full of emotion on the other. The speedometer hit 70 miles per hour as I sped towards Ballarat with no vehicle in sight.

'Jesus, protect this lady,' I prayed. 'Don't let her get hurt.'

I knew the road well. A few miles before Ballarat the road forked. The right fork headed towards North Ballarat, the main road continuing into Ballarat Central. My 70mph hit 75mph but still there was no taillight ahead of me. I would have to make a blind decision. Which fork do I take? I prayed out loud in tongues. I hoped the Holy Spirit would direct me. I approached the fork and swung onto the secondary road heading to North Ballarat. Still there were no taillights. It seemed like a pointless goose-chase.

A couple more minutes and the faintest of taillights appeared in the distance. I reached the car just as it entered the outskirts of Ballarat. It was the landlord's car. I tailed it into the suburbs. It was not too long before it parked in front of a small house. I pulled up behind and flashed my lights. I waited in the car. After a few minutes that seemed much longer, the lady got out of the passenger seat, went to the front door, unlocked it and went inside. The landlord remained parked and so did I. Eventually he pulled out and headed back towards Daylesford. I waited until he was out of sight and then drove on into Ballarat. It was time for pizza.

On the much slower drive back to Daylesford I wondered about my response. I knew the potential for conflict. It could end badly. But I could not stand by and watch abuse like this happen. I was wired by my upbringing to respond. I reasoned Jesus had also wired me this way. I confided in him, 'Jesus, I know you put me right in the middle of this tonight. So, one day you draw me into worship as if this world doesn't exist and another day you draw me in the middle of this crap. It seems all I can do is follow. Is that how it will be for me?'

I imagined Jesus' compassionate smile but giving no answer.

Next morning the daughter placed an extra half fried tomato and ration of bacon on my plate. The landlord avoided me altogether. A week later the first school term ended. I would be finding somewhere else to live for second term.

11

An Unexpected Road

Location: The Mansions, Malmsbury
Date: 1974-75
Event: Finding community

The fog was already settling over Daylesford Lake as I parked my car. There was no one else in sight, as I expected and wanted. The chill of the winter night kept people rugged up inside. I got on with what I had come for. I needed time with God, and the outdoors were my cathedral. I took a deep breath sucking in the silence, and breathed out slowly. 'Lord, here I am. Speak to me.'

The Spirit formed words within me. I sent them echoing out across the lake gently dispelling the stillness of the evening. I listened to each phrase and waited. A thought eased into my mind, 'Drive to Malmsbury.'

I allowed the thought to remain for a few seconds before, 'Are you sure about that?' I said out loud. 'Driving on that winding road on a foggy winter's night is not a good idea.'

I sat silent for a couple of minutes looking over the lake. I turned the key and started the engine, drove out onto the main road and to the intersection. A right-hand turn led towards Malmsbury. I paused, put on my lefthand indicator and turned in the opposite direction towards Ballarat. I said to myself, 'Okay Barry, if you are going for a drive at least you know a pizza awaits you in Ballarat.'

As the last lights of Daylesford faded in my rear vision mirror the certainty of a pizza became less appetising. A nagging thought tugged at my mind,

'If you don't go you won't know if it was the Spirit. What have you got to lose?' I slowed the car, made a U-turn, and headed back the way I had come.

The kilometres passed slowly as I tentatively made my way through dense clouds of fog that reduced visibility to less than a few metres. Much to my relief, a roadside sign eventually came into view welcoming me to the small township of Malmsbury. The road swung under a railway bridge and to a T-intersection onto the main Melbourne to Bendigo Road. As I approached the junction I saw a large two-storey bluestone building on my right. Painted high up on the wall facing the Calder Highway were the words, *The Mansions – 'Jesus is the Way, the Truth, and the Life'*. I immediately knew why I had come.

I remembered this place from a brief visit with Jeff a year earlier. Jeff told me the story of the local Anglican minister being baptised in the Holy Spirit and speaking in tongues. It caused a stir in the press at the time. A Melbourne tabloid newspaper gave it front page headlines. The ABC sent a reporter to do an interview. The Bishop was at a loss with what to do with the unwanted attention. He sided with *the noise*. The young Anglican minister became a priest without a parish. He determined not to abandon his ordination or his new experience of God. Now without any income from the church, he moved with his family into an abandoned and derelict bluestone double-storey building from a previous era, called *The Mansions*.

I parked the car, braved the winter wind, and went to the front door, knocked and waited. A medium sized, middle-aged man came to the door.

I introduced myself, 'Hello, my name is Barry. I am a school teacher from Daylesford.'

The response was equally straight to the point. He extended his hand and said, 'I am Ron Wood. What is it that you want?'

I heard myself asking, 'Do you have a Bible study?'

'Yes,' he replied. 'We have one tomorrow night. It is on every Wednesday.'

'Can I come?' I replied.

'Absolutely! You are welcome. Look forward to seeing you tomorrow night.'

I drove back home amazed by the string of events. It began with an urge to find a quiet spot to pray in the Spirit. Then there was a thought, an uncertain response, then cautious obedience to the thought. The result was an invitation to join a new community.

The next evening I travelled to Malmsbury, along a road already feeling familiar. Jan Wood welcomed me. A large slow-combustion stove warmed the kitchen as Jan poured me a cup of tea. Ron came and went as he prepared for the evening. Their three young girls warmed themselves in the kitchen before they headed to bed. I immediately felt at home.

A little later, Ron stood next to an overhead projector with its image projected onto a white screen. 'Tonight we are starting a new series,' he began. 'We will study each of the nine fruits of the Spirit listed in Galatians chapter 5. Tonight we will look at the first one, *Love*'.

There were six of us present including Jan. The group was smaller than I expected, but its small size only deepened the sense of privilege that I was feeling. I was being personally discipled by a veteran of the charismatic renewal that was impacting the main denominational churches.

I left *The Mansions* later that evening knowing that the Holy Spirit had taken things into his own hands and provided me with a spiritual home. Anticipation was already building for the following week's teaching on the place of *joy* in the life of a Christian.

There was another natural reason I felt at home. Ron and Jan were country people. Ron was raised in Moama, some 30 miles upstream from my birth place. When Ron spoke about faith he used the imagery and everyday language that I understood. For some, Ron's directness could be off-putting, but for me his no-nonsense approach was like fresh air.

My first year of teaching was an eventful one. After two stimulating terms at Korweingaboora Primary School, the Education Department moved me to Daylesford State School to fill a temporary position. A class of

36 five-year-olds in their first year at school awaited me. It was chaotic, exhausting, and a lot of fun.

Towards the end of the year I was eligible to apply for a permanent teaching position, rather than fill temporary vacancies. I pondered the decision. I asked Ron his opinion and got a lesson that would follow me all the days of my life.

'Ron, I am wondering if I should apply for a school position near Malmsbury. What do you think?'

He looked me straight in the eye and responded, 'Why are you asking me?' Then he chuckled, 'Ask Jesus. You know him as well as I do!'

I felt an immediate sense of relief. The lesson was obvious. I was looking for the easy way out. Ron was not about to fall for it, nor was he about to give in to his ego and inflate his own sense of importance at my expense. I too chuckled as I walked away with words replaying in my mind,

'Ask Jesus. You know him as well as I do!'

It was a lesson well learnt. Jesus and I were responsible for the decisions I made concerning my life. Ron was not about to take that away from me. I had found a rich spiritual home that assumed God spoke personally to each of his followers.

12

An Unlikely Pair

Location: Euroa, Blue Mountains, Rushworth
Date: 1975 - May 1976
Event: Proposal, marriage and our first home

My appointment to a one-teacher rural school in Costerfield, 13 kilometres from Heathcote brought one distinct bonus. Heathcote, where I boarded, was only 30 minutes drive to Bendigo. Bendigo in turn was where Marg Clarke resided while completing her final year at Teachers College.

Marg had been on my mind all week. I could not sit on it any longer. This time it would not be an accidental meeting while in the company of others. This time I would drive to Bendigo for one purpose alone. I had to talk to her.

One of Marg's housemate answered my knock and let me in. It was a chilly night. The front door opened directly into the lounge but Marg was not there.

'I'd like to talk to Marg. Is she around?' I asked as nonchalantly as I could.

Her housemate smiled and said, 'She's in her little office studying', nodding toward the second door on my left. I knocked on the door and waited for Marg's response.

'Come in,' she called without checking who her visitor was. Marg was seated comfortably at her desk with a coiled electric heater warming her feet. She was surprised to see me, but I could tell she was not disappointed with the interruption. There wasn't room for a chair so I perched on her desk. She welcomed me with some easy small talk. I was keen to get on with my reason for coming. I took courage and got the words out.

'Marg I have come to ask you a question.'

She sat quietly waiting. A few seconds passed before I calmed the storm that was in me and as casually as I could asked,

'Would you be my friend?'

It was not in her nature to rush a response. After a suitable pause that seemed longer than I'm sure it was, she leant back in her chair, smiled and said, 'Yes. I think we can be friends.'

■ Marg recalls

> … I felt a warmth to the question and a smile spreading across my face. I remember leaning back in my chair. I sensed this request was for real and that God was in it, but I was not in a hurry to pursue a relationship. I was enjoying my final year subjects and wanted to do justice to them. I had also been elected as Christian Fellowship President so that took up my spare time. I paused before giving my response. 'Yes, I think we can be friends.' My response was for the here and now. To be a friend was enough for now.

Marg had reason to be cautious. She knew first-hand of my reputation for easily starting relationships that abruptly ended. I didn't end relationships well because of my immaturity. I knew deep inside this friendship was different. She was the one.

Marg and my friendship steadily grew. Within six months we were ready to check out a jeweller in Bendigo for an engagement ring. As we walked out of the jewellers, the Head of the Education Faculty from College walked past. He saw us together and with the backdrop of the jewellers he drew the correct and most obvious conclusion. His reaction was immediate. He stopped, shook his head in disbelief.

'Not you two!' he exclaimed.

He knew Marg as a Grade A student who was conscientious and respectful. It was obvious he saw me in a different light. Almost two years previously he and I had had a marked difference of opinion. With just a couple of weeks to the end of my final year I received a note asking me to come before his education faculty staff. It was an unusual request. As I entered the staff room I was immediately confronted by grim-faced faculty members sitting along both sides of a long table. The head of the faculty stood at the far end. Though he was not a man given to annoyance, that was what I felt coming down the table directed squarely at me. He went straight to the point.

'We don't like what you have written for the purpose statement in your major education assignment.'

I knew what I had written. It had amused me at the time as I belted it out on my Olivetti. It read: *My purpose for doing this assignment is to get the minimum mark required to pass the assignment and to pass the subject, in order to graduate, in order to become a teacher.*

He looked straight at me and gave the ultimatum, 'Rewrite your purpose statement or you will fail the assignment.' He stood waiting for my response. What he knew, and I knew, was that all students needed to get a satisfactory pass in this major assignment to pass the subject. Fail the subject and you don't graduate.

I collected my thoughts. Do I comply or do I fight? My inclination not to back down kicked in. I stood determined at the other end of the table and gave not an apology but my defence. Looking back at the Head of the Department and then to the staff seated, I replied in a calm voice,

'I won't be changing my purpose statement, and here are the reasons. The quality of my work is better than most. It is worth a good mark. Even more importantly my observations on the cognitive development of my subject is my own work, which you can't say for other students you will pass. You must know that students have been copying assignments from previous years with minor changes for years now. The reason they do is because you trot out the same major assignment year after year. Given that, I think my purpose statement is completely okay. I won't be changing it.'

I stood and waited. There was silence from the faculty. The tables were turned. The head of the faculty scoffed and dismissed me with disdain. 'Get out of here,' he retorted.

I left surprised by my own recklessness. I had put my graduation on the line over one simple statement. But I was wired to fight and not back down. I would wait and see how it played out. My paper was handed back to me a few days later. I scanned the final page for the mark. I received a 'D' the minimum pass grade, with no comment. I was delighted. I would graduate.

Perhaps seeing us together almost two years later, brought back the pain of this encounter or maybe he was reminded of the excellence of Marg's work. Whatever it was, these two human beings did not belong together in his mind. What he did not know was what we had in common. We both shared a passion to follow Jesus. It was possibly the only explanation that made sense even to us.

I went into married life without a concrete plan and little idea of how to go about it. Marg's expectations were a little better formed. I carried responsibility lightly. I would stumble into it and then with God's help, trusted we would work it out as it unfolded.

Two weeks before our wedding date, the apartment we were to rent in Heathcote fell through. It was the one concrete plan we had made before the wedding. We knew where we would be living. I was not overly concerned but I knew this unexpected news could not wait to be conveyed by letter. The public telephone was my emergency contact.

Marg was boarding with family friends in Pascoe Vale and teaching at Craigieburn Primary School. They had a home phone. I lined up my coins along the shelf above the public phone in the main street of Heathcote. I rang the number where Marg was staying. It was good to hear Marg's voice at the other end of the line. With love and greetings shared, another twenty cents went into the slot. Long distance calls were expensive. The reason for the phone call beckoned. I broke the news,

'That little apartment we were hoping to live in has fallen through.'

I was totally unprepared for her response. I could not see the tears but I could hear the sobs and felt her disappointment.

'Where are we going to live?' Marg asked in between her anguished tears.

I didn't know what to do with the tears, as tears were an unknown event in the household I grew up in. Ignoring them I replied,

'I don't know where we will live, but I am sure God has it in hand. We will be fine.' It was a genuine belief but one I came to far too quickly given the circumstances and Marg's emotional response.

- **Marg recalls**

    Although I hadn't seen inside 'our' brand-new unit, I was already imagining us settling into it to start our brand-new life together. The unit had sounded perfect for our needs, even though I didn't know where I might be teaching. With my dreams dashed I did not know what to think or to say. The tears came readily. Eventually they stopped and we agreed to trust God to provide.

Twelve months after I had asked Marg Clarke if she would be my friend, we were married. Family and friends gathered at the Euroa Baptist Church to witness the marriage of Margaret Louise Clarke and Barry Ronald Borneman. The Rev Ron Wood, who was now reinstated in the Anglican Church, was our celebrant. We both believed that God had brought us together. We made the promise to love and cherish until death us do part. Marg was 21 and the Dreamer was 23.

With no fixed address and no bed booked for the night, we headed northward out of Euroa with *just married* emblazoned across the back window of our car for all to see. We did not have a care in the world. For the Dreamer it was a perfect way to begin life together. For Marg it was almost perfect, but she would have enjoyed just a little more certainty.

With no prior planning, what does one do on their first night as a married couple? We drove into Albury, pulled into a motel and booked a room for the night. That was a good start. It was time for something to eat. Marg wanted something special.

'Let's get take-away chicken,' Marg exclaimed, 'I haven't had that before.'

'And I know the perfect place to eat it,' I replied.

Fifteen minutes later we found our way up One Tree Hill overlooking the lights of Albury. We snuggled up close on the front bench seat of the old Valiant to enjoy our hot roast chicken and chips. We reminisced over the day's events that had flashed by all too quickly. We drove back down One Tree Hill and to our motel, the Dreamer and his hot chick.

Our honeymoon destination was my secret. However, Marg had already guessed that we were heading for the Blue Mountains. She stayed silent, and let me live out my dream of surprising my bride. Five days of exploring the Blue Mountains was exotic for two brought up on the flat land of Victoria north of the Great Divide. With still no place to live we cruised the longer route back to Melbourne following the coastal road, planning to call in on the Education Department at the end of our honeymoon.

It was Sunday when we arrived in Bairnsdale. Having settled into our motel for the night, we set out to find a church and enjoy some fellowship. It wasn't long before we spotted a car with a Jesus sticker on the back window.

'Why don't we follow it and see where it leads us,' I suggested. Marg loved the idea. It wasn't too long before the car turned into a full church car park as we had hoped. We could already hear the singing and felt the pull to worship.

I always enjoyed worshipping Jesus with others, but there was nothing better than having at my side my new bride who also thought this was the best of places to be, even on our honeymoon. It was a special church service with a young visiting preacher named Steve Ryder. He told his story of his criminal life, time in gaol, Bible reading, and then his encounter with the transforming power of Christ. He was an authentic *Jesus man*, something Marg and I both wanted to be.

A few days later we arrived at the Education Department office in Melbourne to find out what temporary teaching position they had that Marg could fill within driving distance of Costerfield.

The clerk looked over the vacant position still vacant and offered, 'There is a Grade 6 position in Rushworth for one term. It is the only one I can see in your area.' Marg was disappointed, 'I was hoping for an infant grade.

I specialised in teaching the lower classes.' The clerk was sympathetic, 'I'm sorry I can't help with that but maybe the principal might agree to you taking a lower class.' With no other options before us we decided to investigate. Rushworth was familiar to Marg. She passed through it each time she drove from the family farm to Bendigo. Small country towns and country schools held no fears for us.

Full of anticipation we headed straight to Rushworth and a meeting with the vice-principal. The greeting was warm, conversation helpful, but he did not want to unsettle two classes. Marg, with some trepidation, agreed to take the grade six position. Unusual, even for that time, the rest of the teaching staff were all male. As the conversation finished, he added one word of caution,

'Accommodation is very hard to find in Rushworth.'

We entered the office of the *Rushworth Chronicle* to place an advertisement in the weekly newspaper. 'Needed: House to Rent'.

Sharon, the receptionist, greeted us. She confirmed what the Principal had said. There was little chance of finding a rental property in Rushworth. Warm conversation continued as we prepared the advertisement. It gave Sharon enough time to sum us up in the way that country people do. She then ventured, 'My parents have an old house that is empty. It was not for rent but they might be willing to help you if you can't find anywhere else to live.'

'Thanks,' I replied. 'Can you tell us the address? It would be good to have a look before we go.'

We drove by a weatherboard house from a previous era. An outside toilet and wash room stood separate from the house. One factor was in its favour. It was well located not far from the centre of town and walking distance to the primary school for Marg.

As we drove out of Rushworth on the 30 minute drive to the Clarke farm to spend the night, we could already see ourselves living there. We had asked God for a roof over our heads and we had got one. That night we scoured the map and found a bush track to Costerfield through the Whroo Forest. An hour's drive via the main road was reduced to 40 minutes along a bush track. We were excited! In our mind it was no longer a dilapidated house. It was to be our first home. And so when our advertisement failed to produce an alternative, it came to pass.

13

Our First Home

Location:	Rushworth
Date:	1976
Event:	Making a home

Marg was delighted with the old house, or perhaps more accurately, with our new home. There was a spare room for anyone who may need a bed, and a large open fire-place in the lounge which invited a sense of companionship and community. A small kitchen was at the back of the house with a wood stove, which was similar to what we had both known through our growing up years. A wood stack came complimentary from the owner. He was a woodcutter. The only drawback was that we could only get cold water from both the cold and hot taps regardless of whether we had the wood stove alight. A narrow cement path ran from the back door to an outside laundry several metres away where there was a large copper. We would not be short of hot water after all. The outside drop toilet continued the memories of our own childhood. The rent was cheap at $10 per week. In all it was a perfect provision for us.

For Marg, marriage was not just about finding a husband, it was about making a home. Home was a place for sharing conversation and doing life together. *Together* for Marg meant an unhurried conversation after school recounting the day's events and the people she had met, hearing about my day, doing the dishes together, gardening together, doing the laundry and pegging the clothes out together, taking walks together, doing Bible study and praying together. There was only one catch. The Dreamer had not broken from his habits as a single man. He did not do *together*. He did *solo*. It was the Dreamer's default to do *solo* that brought Marg her first tears when after school I got lost in the newspaper and totally missed the cue that Marg wanted to debrief on the day's events and hear about mine. This tension between *together* and *solo* would last a lifetime but it was at its fiercest in the first year simply because we did not yet know ourselves or have the words to understand each other.

■ **Marg recalls**

> *I remember the joys and challenges of my new grade six class. I was feeling very stretched and needed support from my more experienced teacher husband. The best time for me to debrief was immediately Barry arrived home. It was not that we didn't share many things together. It was more that my husband liked to retreat into his world when I most needed to talk. When his retreat was combined with a newspaper then I felt compelled to let my presence and need be known.*

One thing we did agree on was that we would always do church together. Our first priority after finding a house was to find a church. Marg did not want to shop around for a church to see which one suited us best. Meeting and then seemingly rejecting people was not something she wanted to do. Any church would be okay by me. Marg sensed we were to attend the church on the hill. It turned out to be the Church of England.

Marg with her Baptist upbringing and me with my non church background had little to draw on when we stepped into the church. The Book of Common Prayer dated 1662 and an old hymnal were handed to us as we joined the congregation from an older generation. We struggled to know when to stand, when to sit, and when to kneel in an ancient tradition. But our ignorance did not dissuade the young minister. At the first opportunity he invited us home to share a meal with his wife and young family.

We shared our common story of Jesus turning our lives around. The minister despaired that the gospel he preached each week seemed to fall on deaf ears. He confided that we may be the first people to walk through the door to actually know what he was preaching about. Our friendship and trust grew. We could talk about Jesus and the Scriptures freely. But one area was out of bounds. The Dreamer could not talk about Holy Spirit encounters and mysteries of God that took him to another place. Such places were foreign to our new friend. He also considered them dangerous and to be avoided. Rather than disturb our friendship they remained secrets until a future time. It was easier that way.

It did not take long for Marg to befriend and regularly call in on an old lady living alone near the school. I was discovering that for Marg, age, ethnicity or status went unseen in making conversation with others. She connected with the high school principal and his wife and received an invitation for us to join them in a Bible study in their home. Rushworth was becoming our new home.

Marg could see that I related easily with people but did not seek company. She suggested,

'Why don't you play football with the local team?'

I was not expecting it but she was keen to expand my network and for me to burn up my excess energy. I took her up on her suggestion. A brand-new recruit arriving mid-season and playing centre half-forward was big news in town. The team went from most often losing to more often winning. When we narrowly defeated the neighbouring town in the final match of the year, Rushworth supporters were a-buzz. Unfortunately, I missed most of the game. I had kicked four goals well before half time and it caught the attention of the opposition coach. Not long after, an overweight back-pocket player short on football skills but big on thuggery, cannoned into my shoulder at full pace. At the slightest movement a pain shot through my shoulder. Our volunteer trainer had one feel of the shoulder and said, 'Your game's over mate. It's off to hospital for you.' The doctor put my arm in a sling and ordered me to not lift my arm for six weeks. The locals however, had seen enough. The football committee was already making plans for me.

Joe dropped in for a quick visit on his way home from Melbourne. He climbed the roof and tinkered with the water tank. He climbed down and coolly stated, 'You have hot water now.'

He then pulled me aside, out of Marg's hearing. I could see that familiar look of the man of the soil exasperated once again with the Dreamer. He spoke calmly but with inherent authority,

'You have to do better than this.' Turning his head toward the house he added, 'If you think Marg is going to follow you around living in conditions like this you've got another thing coming.'

It was a cautionary comment not for discussion. No response required, and I gave none. For Joe the provision of a house that is worthy of being called a home was a man's responsibility and I had failed. What he did not know was that the Dreamer and his new wife saw this old timber house as God's provision. They delighted in what it provided, not burdened by what it did not. To them it was the best of homes for now.

'Let's go to the pub,' Joe said. 'It will be good to meet some locals before I leave.' I had not once visited the pub since we arrived in town, but it was not an environment in which I felt uncomfortable. Joe paid for my lemon squash, and with a beer in his hand, we casually stood at the bar waiting for someone to come and make conversation. He knew the pub etiquette in a close-knit country town. They know you are there, so you don't push yourself forward. If someone wants to talk to you or satisfy their curiosity, they will. Otherwise you enjoy your drink and go.

We were half way through our first drink when a gentleman around Joe's age came over. Speaking directly to Joe, he said, 'Barry's father I assume?'

They exchanged names. He continued, 'I am president of the Rushworth Football Club. This son of yours is a good footballer, Joe.'

Joe deflected the comment replying, 'There are a lot of good footballers in the country.' Joe was inherently suspicious of personal praise.

The President then turned his attention to me. He said, 'The club committee has decided to offer you the coaching position next year.' It caught me completely by surprise. My time at the club had not been without conflict.

A month before, I stayed on for the BBQ at the footy shed after training. What I didn't know was that there was follow-up entertainment. The comedian introduced himself by saying,

'Give me three unrelated subjects and I will weave a story out of them.' So began one bawdy story after another, laden with every swear word common to rural Australians. I was not the only one uncomfortable with the vulgarity but I was the first to act. As he started on yet another barrage of swearing and crudity I walked across the room between the comedian and the onlooking clubmen and out the door. I was about to get in my car when the coach came running after me.

'Barry,' he called, 'I'm sorry, we didn't know it was going to be that bad.'

I could see his fear of losing the new centre half-forward over a filthy-mouthed comedian.

'Don't worry,' I replied. 'I am here to play football. I'm not here to listen to that crap.'

He nodded apologetically, turned and walked back towards the shed. Nothing was said to me by anyone about that incident, though there would have been talk. Now I was being offered the coaching job.

The president continued. 'We will pay you $2500 a season as well as fill your car with fuel each week.'

I listened without committing on the offer. Joe stood observing. I could tell that he was enjoying the moment. Neither the club president nor Joe knew I had decided to retire from competitive football for good. This was not the time for that discussion. I enjoyed playing sport but it was no longer a priority or a need. In the choice between cricket and football, cricket it would be.

Joe said goodbye to Marg with a hug, and a firm shake of the hand for me. He was fond of Marg. She was smart, capable and level-headed. His son had more chance succeeding with her at his side. It was a much more contented Joe who drove back to the farm.

For Marg, a home needed visitors. Everyone was welcome no matter how short the notice might be. The young Catholic priest warmed to the conversation as we sat around the meal table. It was only a few days earlier that we had met on the cricket pitch.

It was my first game for the Rushworth Cricket Club. Our guest was the opening batsman at the other end. I became curious about who he was as we built a solid partnership. He did not have the mannerisms of a local.

At the break I asked, 'What do you do mate?'

He hesitated, smiled and replied, 'I'm the priest at Saint Mary's.' It was not what I was expecting, but there was something about him that hinted we shared a kindred spirit.

'I exclaimed, I'm a Christian too. It would be great if you come home for tea. We can talk some more then.'

He thought for a moment and replied, 'I would love to.'

As the evening wore on our conversation naturally moved to faith. I asked him, 'Why did you become a priest?'

His answer could have been my own words. He replied, 'Jesus changed my life. He means so much to me that I want to spend my life introducing him to others.'

Wow, I immediately loved this man. There was every chance he would even understand the Dreamer.

It was late when he rose to leave. He confided, 'I did not tell my Father Superior where I was going tonight. He wouldn't understand me visiting a protestant's house. Thanks for a great night.'

We shook hands firmly as we said goodnight. We were brothers in Christ even when strongly held dogma might suggest otherwise. The mystery that God allowed it to be so, was what the Dreamer loved about Jesus. He chooses his friends; we don't choose them for him.

We separately jotted down the names of schools from the Education Department Gazette that had vacancies for the following year, 1977. The places that we had both listed became our final list. With these positions written on separate cards, we placed them in a bucket and drew out a card. The first pick became our first preference, and so forth down the line.

I had been teaching at Costerfield, a one-teacher school for two years and I needed a change. During third term Marg had enjoyed being the sport/art/music teacher but she was keen to take on an infant level class that she had trained to do.

The Dreamer liked the unpredictability of our drawing lots. Marg liked the fact that it helped her to make a decision. We both believed God had the final say, besides didn't they *draw lots* in Biblical days?

And so I became appointed as the Grade 3-4 teacher at Lancefield Primary School in 1977 and Marg as one of three prep teachers at Kyneton Primary School. We were both delighted. Our move this time was organised a few months in advance. An investment house owned by an Anglican minister in Melbourne became available for rent. We jumped the queue, as we were now known as Christians, and Anglicans, and offered first choice. As word of our move spread through the church, we quickly heard that we were not the first ones to move from Rushworth to Lancefield and that we would soon be attending 'Father Elson's church'. Yes, the previous minister in Rushworth now lived in Lancefield. We soon heard from another source that he now preferred to be simply called *Harry*.

14

Hospitality Expands The Heart

Location:	Lancefield
Date:	1977
Event:	An open letter from a real Australian

I could not put the book down even though the reading was painful and an accompanying deep sadness endured well after the book was returned to the shelf. *Bury My Heart at Wounded Knee* by Dee Brown would not lie down since I had found it on Joe's bookshelf. The stories told of broken promises and treaties, of brutal massacres, government duplicity and dispossession were piled end on end. The accumulated weight of the history told from the perspective of the Sioux, the Navajo, the Cheyenne and the Apache as they buckled under the westward expansion of America, left me saddened. The accounts were often brutal and unforgiving, the glimpses of shared humanity dwarfed by a relentless tide of destruction. I am unsure why it takes reading another nation's history to cause you to look afresh at your own but the parallels with the adoption of *Terra Nullius* were painfully obvious.

I wondered about the plight of the Yorta Yorta who had graced the banks of the nearby Murray River and had gathered for ceremonies at Kow Swamp just down the road from our farm. Though I knew little of the local Indigenous history I knew that being from a fourth generation pioneer family, my history and their history were linked, and even with the very best will and intentions, my history brought suffering, dislocation and despair to the first Australians.

So, it was with this in the back of my mind that I was drawn to an article in the monthly magazine, *On Being*. It was written by Ben Mason, the pastor of the Aboriginal People's Church in Kalgoorlie, Western Australia. It was entitled *An Open Letter to Australian Christians from a REAL Australian*. As an Aboriginal Christian leader, Ben wrote of the sense of disappointment when white Christians struggled to live Jesus' prayer in John 17:21 *'That they may be one.'*

Ben dreamed of a different future.

Yet having come from different cultures, there must be a common ground to work and worship in Christ.

Ben implored his readers to take hold of *the privileges and responsibilities in Christ to love one another, not only in theory, but in a practical way.*

Amongst his seven practical suggestions one dot point stood out. He suggested

- inviting Aboriginal Christians to your homes.

I put the article down. I felt an unusual connection with the author even though we lived in different worlds both culturally and geographically. I needed to respond. I showed the article to Marg.

'I need to write to Ben and thank him for his open letter.'

Marg gave a reassuring smile. She was always happy for me to reach out to others beyond my contained world, and even more so to reach out to an Aboriginal Christian.

The next day a letter to Pastor Ben Mason was on its way to Kalgoorlie. In it I introduced myself and expressed my appreciation for his letter. I told him we were school teachers and attended our local Anglican Church. I mentioned our desire to enter into some form of missionary service. I finished off the letter with an invitation for Ben and his family to come and stay with us should they ever visit Victoria.

One day, tired from a day's teaching, I collected the mail from our letter box. I turned it over and read on the back the name and address of the sender. It was from Ben Mason.

14/7/77
Dear Brother Barry,
Greetings in the name of our Lord Jesus.

As I scanned the letter my heart beat stronger.

> *Thank you brother for your letter ... It was a source of strength and encouragement to Bernice and myself to press on in the Lord.*

> *... Please be assured of a welcome should you ever come over and visit us. We have a big house which we are renting from the Anglican Church.*

Ben then addressed the past hurts experienced by Aboriginal people from the negative attitudes of whites, by calling on the power of forgiveness.

> *... We as Aboriginal people must not commit similar sins by taking a negative attitude towards our white brethren for the past, but we must be willing to forgive each other for Christ's sake. All that we do must be for His Glory.*

I sat silently moved by the radical upside down kingdom that Jesus ushered in. Ben was talking about Aboriginal people forgiving white people, and vice versa because our lives must be for His Glory.

I read on. Ben mentioned that in ten days' time he will be in Melbourne sharing on a panel at Bentleigh Baptist Church with Mr Ian Viner, the Federal Minister for Aboriginal Affairs. He concluded,

> *Thank you both for your kind offer of facilities. Lord willing any time I am in your state I will make every effort to come and see you.*

I reasoned that perhaps Ben and his family had already crossed the long expanse of the Nullarbor. They could turn up any day.

I told Marg the news as soon as she arrived home from teaching at Kyneton. She was delighted. The fact that we lived in a small two-bedroom house and had limited space was immaterial. The Dreamer penned an immediate response in his journal,

> *Praise God for the letter from Ben Mason. The possibilities in God's service are limitless ... God we desire your leading. Praise Jesus for all things – life is really beautiful.*

A couple of days later, we arrived home in the late afternoon to find a parked station wagon with suitcases tied to its roof in our drive way. Ben and Bernice and their five children emerged from the car. We greeted each other as old friends.

Marg was prepared. She had asked friends from church if they could stay in their spare rooms. By the time darkness set in, our friends, the Mason family and ourselves were all sharing a hot meal together on a cold Victorian winter's night. However, there was one complication with the timing. The following day, Marg and I were registered to attend a Christian conference in Melbourne organised by charismatic Uniting Church ministers Dan Armstrong and Harry Westcott. The simplest solution was to invite Ben and Bernice to join us while their children stayed with our friends. They agreed. We arrived at the Dallas Brookes Hall to a packed auditorium. As the music started, people worshipped God together with their hands raised. Ben and Bernice stood beside us taking in the surroundings and the atmosphere. Unbeknown to us Ben was choosing to put himself outside his comfort zone. His Christian tradition had taught him to be suspicious of charismatic Christians. Our friendship and our shared hospitality allayed enough of those fears for him to come. He warmed to the teaching and experience of worship. After the conference we returned to Ben and Bernice's comfort zone, spotting koalas at Hanging Rock, sharing stories and enjoying each other's company.

Some years later Ben told us that this visit prepared him for what was to happen four years later. In the late '70s the Holy Spirit swept through Elcho Island in Arnhem Land and in the following years on through various Aboriginal communities including Central Australia. Ben Mason became a significant leader in this movement.

The ease of the visit from Ben Mason and his family reignited in Marg something that was close to her heart but which she had put aside when marrying the Dreamer. Through her teenage years Marg had wondered if God might call her to work alongside Aboriginal Christians. This motivation saw her take Aboriginal Studies as a major at Teachers College with a self organised study trip to Alice Springs. If she remained single, teaching always had the potential to take her further along this road. With marriage she put that dream aside, at least for the time being. Now as she saw her husband connecting with Ben and experiencing the delight in getting to know the Mason family, she dared to dream again.

By offering hospitality to strangers, the missionary flame burnt brightly in Marg and a spark was lit in me. Our world had been expanded by our friends from Western Australia and it confirmed a death blow to the possibility that we would spend our life teaching in the Victorian Education system. What was next for us we were unsure, but change was in the wind.

We checked out teaching positions in various Aboriginal communities around Australia, even as far afield as Coolgardie in Western Australia. However, the more we thought about it, the greater was our growing realisation that we were unprepared for what was ahead. I was particularly aware of my lack of Biblical knowledge. What started as an *unsettledness* in the status quo stirred by indigenous issues and new Aboriginal friends morphed into something much more. We decided to resign from our teaching positions at the end of the year and apply to study at a Bible College.

It was quite unexpected and it was not going to be easy for others to understand. We both enjoyed teaching and the opportunity to invest our efforts into young lives. We were setting ourselves up financially for the future and there was no personal stress or pressure pushing for change. On the contrary we were very content and happy with our lot in life and that was evident to those around us.

15

A Day Of Reckoning

Location:	Lancefield
Date:	1977
Event:	Resigning from teaching

We counted down the 200 kilometres of the trip from Lancefield to Leitchville for Joe's 50th birthday. Our Valiant that had recently begun giving us some difficulties, was running smoothly as we headed on past Echuca with 50km to go. In high spirits, Marg and I broke out in song,

Thank you Lord for this fine car (X3)
Right where we are
Hallelujah, Praise the Lord (X3)
Right where we are.

It was then that a massive thump was heard from the back of the car. The vehicle slowed and began to labour. Its day of reckoning had arrived 40 kilometres short of the farm. On our honeymoon the garage mechanic had told us emphatically, 'I wouldn't trust the car to get you back to Victoria. Replace it as soon as you can.'

Fifteen months had passed and it was still our car. We looked at each other and instantly agreed on our course of action. Nothing had changed. We would keep on thanking Jesus for this fine car, thumping noise or not, all the way to the farm. And it did thump and labour as we sang and drove on slowly, eventually limping down the driveway to the farm just as the party was starting.

It was a joyous event with my former cricket mates ensconced around a beer keg and longterm friends on the front verandah telling stories and reliving our victories. Phyllis was busy in the kitchen and making sure our guests were well fed. Everyone knew everyone else, and had done so for a long time. Eventually Herb Alpert and the Tijuana Brass filled the lounge room from His Masters Voice record player. With a few beers under his belt Joe was unstoppable on the dance floor, while Phyllis maintained all the decorum of a ballroom dancer. As the night made its way towards morning, guests came one by one to thank Phyllis for her hospitality before they headed towards their cars shouting back farewells to Joe. It was a perfect night amongst neighbours and friends.

Next morning over a leisurely breakfast I raised the topic of our car. 'Our old Valiant is dead. It won't get us back to Lancefield,' I said.

Joe weighed up the statement and found his own solution, 'I'll give the local dealer a call. He sometimes has a couple of second-hand cars in his yard. I've just bought a tractor off him so I think he owes me a deal.'

The call was made and Joe declared the problem solved. 'He has a three-year-old Toyota Corona that has just been traded in. Excellent condition, one owner and only driven around town.'

Marg and I looked at each other. That was exactly the model we had in mind. This was Joe's territory where deals were closed by a handshake and transactions are monitored over a life time.

'Stay in the car,' he told me as we limped into the dealer's yard in the old Valiant. Joe was ready to make the deal and he wanted no distractions. Local businesses were built on loyalty that relied on finding common ground. The deal was done within five minutes without inspection of either vehicle and cemented with a handshake at the door. How he managed to get $800 for the old Valiant I will never know. The mustard-coloured Corona was perfect for us. Joe had delivered again for the impractical Dreamer.

Milking the cows that evening provided an ideal context for a potentially difficult conversation. There was always a cow to divert your attention when needed but enough small interludes where conversation could be shared and mulled over. I put it as innocuously as I could in what I thought was a matter-of-fact tone.

'Joe, I have been thinking about going to Bible College to study. I don't really know a whole lot about the Bible and I want to know more.'

Joe took the milking machine off a cow nearby, let it out of the bail as another cow followed in to be milked. At the next break in the milking he summed up his thoughts.

'It won't put food on the table. That sort of study is like a hobby. You should cement your career first, buy a house, and look after your family. That is your first responsibility.' Both Joe and I went back to milking giving time for the comments to settle.

At the next interlude Joe, perhaps recognising that this was no longer a son to be told what to do but an adult to be reasoned with, offered his best effort at a conciliatory way forward, 'If you really want to do it, then do it later in life after you've raised your children.'

The Dreamer said little in reply. He respected Joe's advice. It was both fair and reasonable. Joe was satisfied that he had put a good case and once again felt he had rightly directed the Dreamer in the way that was best for him, his wife and future family. Dreams rarely pass the *reasonable* test, and they didn't pass this one!

It had been a big weekend for all. Before we left, Phyllis suggested that I should speak with my school principal before I made any silly decisions. She was sure his advice would side with hers and ensure her son didn't throw away his career.

For Marg and I the pros and cons were equally balanced. We were of a generation that believed in following our dreams but respected our upbringing and the need to dig into the soil and establish our career and home. But the pros were not all about passion. It was also logical. If an education degree was foundational to being a teacher, we reasoned that a few years studying the Bible was foundational to living life itself.

There were two major hindrances that stood in the way of making the final decision. First, I was young and second, it seemed presumptuous. As Joe said, philosophy or theology is for older, more mature people. It looked and seemed like I had tickets on myself. Such an accusation struck at my identity as a country person. It was okay to be reckless at times but never bigheaded.

We heard Barry Chant, who had just founded Tabor College in Adelaide, was guest speaker at a weekend church camp not far from Lancefield. It was too good an opportunity to miss. Tabor was one of the Bible Colleges that we were attracted to. We joined the Saturday morning session with a small gathering of about 50 people. Barry began his meeting in an unusual way. He said,

'Before we start I would like to give a Scripture verse for each of you who has joined the camp today. I am trusting the Holy Spirit to give me the verse so I prefer to do this when I know nothing about you. If you are new today just raise your hand.'

Marg and I both raised our hands. He did not know us and we did not know him. There was nothing to lose. When it came to our turn, Barry asked our names then followed by asking me a simple question. 'Do you know what your name means?'

'No,' I replied.

'Well I think it is important for you right now. It means to be as straight as a spear or an arrow, and head straight for the mark neither deviating to the left nor the right. The verse I have for you is 1 Timothy 4:12, *Don't let anyone look down on you because you are young.*'

He paused then asked, 'Does that have any relevance for you?'

I nodded, silently amazed at its precision.

He then gave Marg 'Luke 1:37, *With God nothing is impossible.*'

■ Marg recalls

> Barry's word was really clear to me. My verse laid to rest my concern about my ability to conceive. It was something I had kept to myself and it showed me how much God knew and cared for me.

The principal of Lancefield Primary School was a man I respected. Peter was a career educator who shared a love for children. He was also a warden at the Anglican Church where we attended. We were colleagues and family friends. When I asked his thoughts on us resigning from teaching he shared his advice from personal experience.

'The longer you stay teaching the harder it will be to leave the security of a weekly income. Once you start a family and get a mortgage it will nearly be impossible for you to do what you plan.' He went on, 'If you don't do what you want to do now, while you are young, you might find yourself trapped.'

I immediately understood the message. This decision would not get any easier with the passage of time, it would only become harder. It was now or never. His answer confirmed what we were thinking deep down.

My school principal was not the only one advocating a radical decision. Father Harry, who now preached from the aisle and not the pulpit with a sparkle in his eye and a contagious passion for Jesus, put it this way, 'I was made a Christian when I was baptised as a baby, and I became one last year.' The Holy Spirit had surprised Harry late in his years as an ordained clergyman. Harry was certain that Anglican ordination was the road for me.

The altercation with Joe was short and to the point. He and Phyllis called in for a short visit on their way back home from a visit to Melbourne. I took the opportunity to tell them of our decision.

'I have decided to resign and go to Bible College next year.'

The shock was too much. Joe exploded,

'What do you think you are doing, you idiot! If you are going to do that then don't you bother coming home.'

His outburst was directed fully at me, not at Marg. Marg was immediately worried. She did not like conflict and this was serious. I was silent, holding my thoughts to myself. I interpreted his rebuke as coming out of concern but delivered in anger. In the same situation as a father, I would give the same advice only perhaps not delivered with the same trademark directness. Joe was once again trying to knock the Dreamer out of me to protect me (and my family), from self-inflicted harm. His declaration 'not to bother coming home' was for effect. I knew Joe and Phyllis' home was always open to us and always would be. Besides the front door of the farm house was never locked.

As Joe drove away, he did not know how closely I was marching to a different drum. If he did, he may have understood. My future was now directed by the Living Word who spoke the world into existence. The words to the song *I have decided to follow Jesus* had become my personal anthem and the embracing challenge, *though none go with me, still I will follow.*

I applied to Ridley College just as applications were closing. It was accepted. However apartments on campus for married couples were already full. The principal mentioned an advertisement he'd just received for *house parents* at a halfway house run by Brunswick Uniting Church as a possible solution to our need for accommodation. We applied and to our surprise we were accepted for the position. We found out later that no one else had applied!

What we didn't know was that we were embarking on the biggest culture shock of our lives. We traded a small country town where I walked to school, walked to the newspaper shop, walked to the cricket ground and walked to church, for the foreign world of inner-city Melbourne with its hustle and bustle and clanging of trams along Sydney Road. We traded quiet nights preparing for our next day's class for five young men escaping dysfunctional homes, juvenile prison, or life on the street. We traded control of our private life for an unpredictable public spectacle. And at Ridley, I traded our everyday rural language for Greek terms and previously unheard-of theological discourse. And then in a very short time the underbelly of society came to our door. We barely survived *the pressure cooker* that was our first year in Melbourne, but it was a learning experience never to be forgotten, and even came to be treasured.

A DAY OF RECKONING

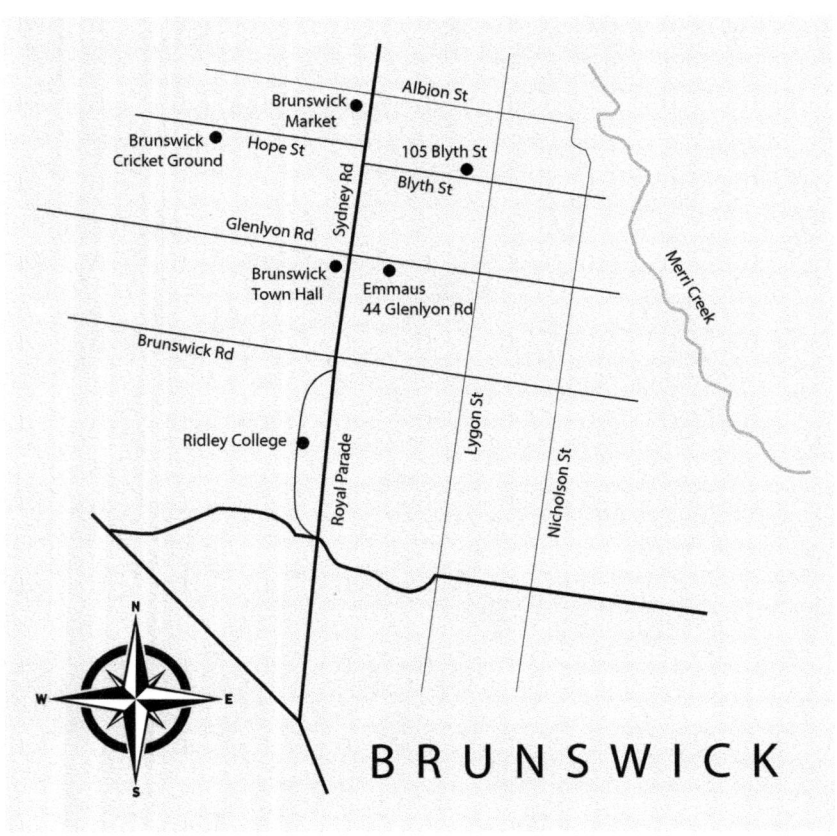

16

Hidden Dreams Of A Hitman

Location: Emmaus Halfway House, Brunswick
Date: 1978
Event: Unexpected drama

The Dreamer was enjoying his daily refuge of a long hot shower that cleaned the body and stimulated the mind. Marg knocked and opened the door interrupting my next random thought.

'A man is here in the lounge wanting to talk to you. I can't look after him as I need to get on with cooking dinner.'

I quickly finished my shower, dressed and headed to the lounge room. There stood a well-built man in his early 30s, smartly dressed in a suit: not the usual scruffy teenager who frequented our place. He introduced himself as Allan. That was easy. Same name as my father. He asked if we could speak in private. The only private place in the house was our bedroom. We went in and sat on the end of the bed. He spoke first as someone on a mission. He looked me in the eye and asked, 'Are you a Christian?'

'Yes,' I replied.

The reason for this question became clear as he briefly filled me in on his situation. 'I have just got out of prison. I shared a cell with *a lifer* who was a Christian. He told me if I was ever in trouble and needed to trust someone then go and find a Christian.'

He paused and looked at me before asking, 'Can I trust you?'

I nodded.

He took a folded single sheet of paper from his coat pocket, paused for a moment, then handed it to me.

'Could you read this note?' he asked.

In my hand I held a scribbled note on unlined paper. I read it in silence.

> *I am planning to rob a bank. The reason is to get out of the mob. If I rob the bank and give money to the Boss it will show I am serious about starting a new life. I just want to live a normal life.*

I finished reading and calmly handed the note back.

'Sorry I can't accept this note. I can't help you.'

It was not the response he was expecting. His whole body stiffened as he sprang to his feet, poised for action. He was no longer asking but demanding.

'Why can't you accept it? I was told I could trust a Christian. That was obviously bullshit. You can't trust anyone.' I held his gaze and responded with all the authority I could muster.

'I can't accept the note because you have just made me an accessory to a crime. If I keep this note I am as guilty as you are. You can't walk in off the street, hand me this note and think I can just go along with it.'

As my reasoning sank in, I could see him slightly relax. I went on, 'If you want to tell me your story, you can stay for dinner and we can talk later.'

We talked into the evening as I weighed up every word to make sense of the note. The question swirling in my head was, 'Is he who he says he is?'

As his story unfolded it became more improbable yet he told it with conviction.

'My own father was killed on the wharfs when I was young. The mob is all I know. I became a *hit man* which is why I finished in gaol. I was sentenced for 14 years but was released in seven years. The mob paid someone off to get me out as part of an early release scheme. While in prison I shared a cell with a lifer who had become a Christian. I then got to thinking I don't want to carry a gun all my life and always be looking over my shoulder.

This is why I am here. I have got to do something to show the boss that I just want out and I am not setting up my own business.'

I asked, 'There must be another way for doing that other than robbing a bank? I can't see how that helps.'

Allan thought for a while then added, 'It might work if I present the boss with a machine gun.'

'Well, a machine gun is a better option than robbing a bank,' I responded with more enthusiasm than it deserved. 'Excuse my ignorance, but can you actually get a machine gun in Brunswick?'

'I reckon I could.' Allan responded as if it was as easy as buying vegetables at the Brunswick Market.

Throughout the night we came at the problem from different angles. Around midnight while sitting in his suite in the Victoria Hotel in Little Bourke Street I made an offer

'I have $800[1] in our bank savings. If that will help with the purchase of the gun you can have it.'

I waited for his response.

'That will help,' he replied.

From that moment I was convinced he was a fraud. When I got home I filled Marg in on my plan. I explained, 'I have agreed to meet him tomorrow at 10am at the front of the Brunswick Town Hall. The plan is to draw $800 from our account to give it to him so he can purchase a machine gun. He says the machine gun will convince the Boss he is not setting up a racket in competition. But I think he is a fraudster. His story does not add up, so at 7am we are driving to the Criminal Investigation Bureau (CIB) in Russell Street to report him. They can nab him when he turns up to meet me. That will take one more con artist trying to take advantage of Christian compassion off the street.'

It was right on 7am when we pulled up outside Russell Street CIB and went in. Our brief story to the lady at the front desk was sufficient for us to

---

1. Equivalent to $4,000 in 2023

be led into a small office. We were seated in chairs in front of a desk when a CIB officer walked in and welcomed us.

'Tell me again what you have to report,' he said warmly. When I had finished my story and given my assessment he agreed, 'It does sound like a con job. We will pick him up when you meet with him.'

A second officer entered with a large A4 folder. He placed it down in front of us and casually said, 'Before you go could you look through this folder to see if you recognise the person?'

The officers went about their business as I perused each photo. One face suddenly caught my attention. He was remarkably like the gentleman with whom I had spent several hours the previous night. I tentatively told the officer, 'I think that's him.'

Suddenly mayhem erupted around us. The detective called in others and in no time the room was buzzing with activity.

'Can you reconfirm that this is the man?' another senior detective asked.

'Yes,' I replied, 'it is definitely him.'

Listening intently, I was flabbergasted by what I heard. The name I knew him by was an alias. He was connected to the notorious gang involved in the 1970 Mayne Nickless robbery, the largest heist at the time in Australian criminal history. He was under surveillance since he was released from Long Bay Gaol a few months previously. They had monitored him when he flew from Sydney to Melbourne and followed him from the airport to St Kilda. Two weeks ago he suddenly disappeared.

They were puzzled by my story and unable to tie the threads together. The detective exclaimed, 'Why would he turn up at someone's place in Brunswick. It simply does not make any sense. What is he up to?'

The Dreamer thought he knew the answer. Just maybe he wanted to get out of the mob. Just maybe he arrived at our place because he *was* looking for a Christian he could trust.

The detectives plotted their next move. A surveillance team would be immediately dispatched to the Victoria Hotel. They turned to me, 'Do you remember the room number?'

'No I don't,' I replied, 'but I think it was the fifth floor.'

A phone was thrust into my hand with the dial tone already ringing.

The officer gave me direct orders, 'Ask the receptionist to put you through to his room. Tell him you won't be meeting him this morning.'

'Victoria Hotel. May I help you?' came the pleasant voice from the other end of the line.

I took a deep breath, 'I am wanting to contact Allan J. Could you please put me through to his room?' My mind was racing. I still had no idea what I would say once he took the call.

Half a minute later the receptionist was back on line, 'I'm sorry but we don't have a gentleman staying here by that name.' I almost shouted *hallelujah!*

Without pausing the officer outlined the next course of action.

'Come with me and identify the room. Once you have done that it will be over for you. We will take care of it. You can go back home as if it never happened.'

Once back at Emmaus, Marg and I both took deep breaths. It was not clear to us what our next move should be. I considered the police advice and understood why it was given. I recounted the events of the past twelve hours. Most of this man's story was true though not all of it. What weighed on my mind were his words, '*I was told I could trust a Christian.*' If I abandoned him now it was proof this was not the case.

I said to Marg, 'I think I will still go and meet him at 10am. What do you think?'

Marg put the decision back on me, 'If you think that is what God wants you to do then you should do it.'

'What a gutsy wife,' I thought. 'She trusts God enough for me to meet an underworld hitman with unknown consequences.'

'I am going,' I replied.

As I prepared to leave, a friend of Marg's from Ridley dropped by for a casual visit. Perfect timing. Marg had someone to share the story of the knock on the door, the note about robbing the bank, the money for the machine gun, and the chaotic events of the morning. Then perhaps the question, of all the doors in Sydney or Melbourne, 'Why did he knock on ours?' Together they talked and prayed for my safety and for God's intervention.

- **Marg recalls…**

    The first thing that Allan told me the night before when I had answered the front door bell, was that the lady from the church up the road had sent him to us because we were Christians. Her husband was out at the time and she was home with their young children. So right from the start I felt there was an authenticity to his story and I didn't think that the risks to Barry were too high. I trusted his judgement but I certainly felt a lot better for having good company, to share the story and pray while he was gone. I saw Gill's timely arrival as a special gift from God for me.

As I approached the established rendezvous point outside Brunswick Town Hall, I saw the hitman pacing at the corner and looking in different directions. I tried to minimise in my mind the risk I was facing. He likely carried a gun, but I surmised he would not waste a bullet on me. I resolved to tell him the truth and see what happens next.

As I crossed Sydney Road, he turned towards me, his face etched with tension. Without greeting him I said, 'Sorry mate but I have just *dobbed* you in to the police.' The verbal interaction came in quick fire.

'What the hell have you done? I was told I could trust a Christian,' he yelled at me.

I shouted back, 'Yes and I should trust a con artist. You give me a false name, half a story and think I should believe you.'

He began walking away, yelling at me. I followed him, raising my voice, 'Tell me half a story like you did and of course any right-minded person would go to the police.'

After a couple of hundred metres the yelling back and forth was exhausted. We walked for a while not saying anything and not going anywhere in particular. As the steam settled, I asked him, 'Do you want to talk? I am still here to help.'

He nodded. 'Let's find a coffee shop.'

He insisted on sitting in a chair facing the front door with me between him and the entrance. He said it was just in case someone came gunning for him. He was tense, his eyes scanning the scene, darting to and fro.

'This is how my life is,' he said. 'Every moment of the day I have to be watching in case someone is coming for me. This is why I want out.'

For the first time I saw and felt firsthand what he was talking about. He did not ask for it but I offered it.

'Is the $800 in my bank account still useful to you?'

'It could help,' he replied. 'I don't know exactly what the machine gun will cost or if I can get one.'

'You can have it,' I replied, 'but under a couple of conditions.' He waited to hear what they were.

'I want a signed declaration from you that you borrowed the money. It needs to be backed up by your signature and a finger print. If you are willing to do that I will loan you the money.'

I was expecting a counter argument but I got none.

'I will do that,' he said quietly.

An hour later in my wallet was a photo of my new friend taken in a photo booth. It was attached to a statuary declaration form from the post office with his signature and fingerprint confirming a loan of $800. We parted company at the bank with my money in his pocket and his personal details in mine. The exchange was done.

Marg's friend had left by the time I arrived home. We sat close and enjoyed the quiet of each other's company. There was not much to say. Normality never felt so good.

That day, an hour before midnight, the doorbell rang. A doorbell at that hour of night in *a halfway house* was rarely good news. One of the young men in the house answered the door. I could hear footsteps coming down the hallway followed by a tap on our door. I opened it, and there stood the jubilant and smiling face of Allan J – or whatever name he was going by now.

'It worked,' he said. 'I am free. I no longer need to carry a gun.'

He perched himself on the end of our bed as if it was his own and told us the events of the day, the details of which are best left out of this book. I listened with doubt about the optimism he shared. Forty-five minutes later we shook hands. He walked away out of our lives and into the night. I had no expectation that we would see him again.

Eighteen months later I picked up the phone and was surprised to hear a voice that I still remembered well.

'It's Allan here mate. I am doing okay.'

'That is great!' I said, not knowing if it was true or not.

And as if to read my thoughts he added, 'And I don't need to carry a gun anymore.'

'Just wanted to let you know I am okay and thanks for helping.'

'Thanks for ringing,' I replied, 'and all the best'.

He hung up the phone. He was gone. That was the last time I heard from him.

The practical man of the soil was challenged by the events. Was it about being Jesus' representative?

Was it about learning to let go of our finances?

Was it about conquering fear?

Was it about something that had nothing to do with me? There must be reasons and lessons to learn.

But Jesus didn't answer my questions. I simply received an assurance that I had done okay. The Dreamer understood some things are best left as a mystery even when you want an answer. Neat packages and clear answers are sometimes out of place.

17

Entrenched In The Soil

Location: Emmaus Halfway House, Brunswick
Date: 1978
Event: Inner suburbs culture shock

The first year in Melbourne found us in an environment where young men's dreams were more often shattered than made. One of our young men got drunk, became violent and physically threatened me. I wrestled him to the floor and held him down. He struggled, spat in my face and cursed me until the police arrived.

It was not the first time he had threatened me. He broke the *no alcohol* and *no violence* rule more than once. I asked him to find other accommodation, which he did. However, he still liked to visit after work and always received a warm welcome. One night he went back to his lodgings, got into an altercation with an older man who died as a result. He was charged with manslaughter. He did not need to find another place for accommodation. We visited him in Pentridge Prison.

Another hardworking resident lost his savings from illegal gambling. The curse was pinball machines at a nearby café in Sydney Road. This event would previously have sent him back on the streets and destitute except our house was still home for him. His hope of independent living remained in jeopardy because of this addiction.

Another of our young men feared reprisal from a bikie group and sought our protection should they show up. However, with him it was hard to know if it was in his mind or based on fact. His underlying insecurity acted itself out by being loud, aggressive and clambering to be the centre of attention.

When any of the men lost jobs, new ones were difficult to find for unskilled workers. It was in the early days of the decline of the manufacturing industry in Melbourne. They went to job interviews with over inflated hopes only to have them dashed. Their conversations were bare-boned and consumed by immediate needs. Big dreams only extended a few weeks into the future. This was our home and world we lived in. A home where dreaming was a forlorn luxury. It was all soil and with that the Dreamer struggled. Personally and spiritually I often felt hemmed in by the concrete and the crowds that surrounded me.

Marg survived by embracing the needs of the people around her. Marg was enlivened not by dreaming of new futures but by being a doer and carer of people. She held the household together and extended her borders to include neighbours, shopkeepers, and whoever crossed her path. The canvas she saw God in and drew pleasure from was a canvas full of people of all colours, ethnicities and walks of life.

The canvas that I found God in and gave me life was more often a blank canvas waiting to be drawn on. As amazing as the year was, and the experiences it brought us, it was not sustainable. The canvas was full.

Marg and I came home late after one of our rare nights out together. We had little time to appreciate the evening. The boys had an out-of-control time of fun in our absence. Toilet paper littered the rooms, chairs were in disarray, and an assortment of clothes and objects that could be hurled at each other lay where they had fallen. Perhaps these young men thought they would clean it up in the morning but I didn't give them a chance to explain. My fuse was lit.

I pulled each one of them out of their beds and demanded that they clean up the mess now. They had seldom seen this look in my eye. I was not to be crossed. In silence they did as required and when they had brought enough semblance of order they retreated to their rooms. I also retreated to our room still not in a mood for consoling anyone, nor myself.

Next day Marg and I took ourselves away for some space. We had the key to a friend's house for such an occasion. When they came home to find us there they prayed with us. For the first time in my adult life I hid my head in my hands and wept. I thought of all that Marg had given and gone through, and the pain of being a father and mother, a brother and sister to *rejected* teenagers trying to find their way in the world. The tears cleared the fog and released the pain. We returned an hour or so later to Emmaus a place that had become our home. The household was back to its normal loud self. All had been forgiven.

There was much that we loved about our home. Every night we sat around the dining table eating together, animatedly talking about the most trivial subjects and occasionally the meaning of life. There was always someone to join you for a game of billiards, or an extra seat at the table for friends and visitors. We especially enjoyed Geoff's company one night each week. He brought some semblance of normal conversation. In many ways we were all enriched but it was time to close *Emmaus Halfway House*. Together we discussed what each one's next step might be. One by one new accommodation was found. Hope for a better future remained. The pitfalls of life still lurked.

Our move into the semi-detached house at 105 Blyth Street, one block north of *Emmaus*, came with much anticipation. I needed time to dream again. Marg needed a place to make into *her* home along with opportunities for two-way relationships where she could receive and not feel like she was always on the giving end. The small backyard was soon graced by a rockery and veggie garden. The extra bedrooms left opportunity for guests. One of the young men came with us for a short while until he found his feet. It was warm and cosy and ideal for putting life back on a more stable course. We replaced random visits with a Friday night open house where soup or pasta was always on the stove. People came and went at their leisure one night of the week rather than any night of the week. Marg and I led a home group that was not too dissimilar to Christian Fellowship at Teachers College, only a slightly older version. At its essence was hospitality, shared meals, Scripture and prayer. It became our church. Over the following two years half a dozen people made our home a place to temporarily lay their heads, to gather their thoughts and dreams before moving on elsewhere.

Creating home allowed us time to breathe again and for the Dreamer to dream again. The storm clouds had passed as we enjoyed some time in the sunlight. The Spirit moved with awe and reverence at the Easter Camp at Ocean Grove touching lives and showing us his love. We were filled with thanks and to add to the joy Marg became an expectant Mum for the first time.

18

Dreaming Of Cricket

Location: Brunswick Cricket Club
Date: 1979-80
Event: Return to the cricket field

Somewhere in the twilight zone between a deep sleep and wakefulness where dreams came easily, I saw myself walking into the club house of the University Cricket Club. I held my *Shaw and Shrewsbury* cricket bat in my hand for comfort. A group of young men stood nearby in their white cricket trousers and cream, sleeveless, cable knitted jumpers. The tallest of the group looked in my direction briefly but no welcome and no introductions were given. I stood waiting. Eventually one of the group called out in my direction, 'Are you a bowler or a batter?'

'An opening batsman,' I replied.

'We don't need any more batsmen,' he called back. He returned to his conversation.

I had come to test myself in district cricket, the highest grade in Victoria. I had also come to be part of a team. But here in my dream there was no interest in an outsider challenging for a batting position. It was individual interest first and team second. Just as I concluded, *This is not the place for me*, I was pulled into another scene.

I saw myself walking into the Brunswick Cricket Club. I was again holding my trusty *Shaw and Shrewsbury* cricket bat. It was the only thing that indicated I might be a cricketer. In the far corner of the room a group of cricketers stood talking together. A short man, slightly older than the rest, looked in my direction. Without hesitation he broke from the group and walked towards me with an outstretched hand thrust towards me.

'Have you come for a game of cricket?' he asked.

'Yes,' I replied.

'Then come and meet your new team mates,' he said, beckoning me towards the group.

I awoke with a start. The previous week I decided to return to the cricket field after missing a season while living at *Emmaus*. The question that swirled in my mind through the week was not would I play, but where should I play? Now this dream. It was ridiculously specific.

The question that confronted me now was, 'Do I take notice of the dream?'

It might seem automatic to do so, but I dreamed easily in my sleep. Every dream was not a stimulus for action. For me they were just dreams, an unconscious reworking of the mind. There would likely be another one tomorrow night, easily forgotten and immaterial. The only way to find out was to act. I rode my bike down Victoria Street and into the Brunswick Cricket Ground. A number of players were already out training in their cricket whites. I wandered out towards the group of players on the field. An older man dressed in his white cricket gear, broke from the group and came towards me with his hand outstretched and introduced himself.

'I'm Blair Hillhouse, captain and coach of the first eleven.'

'I'm Barry. I'm from the country looking for a game of cricket.'

'You are most welcome to join us. Come out and meet the players.' One by one he introduced me. A warm hand shake came from an older man in his mid 30s.

'Johnny Swanson,' he said.

I recognised the name. Without any fuss or hint of snobbery I was welcomed by a former Victorian State cricketer and member of the Australian Baseball team. With introductions finished, Blair said, 'We have four grades. There will be a place for you. Training starts from 5pm on Tuesdays and Thursdays. See you at the next training session. We train in our whites.'

I rode my bike home in high spirits, skimming across the tram lines. So the dream did mean something. It was so vivid, yet the dream was only about cricket. It added to the mystery of God whom I had chosen to follow. I felt like he had something to do with it. Eight years earlier I had been willing to give cricket up in his name, and now he was saying, 'Go enjoy yourself on the cricket field.'

I was selected as an opening batsman in the Brunswick second eleven for my first match. I had not played in 18 months but the eye was good and the feet were moving. I scored a century not out in the first innings followed by an unbeaten half century in the second innings. It was the sort of batting that normally only happened in my dreams. I was promoted to first grade for the next game as an opennirg batter. The club and my team mates were everything I had hoped for.

We finished the season on top of the sub-district ladder. The first team played the fourth team to go into the grand final. We were up against Dandenong whom we had beaten easily a few weeks before. The first day was washed out. If there was no result we went into the grand final. On the second day the umpires decided to force a result with a significantly reduced overs game on an unplayable wet wicket. It turned the result into a lottery. We lost.

The cricket season started well but didn't finish as I had hoped. But the finish did not diminish the intrigue behind how personally interested God was in all aspects of my life – even where I play cricket!

19

Unto Us A Child Is Born

> Location: Brunswick
> Date: January 1980
> Event: Adding to our family

One year after we moved to Blythe Street our first child was born. The greatest difficulty Rachel ever caused were Marg's labour pains. She was welcomed home and settled in with minimal ripple effect on the household. Sleeping was what Rachel did well and crying remained an unlearnt art for her. She accompanied us wherever we went without a fuss. Granddad Joe and Grandma Phyllis delighted in the daughter they never had, and of course Marg's parents loved their first granddaughter.

I will not tell Rachel's story here except to say that for Marg and I, to join with the Creator in bringing his precious child, and ours, into the world is as profound an experience as a human can have.

■ Marg recalls

The word from Barry Chant two years previously had calmed my anxiety about child birth and allowed me to move on with life and live each day as it came. It was not a difficult pregnancy but it was not an easy labour. My exhaustion was immediately superseded by joy and exhilaration when Rachel arrived. She was God's gift to our family.

A thanksgiving service for Rachel was held in her fifth month. Together with our friends we sang a blessing over her. It was the Prayer of St Francis.

Make Rachel a channel of your peace.
Where there is hatred, let her bring your love.
Where there is injury, your pardon, Lord.
And where there's doubt, true faith in you.

Make Rachel a channel of your peace.
Where there's despair in life, let her bring hope.
Where there's darkness, only light.
And where there's sadness, ever joy.

   Chorus

   Oh Master grant that Rachel may never seek.
   So much to be consoled as to console.
   To be understood as to understand.
   To be loved, as to love, with all her soul.

Make Rachel a channel of your peace.
It is in pardoning that we are pardoned.
In giving of ourselves that we receive.
And in dying that we're born to eternal life.

20

An Oasis

Location: Ridley Theological College
Date: 1978, 79, 80
Event: Theological and Biblical Studies

1978

'Everyone is a theologian,' proclaimed Dr Charles Sherlock. 'The only question is whether you are a good one or a poor one!'

So began my first lecture in theology. Dr Sherlock warmed to his task. Words flowed at break-neck speed. Not ordinary everyday words but words that came from a language not my own. He spoke of the *parousia* here, and the *eschaton* there, assuming a vocabulary in his hearers that had never been heard on a football or cricket field, a cattle sale-yard, or a pub anywhere in Australia. Fortunately, I was hidden away at a desk at the back of the lecture room. I was hoping no question would come my way. I had little idea of what he was talking about. The coffee break could not come quickly enough.

As the weeks and months followed, the words *parousia* and *eschaton* and other theological concepts rolled off my lips more easily. I may have started to sound more like a theologian but I doubted that it made me a better one.

1979

We all stood beside our desks as the diminutive Dr Leon Morris, world renown author and evangelical scholar and Ridley College principal, entered the lecture room with his academic gown flowing. I was now in my second year but familiarity had not born contempt. I still felt the privilege of studying at Ridley, and none more so than as a student under Dr Morris.

The only lecture notes he carried was his well-worn Greek New Testament. Once he reached the podium I sat back in my chair along with the other forty or so students. *Doc Morris*, as he was affectionately referred to, opened his Greek New Testament to the letter of Romans and turned to the verse where he had finished his previous lecture. His familiar pattern followed. Word by word, phrase by phrase, verse by verse he translated and annotated the Greek text. No difficult passage was avoided. All were subject to his scrutiny.

His scholarship did not give way to arrogance. His famous refrain was a cautionary note to those students who might err in that direction Frequently he would say, 'Let the text address you, don't you address the text.' He modelled a rare combination of a sharp academic mind while coming to the text humbly and allowing the text to speak for itself.

When Dr Morris indicated that a particular phrase used by Saint Paul was ambiguous for a number of reasons, a fellow student, prone to voicing his own theories, rose and spoke,

'Dr Morris, perhaps what Paul really meant to say here ...' He got no further. A button had been pressed in Dr Morris.

'Young man,' Dr Morris interrupted him in a tone we rarely heard. He had the full attention of the student and everyone else in the class. My ears pricked up. In a measured voice and articulating each word clearly Dr Morris drove home his point.

'We are not interested in what Paul *may* have meant to say. We are interested in *what* the text says. Sit down,' he commanded.

Dr Morris was not defending himself, he was defending the text. No single event better summed up for me, and no doubt my fellow students, Dr Morris' approach to Scripture. The Bible text is not only to be taken seriously, but is not to be tampered with to alleviate apparent inconsistencies and ambiguities. The text received is the text we work with.

1980

When Dr Colin Kruse entered the room we didn't stand but remained seated. Traditions were changing at Ridley since Dr Morris had retired mid-way through the previous year. Dr Kruse's approach was closer to a mentor than a lecturer, an older wiser brother than a father, a co-learner than an authority. The tradition of humble attention to the text however, did not change. For that reason perhaps, I should not have been surprised by Dr Kruse's question, but for a few seconds it stunned me.

In Ridley tradition we were following, verse by verse, both the Greek text and English Revised Standard Version (RSV) of 1 Corinthians. We came to Paul's comment in 1 Corinthians 14:18, *I speak in tongues more than you all*. Dr Kruse paused his lecture and looked over towards me. He asked, 'Barry, could you explain to the class what happens when you speak in tongues? I think you have more idea than me.'

I was sure that Dr Kruse knew more about the meaning and use of the Greek word *glossolalia* than I did. But here he was not asking about academia, he was asking about experience. I did not think that I was obviously *charismatic*, but in an evangelical Anglican College, perhaps it was more obvious than I thought. Like Paul I could say, *I speak in tongues more than you all*.

I replied, 'It's not complicated. I speak in tongues most days using my normal every day voice. I have total control over when I speak. What I don't have control over are the words I speak. I see it as the Spirit speaking about things he understands better than I do. It is that simple really.'

Dr Kruse thanked me for my explanation and continued with the lecture. He was totally comfortable not having all the answers.

Our experience of Ridley was the best of days. Marg and I came as country people and now embraced inner city living. We came as a young married couple and now were parents of Rachel. We came naive about society's ills and now had experienced the underbelly of society. The study of the Scriptures, theology, and church history was all I could have hoped for. New friendships among fellow students enriched our lives. We came with optimism and faith and that optimism and faith remained. It was an oasis. We were unsure of what awaited us beyond the oasis, but it was time to find out.

21

Elimination

Location: Brunswick
Date: 1980
Event: What's next?

We knew God had a paddock for us to play in. We just did not know which one! We proceeded by a process of elimination rather than illumination, and not by drawing lots as we had some years before in seeking teaching positions. The most obvious pathway that needed eliminating was a vocation as an ordained minister in the Anglican Church.

Three years earlier, our minister Rev Harry Elson came to our home in Lancefield to specifically deliver his message. He had gone straight to the point, 'Barry I believe you should consider becoming a priest. Ordination is the highest calling and I think it is right for you.'

Satisfied he had delivered his message, Harry departed leaving me to my own thoughts. On an impulse, I opened my Bible randomly and rested my finger on Ezra 6:7. *Leave this work on the house of God alone.*

'God, does this mean what it appears to mean?' I asked out loud. 'Unless you tell me otherwise, I will *leave this work on the house of God alone.*'

It was not only Harry who made an assumption of where my future might lie. Word was already seeping back to my home town Leitchville. The Leitchville State School Centenary celebration committee needed a clergyman to lead the Sunday morning community church service to be held on the football oval. Aunty Jean, a stalwart of the Leitchville Church of England, suggested they ask Joe and Phyllis Borneman's youngest son. He was studying at Ridley College which was credentials enough for a country town. The request came from Aunty Jean through Phyllis, and I accepted.

On the morning of the service, Phyllis was keeping herself busy in the kitchen while giving me last minute advice.

'Now make sure you mention the community spirit and how people help each other out in hard times.'

My reply was deliberately evasive. 'It's okay, I know what I am going to say Phyllis.'

Phyllis re-opened the subject again as she gave me bacon and eggs. 'You don't want to be too religious. It is about the community spirit that holds us together.'

'It's okay Phyllis, it's all in hand.' I responded in a light-hearted manner.

My reply was not meant to satisfy her. I enjoyed her uncertainty about what I might do or say. Phyllis was about to try one more time to influence her son's thoughts when Joe lifted his head from behind *The Sun* newspaper and added his clear perspective.

'His job is to preach the bloody gospel and nothing else,' he stated plainly. With that he walked out of the kitchen and down to the shed. Phyllis and I looked at each other with equal surprise. After a moment of silence, Phyllis returned to the breakfast dishes. I assured her, 'It will all be okay Phyllis. You won't have anything to worry about.'

Though I didn't see Joe's reaction coming, it fitted a pattern I had seen before. He had a simple motto, 'If you are given a job to do, you do it.' The job of the church was to preach the gospel. He understood that and expected the church to do it.

A large crowd of men, women, children and dogs from the dairy farming district spilled out across the oval. Those who had not sighted the inside of a church for some time stood or sat in their fold-up chairs at a distance. The brave and the church faithful sat in the provided seats closer to the front. Hymns were sung, the Lord's Prayer recited then I was invited to speak. I looked around at a relaxed crowd of every age. I recognised relatives, school friends and sporting mates. They were not here to hang on every word I spoke. It was simply another event in a long string of functions to help people past and present to connect. I shared my story of Jesus meeting a local boy, and preached the gospel as best I could in the local language, on the local sacred space, the football ground.

When the service was over, I was given the honour due of an invited minister. A steady stream of people came forward to shake my hand. Many thanked me for my message. It seemed they knew what I was talking about. I realised that while I had not seen the inside of a church in my growing up years, it was wrong of me to think that disinterest in Jesus defined my local town. A few of Phyllis' longtime friends greeted me with a twinkle in their eye, and went out of their way to compliment Phyllis on her son's efforts. With the family reputation not sullied, and perhaps enhanced, Phyllis left without any of the concerns she had come with. Meanwhile Joe, perhaps satisfied that the gospel was preached, ambled off to catch up with a few mates.

My appreciation for rural communities, and respect for Ron Wood and Harry Elson, meant I could not outrightly reject the possibility of ordination. I needed more confirmation than to rely on a text that appeared at the end of my finger some three years earlier. I wrote to the Bishop of Bendigo Diocese asking for his guidance. Two weeks later Marg and I stood at the front door of the Bishop's home and knocked on the off chance he was home. We didn't have an appointment. We were in Bendigo to attend the funeral of Jeff's father, my friend who had baptised me.

The door opened and a tall man with a friendly disposition stood before us. I immediately felt at ease. 'I am Barry Borneman. This is my wife Marg. I am wondering if you have any time to talk with us?'

'Yes I do,' he immediately responded. 'Come through to my office.'

Conversation was easy. Once he heard of our connection with the Rev Ron Wood, he moved the conversation on in the direction he wanted to go. In a calm and non-judgmental tone he asked, 'Barry, do you speak in tongues?'

It was not a question I was expecting, but not one I was afraid to address. 'Yes, I do,' I replied in a matter-of-fact way.

The Bishop looked directly at me, 'I don't speak in tongues. Is that a problem for you?'

My reply was genuine. 'No, that is not a problem to me.'

He smiled and moved onto his next line of enquiry. In the next hour all that needed to be said, was said. His parting words were delivered with genuine affection. He summed up his thoughts.

'The Anglican Church is a broad church. We need people like you with your background. I will support your application. However, the decision is not mine to make. You will need to go through the Melbourne Diocese Selection Committee.'

I had expected the door to be closed but instead we drove back home from Bendigo with the door open and a Bishop we felt we could work under. The Bishop had moved our dial from a 5% chance of considering ordination, to an even 50% chance.

For me, the Melbourne Diocese Selection Retreat Weekend got underway in the most absurd of circumstances. I just happened to find myself standing with three other men. The two younger men were dressed in black. The much older man wore a purple shirt and white clerical collar. He was a Bishop from Queensland. My dress code was casual. A waitress, carrying a variety of drinks on her tray approached us. 'Drinks gentleman,' she offered.

The three gentlemen took glasses of red wine. I opted for orange juice as a counter culture statement. The shorter man dressed in black made a comment to the Bishop about me being from *Ridley grey* as he looked at my orange juice. He was from Trinity College. I was the odd one out.

Then he turned his full attention to the Bishop. 'Bishop,' he said in his most cultured voice, 'How many times should you genuflect before the altar when taking a communion service?'

I held my composure and refrained from suggesting six, the number of cricket balls bowled in an over.

The Bishop gave the question his full attention and walked his way through the communion service satisfied that he had counted correctly. This set the scene for the young man to show his credentials. 'Bishop,' he said, 'I believe you were one genuflection short when you led communion at St Michael's on Sunday.'

The three of them laughed as they recounted the service. They searched to find the exact spot where the Bishop may have erred. The pleasure found in the conversation beamed across the faces of the two young men.

I downed my orange juice, looked into the bottom of the glass and said to no-one in particular, 'I am ready for another juice.' In reality I probably needed a whisky. Aided by an empty glass I made my departure, totally bemused by what had occurred. It was going to be a fun weekend.

The Bishop introduced himself as we sat across from each other in a small room. Its comfortable lounge chairs simulated the casualness of a fireside chat. I was unsure if he remembered me from the previous day. He opened with a general question, 'As a priest, what do you see as your main role?'

The Dreamer imagined himself back in Leitchville where the community was more likely to congregate at the football oval or at other sporting clubs rather than the church. I paused a few seconds and started, 'It would be important to find a way to connect with the people. They are very suspicious of outsiders in these well-established rural communities. I know this because I come from one. The challenge will be to build enough trust to share Jesus and make a difference. I would probably start helping out with the sporting clubs in town.'

As I answered, my enthusiasm for the challenge increased and I could almost see myself in a small town doing just that. Enthusiasm however, has a way of losing track of time.

The Bishop interrupted me. 'You have been talking about the ministry of a priest for five minutes and not once have you mentioned the sacraments.'

My reply was immediate and uncensored. 'Hang on Bishop! What good are the sacraments if there is no one who believes?' Time was limited and this was not the time for theological debate.

The Bishop graciously let my response go and moved onto a new topic. 'Barry, tell me about your baptism.'

'Well my mate baptised me in his bath.'

He beckoned me for more detail.

'I had been a Christian for about two years but I had not made it to church yet. When I read about baptism in the New Testament I thought I should obey the command. I went to my friend and asked him to baptise me. He said he couldn't find a reason not to. He filled up the bath and I got baptised right then. As it turned out he didn't fill the bath up high enough so I was half-immersed, and half-sprinkled. Best of both worlds.' The Bishop looked perplexed.

'It's okay', I assured him. 'My baptism is good enough for Jesus and I reckon good enough for the church.'

Our interview ended. He had other candidates to interview, including the two young men in black.

Marg joined me on the second day of the two-day selection conference. Late in the afternoon a written assessment from the selection committee was handed to me. It spoke warmly of my vibrance of faith and experience of God but then added an observation that, *Barry is not a child of the church*. It recommended I spend two years working in a local Anglican Church, or with an Anglican mission, to become more familiar with the workings of the church. I could then be considered for ordination again. It was not a closed door nor was it an open door. The evaluation was perfect. It was protecting the church from the Dreamer, and it was protecting the Dreamer from the church. We left the weekend knowing that ordination as an Anglican minister had been eliminated from our next steps.

22

Illumination

Location:	Brunswick
Date:	1980
Event:	An unexpected turn

With ordination eliminated we continued to search out which paddock we were to work in. For the Dreamer the options were many, but for Marg they were more obvious. Aboriginal ministry had been her dream for a number of years. She could always see herself involved, but now she could see a place for her husband as well. She knew that the newly established Nungalinya Bible College in Darwin was advertising for lecturers. She was sure her husband had something to offer with a degree in theology matched by teaching credentials. Before that option had barely been voiced let alone actioned, the unpredictability and impulsiveness that always lurked in the background with the Dreamer set another course.

The Dreamer scanned the Ridley student notice board. An all-day mission event for the coming Saturday caught his eye. A thought lodged in the back of his mind that he should attend. Saturday brought blue sky, sunshine and a gentle breeze on a perfect spring day. The newly-turned soil of the veggie patch beckoned as the spring planting began. Lunch time came and went. It was early afternoon when the Dreamer remembered the mission event. He downed his garden tools, grabbed his bicycle and called out to Marg, 'I won't be long. I want to check something out at Ridley.'

The three kilometre ride to college, down Blyth Street, left onto Sydney Road and merging into Wellington Parade was a daily routine. A hard right into Lever Street, before the Carlton Football Ground, and then left onto the cobbled laneway at the back of Ridley saw me arrive in good time. I leaned my bike up against the brick wall. A small group of students were enjoying an afternoon coffee break in the garden by the old bookshop. I noticed a tall middle-aged man step out of the Stanley Lecture Room. I assumed he was one of the visiting lecturers. I walked directly up to him and said, 'Good day mate! What is happening here today?'

The gentleman responded, 'We are from Wycliffe Bible Translators. He thrust out his hand and said, 'I'm Frank.'

'Hello Frank. I'm Barry. I'm a final year student here at Ridley.'

There was a small pause. I felt a need to fill the space.

'Does Wycliffe have any need for school teachers? My wife and I are both primary-school trained.'

Frank's interest now heightened, he responded enthusiastically,

'I am a teacher myself. I can tell you we have a need for teachers in Darwin and Papua New Guinea right now.'

'Well, we may be interested in helping,' I heard myself say.

'Then let's talk when you're ready. Here are my details.' He handed me his business card.

The transaction was done. It had taken no more than a minute. I jumped on my bike and headed back at full speed the way I had come. I couldn't wait to tell Marg about this bizarre conversation that I dreamed was orchestrated by God. I pulled the bike into the back shed, regained my breath, and headed into the house.

Marg enjoyed the leisurely pace of our Saturdays at home. With another pair of hands around she had the chance to catch up on household chores, and if it was fine do some gardening. Her life as a young mum and a part-time theology student was otherwise full. She was suitably calm when the Dreamer entered the kitchen. Casually he said, 'I just offered for us to go teaching with Wycliffe Bible Translators.'

'You have *what?*' Marg retorted breaking the serenity that up until that moment had engulfed the day. She was completely unimpressed.

'What was the point of completing a three-year theology degree if you're just going back to teaching again?'

It was not a question for answering. It was a statement rejecting the proposition. Marg had seen her husband as a Bible teacher supporting Aboriginal Christians, not as a school teacher albeit in a mission context. This seemed like a complete U-turn.

The Dreamer did not have a logical explanation. His only answer was that he had a hunch that this is what they should do. I rarely used God's name to support a decision and this was no different. I could not categorically say this was God's leading. It may just be the Dreamer and his own imagination. All I could say was it might be God, so we needed to at least give it a chance.

Marg and the Dreamer maintained a wide berth for the rest of the afternoon keeping themselves busy in their own patch of the garden. It was not the time to talk. It was time to process the Dreamer's latest crazy idea.

■ Marg recalls

> *I was totally caught off guard. I was very sure that the new Nungalinya Bible College that had opened in Darwin was our destination. I was so shocked it was a day or two before I was ready to talk about Barry's latest idea.*

Marg's one consoling point was that she was attracted to this man because of the Jesus factor. While this return to teaching did not make sense to her, she was open to the possibility that Jesus could be in it. Little by little the needed assurance came in the following days. She agreed we should explore this direction.

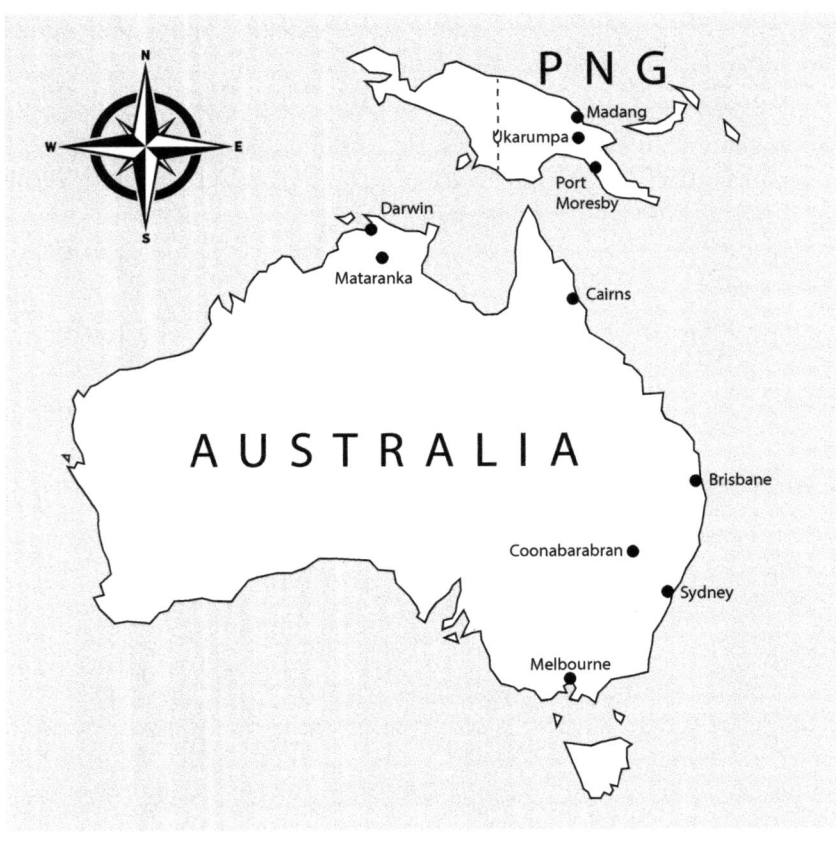

23

No Salary!

Location:	Melbourne
Date:	October-December 1980
Event:	Joining Wycliffe Bible Translators

Ed and Laurel Bentley welcomed us into their interview room with a firm shake of the hand and broad smiles. They immediately put us at ease. Ed and Laurel were legendary Wycliffe pioneers and exuded a faith that was contagious. They lived the Wycliffe motto, 'Nothing is impossible for God.' Ed outlined the options, 'We have two teaching positions that need filling. One is in Darwin at Mararra Christian School. The other is at Aiyura International Primary School at Ukarumpa in the Eastern Highlands of Papua New Guinea. We are happy for you to make the choice.'

Marg and I looked at each other without a clear answer.

'How long have we got to make the decision,' I asked.

'A couple of weeks,' Ed replied. 'But the PNG position is urgent. They would want you there by the first week in January for orientation.'

After the interview, Ed and Laurel prayed that we would know what decision to make. The decision was not clear cut. Taking a teaching position in Darwin appealed to Marg. It brought her closer to the dream of working alongside Aboriginal friends. Her visit to Central Australia at the time of our engagement had continued to fan this flame which had been lit in her teen years. For the Dreamer the lure of PNG was stronger. He would say it was intuitive, a hunch from God, but God may have tapped other reasons lying deep in his subconscious. Phyllis' uncle and an aunt had spent their working life in PNG. Her aunt had worked at the Lae Telephone Exchange and her uncle as a miner, a government patrolman, and general tradesman. Joe's father had gone as a foot soldier to the same country after returning from the campaign in the Middle East. There was something alluring about Papua New Guinea.

After prayer, the idea of teaching with Wycliffe in PNG grew on us both. It felt like a watershed moment. In our Christmas letter we wrote:

> *Though it seems strange to return to teaching after three years of theological training, we have continually felt reassured that this is where God has called us, and though we don't know what the future holds, we have no doubt our experience in PNG will further mould us as servants of Christ and profoundly affect the direction we go.*

Those words proved to be prophetic. Little did we know that this chance encounter, this hunch, would determine the paddock that we would work in for the rest of our working life.

There was one other factor that hung over our decision. Wycliffe did not provide its workers with a salary, or a living allowance, nor travel funds. We were volunteers who covered all our own costs for the labour we provided. In our interview with Ed and Laurel, Ed called it, 'living by faith'. The only catch for Barry, the man of the soil, was that, 'living by faith' was synonymous with living off other people. Asking for handouts was not what a Borneman does. That was called 'bludging'.

My answer to this dilemma was simple. The two-year volunteer work with Wycliffe was not *living by faith* but a self-funded overseas adventure. Many young Australians went to see the world before settling down. We were doing the same. This was helped by the fact that we still had money in the bank. We had not expected this to be the case. The weekly allowance and accommodation provided in the first year at *Emmaus Halfway House* had helped. Driving a delivery truck for six weeks over Christmas holidays helped. An early morning cleaning job at a jeans factory paid for theological books. Marg's occasional catering service, and boarders helped with our food costs. There were specials offered near closing time on Saturdays at Brunswick Market! Our simple lifestyle eased any expenditure pressure.

We reasoned that our savings had been kept for this purpose. I decided the challenge of *living by faith* or *bludging off others* would wait for another day. However we had some friends who knew more about mission than I did and joined us in our adventure by regularly sending finances our way.

Just after sunrise, we said our final good-byes to Marg's Mum and younger sister. Her Dad started the engine, put the car into gear and we headed out of Shepparton for the Melbourne Airport. By the end of the day we would be in Port Moresby, the Papua New Guinea capital. Our itinerary was straight forward. We would take a domestic flight to Sydney then connect to our international flight to Port Moresby. With time to spare in Melbourne, I exchanged our Australian dollars into PNG Kina. We would not be needing Aussie dollars for another two years.

The transfer from the Sydney domestic terminal to the international terminal was more complicated than we had envisaged. By the time we lined up at the Qantas international counter it had already been a long day. Fortunately, Rachel was an easy traveller. She didn't know how to complain. Unfortunately the air traffic controllers had not learnt from Rachel. Instead of actioning our boarding pass the gentleman informed us that the air traffic controllers had called a sudden strike. All international flights were cancelled. The next flight to Port Moresby was scheduled in three days' time. Qantas took no responsibility for passengers on connecting flights. We had to find our own accommodation for those three nights.

The news drained whatever energy was left in me. Our PNG money was worthless in Sydney. We did not have legal tender for a taxi or a hotel. For all my careful planning and independence, the experience of *living by faith* that Ed and Laurel had talked about was upon us much earlier than we anticipated. A silent cry went up, 'God we need your help.'

With our luggage at our feet, a daughter in the stroller and an anxious look on our faces it was not difficult to ask the lady at the Qantas desk to use her phone. We held out hope that the only people we knew in Sydney would answer their phone. Marg reached into her bag, retrieved her phone book and looked up their number. I dialled but there was no answer. Our friends from Lancefield days were not home. There was another possibility. We found the Wycliffe NSW Office in the White Pages. I dialled the number. Again there was no answer. Where else could we ask for help? We sent up another prayer. 'Any ideas God?'

'Mascot Airport! That's it! At least we know where we are. We're in the suburb of Mascot.'

'Why not give a church a call and see if they can help us,' Marg suggested.

I was hesitant. I did not want to call on a stranger. Marg could not see the problem. One more flurry through the White Pages and we found the phone number for the Mascot Uniting Church. I rang the number without a lot of confidence. I heard the click of the receiver being picked up. 'Hello, Mascot Uniting Church.' It was a man's voice.

I replied with more urgency in my voice than I wanted, 'Hello, you don't know me but I need your help.' At that moment I was half expecting the phone call to be terminated, but instead a voice of encouragement followed.

'Go on,' he said in a tone that sounded like he meant it.

'My wife and I are with Wycliffe Bible Translators. We were meant to be on a flight to PNG but we are stranded in Sydney because of the air traffic controllers' strike. I have exchanged all our money for kina and we don't have money for accommodation. Is there any way you can help us?' It was done. I was now a bludger and a beggar!

His answer was immediate. 'No problems. I'd love to help. I'll be around to pick you up in 20 minutes. I'll be in a white van so I have plenty of room for your luggage.'

I got off the phone and gave Marg the thumbs up. 'He is coming to pick us up.' Our tiredness disappeared in a flash. We were young excited adventurers all over again. It was a jubilant, smiling couple and their contented baby waiting at the pickup zone for a white van to appear.

The minister's welcoming response on the phone was matched by a bigger welcome in person. His wife and teenage children were away for a few days visiting family. He was joining them the next day. He had a big empty house to himself with plenty of room for a young family. He also knew Wycliffe. He had previously been a *Flying Bibleman* with the Bible Society in the North of Australia. The fellowship was sweet.

The next morning after a wonderful sleep we rang our friends again. This time they answered their phone. They were more than an hour from the airport but were ready to help. Two hours later, Denise picked us up. Driving back from Mascot to their place we passed the University of New South Wales. It jogged a vague memory in Marg's mind.

'That's where the Wycliffe staff will be. They run a Linguistics School at New College each summer!' Denise turned and drove into the university grounds. New College was not difficult to find. We approached the school administrator and introduced ourselves. He was an administrator by name and an administrator by action. He liked to solve problems. With introductions barely finished he said, 'We have a spare room in the dormitory. You can stay here. I will add your names to the meal list if you like.'

'Please do,' Marg said.

'I will arrange someone to take you to the airport, so you don't need to worry about that.'

It was more than a roof over our head. We were joining a community of like-minded young people studying to be Bible translators, or something similar. Denise was pleased that we had found a home. We deposited our luggage in our room. As Marg settled in with Rachel, I went to explore the surroundings. My eyes were drawn to cricket nets in the distance. I could see the distinctive figure of Australia's new opening bowler Geoff Lawson rolling his arm over in the nets.

The Dreamer pondered this unexpected set of events. Is this what *living by faith* looks like? On the very first day on this adventure, circumstances left us trusting God for our provision. What he gave us was far, far better than what we could have done ourselves even with a pocket full of cash, and I got to see Geoff Lawson limbering up in the nets!

24

New Soil

Location: Port Moresby
Date: 1981
Event: Adventures in a new world

The front gate of the Missionary Guest House was firmly secured. All residents were advised to stay in for the night. New Year's Eve may normally be a cause for celebration on the streets but not in Port Moresby with its reputation for unpredictable revelry. It started slowly with a few firecrackers here and there. As the night progressed the city's noise elevated to a crescendo towards the appointed hour. It seemed the whole town was out walking the streets. Some intoxicated, some not. Some looking for mischief, others at peace. It was our first night in Papua New Guinea and we welcomed the New Year sedately behind those locked gates.

Morning tea time next day, Marg beckoned me over to meet an older couple she was talking with. 'Barry, meet Murray and Joan Rule,' she said.

They warmly greeted me. Then came the invitation, 'We would love to show you the sights of Port Moresby. We have plenty of room in our van,' Murray offered. Marg was excited by the opportunity. Half an hour later, Marg, baby Rachel, myself and Denise, a volunteer Australian high school teacher, piled into their van for the tour.

As we passed the guards and drove through the opened gate Murray informed us, 'We are heading up to shanty town first.'

Shanty town was not where we would have wanted to be the night before. It earned a reputation, rightly or wrongly, as an unruly place and unsafe for outsiders. The further we drove in along a dusty winding road gouged by intermittent flooding, the more it felt like the wrong place at the wrong time. Groups of strong and wild-looking young men stood in front of housing made of corrugated iron and hessian bags. They stared at us as we slowly drove by.

'The Huli are up this way,' Murray said. He pulled the van to a stop on a patch of bare ground and turned off the engine. He called out to a group of young men huddled nearby. It was not English he spoke, or Tok Pisin, but a highland language called Kaluli. The young men immediately looked up. As if under someone's command, they turned and relayed a message further into the bowels of shanty town. A small group of men, women and children emerged, no longer with a look of suspicion but with wide smiles, animated voices and a warm welcome. I did not understand a word of the conversation that followed except I felt the warmth of acceptance.

We got out of the van and followed our new friends into the shade. It was our second day in PNG and we knew this special experience was nothing to do with us. It had everything to do with the power of language and years of service given in love by this legendary missionary couple. Life did not need to be lived behind locked gates.

The following day it was with a mixture of relief and excitement when we saw a small township below us comprising iron-clad roofs and brown dust roads. The pilot pointed in its direction, dipped his wing and circled the town. 'That's Ukarumpa,' he yelled over the engine noise. 'It's 1500 metres above sea level.'

My first impression was its size. It was larger than I expected. Much bigger than my home town of Leitchville. It also sat in stark contrast to the grass-roofed huts of the surrounding villages.

The pilot expertly landed the single engine Cessna on the long, wide airstrip. We stepped out of the plane to be welcomed not by the humidity and heat of Port Moresby but the invigorating temperate climate of the equatorial Eastern Highlands. A small crowd of *expat* onlookers watched from behind the fence, waiting to greet the newcomers. An Australian came up to us and introduced himself.

'Stephen Head,' he said, shaking my hand. 'Who's meeting you here?'

'I don't know,' I replied.

He looked slightly confused. Then he asked, 'Who do you know at Ukarumpa?'

Marg answered, 'We don't know anyone here, except for Denise travelling with us.'

He repeated what Marg said for clarity with a quizzical tone, 'You don't know anyone here?'

We both nodded. Stephen added, 'Amazing! I have never heard of someone coming without knowing at least one person here. Well, it's great to have some more Aussies around. You'd better come to our place for a meal once you've settled in. There'll be a meal roster for you for the first few days so you will quickly get to know people anyway. And being a school teacher, the parents will be keen to get to know you too!'

And so our welcome to life at Ukarumpa began.

25

A Red Account And The Classroom

Location:	Ukarumpa, EHP
Date:	1981-2
Event:	Aiyura International Primary School.

There was a knock on the front door. I opened it and two boys stood before me. The more confident of the two opened the conversation with, 'Hello Mr Borneman, we would like to introduce ourselves. We will be in your grade six class.' I was taken aback for a few seconds before saying, 'It's good to meet you. Come in.' Ten minutes later they left and went on their way satisfied that they had sussed out the new teacher. It was clear this was their classroom as much as it was mine. It was indicative of what was to come as Theology, New Testament Greek, and Church History studies were parked on a back burner and replaced by an old friend.

Before I had time to settle into teaching I was unsettled by an unexpected quandary. As I opened our first monthly finance statement I was not anticipating anything out of the ordinary. I read it, and as the reality slowly sank in. I blurted out to Marg,

'Our account is in the red.' I was confused. 'Didn't we put funds in our Wycliffe account in Melbourne to cover the costs of the first few months?' Marg was more interested in her letter from her mother than a conversation about finances. She brushed me off.

'There has to be an explanation,' she said and returned to her letter.

Next day I made my way to the finance office. I asked the manager,

'Could you explain our finance statement to me and why we don't have any income?'

The finance manager patiently looked at the statement and offered to get back to me later in the week. When he did so, he spoke with an obvious sense of relief on his face which showed also in his voice.

'It's okay,' he said. 'We found your missing funds. Your money from Australia comes to us via the USA. It looks like yours went into the account of a Wycliffe team in South America with a similar name to yours.'

'How long before the money comes through to us?' I asked.

'The funds will be reversed back to the USA at the end of the month, then it will be another month before it is transferred into your account here.'

The mention of the *red account* replaced the short-term shock with a longer-term challenge. In the short time we had been in Ukarumpa, our expenses for food and rent were greater than what we anticipated. With a quick calculation I concluded our savings and small amount of donations from Australia would not be sufficient to meet our financial needs for two years. With no means of earning income in PNG we had no option but to embrace *living by faith* and *trusting God for the impossibl*e whether we were ready to or not.

Jeff Bailey was a knock-about Australian who seemed to have more local friends than he had *expat* friends. He previously had worked as an agriculturalist at the nearby Aiyura Research Station and later in life joined SIL. Jeff was the leader of our Orientation Course. He also initiated community development projects in remote villages.

Jeff came to see us with a straight forward offer. He said, 'I have friends at Aiyura Ag Station going back to Australia for three months. They need someone to look after their house. I think it might suit you since it's just up the road from the school. And a car, veggie garden and a gardener come with the house. Let me know by the end of the week if you will take it.'

The decision to accept the offer was not straight forward. Marg's roots had already gone down. It would mean moving away from Anne, her new Canadian friend who lived just up the road with a daughter Rachel's age. There were potentially increased security risks that came with not living on the mission base, but there were advantages. It was walking distance to the school AND it came without any rental cost.

Anne invited us to join the Bible study group they were enjoying on Wednesday nights. Although we had not been before, Marg stated that these were the people who we would ask to pray specifically to help us with this decision. Towards the end of our first meeting an opportunity was given for prayer. We took it.

As our new friends prayed asking God to make the decision clear to us, a thought came strongly to Marg's mind. Having a car was great, but it was not much use if there was no child seat for Rachel. She decided a car seat was her sign from God. No car seat then we don't go. I was less convinced of its importance as compulsory car seats for children were not the law in PNG.

The next morning two of the ladies who were part of the group who prayed that night, came to our door. They handed a written page to us. Janet explained what had happened.

'Last night, when we were praying for you I experienced something I had not experienced before. God gave me pictures and words directly for you. When we got home I wrote them down.'[1] Marg read the page with tears welling up. God was speaking directly to her.

■ Marg recalls

Each line addressed some aspect of my uncertainty that came with moving house again and living off the mission base. God gave me a peace about it.

With Marg now ready to take the next step I ran down to the Bailey's house. 'Jeff, we would like to take up the offer.'

---

1. We unexpectedly spoke with Janet again 32 years later when on Sabbatical in North England. She told us the experience she had of getting pictures and verses for us was still a vivid memory.

Jeff was delighted. 'By the way', Jeff added, 'they have one of those new-fangled car seats.'

A week later we picked up the keys to the car and to our new home at the Ag Station. Marg placed Rachel in the car seat without a hitch. It was identical to the one we had left behind in Melbourne.

For the next three months we lived simply. The veggie garden met most of our dietary needs. Our money from Melbourne came through. With no rent to pay, our red account quickly corrected itself. We put aside savings for a motor bike for me to ride to school, and for some holiday time later in the year. And there was another added bonus. Because we were walking distance to the school, Rachel, not long having had her first birthday, often came to class with me. The girls took great delight in caring for her and sharing her around as they did their classwork. Rachel became the Grade 6 mascot.

A class of high performing students from seven different countries was the Dreamer's delight. Education became a collaborative effort expanding beyond the curriculum. Together neither student nor teacher shied away from academic pursuit, creative endeavours or simply having fun.

So it was that a science lesson was introduced by a Mad Professor dressed in his night gown, night cap, and long socks who insisted on the students

standing on their desks and being ready to spurt out their latest scientific observation or knowledge when asked. The standard reading curriculum was replaced by books of the students' choice that saw *Tolkien, Watership Downs* in English and German alongside the *Famous Five* enter the grade six reading syllabus. So it was that the school classroom took place for a week at a camp site an hour's drive away where students were immersed in practical maths, screen printing, videoing, and whittling bush shanghais along with the fun of camping and living together.

Simultaneous equations entered the maths curriculum for the most advanced mathematicians, and Aussie Rules football, and cricket for both boys and girls were added to the sports for the year. The word INITIATIVE in large bold writing was strung across the back wall as the class motto for the year. I proclaimed that Initiative gone wrong was better than no initiative at all. So it was that history lessons culminated in 'dress up days' and assemblies became excuses for dramatic plays. In any given week concentrated work of dictation, creative writing, spelling or maths tests could be rewarded with a splash of initiative by either teacher or student. Prime amongst them was the *kidnapping* of the Grade 1 class to the grade 6 room while on their way to the library. After all it was April Fool's Day!

It was in the midst of all this *education* that Marg cried out one night, 'What happens when the ideas run out? I'm exhausted just looking on. The children must be too!' The Dreamer was certainly immersed in the world of children's education but another world was gradually opening up. The parents, wanting to check out the Aussie teacher with his unorthodox classroom, invited us for a meal here, or a door stop conversation there. We heard first-hand about the world these families were immersed in, of Bible translation and literacy among the remote tribes of PNG. The seeds to our future work were being sown.

By the time we returned to Australia two years later, our income and expenditure balanced perfectly. *Living by faith* provided us with not a dollar more nor less than what we needed. It was *manna* from heaven. In our last days at Ukarumpa some friends gave us a generous $200 gift 'to help set up house' when we got back to Melbourne. God was looking after us one step at a time.

26

New Life And New Direction

Location:	Ukarumpa, EHP
Date:	1981-2
Event:	Growing family and illness

The night security guard from the local village was not to be messed with. Each night he patrolled the Ukarumpa streets dressed as a traditional warrior with his bow and arrow poised. No unusual sound, unexpected movement or detail missed his attention. As he passed by our house the front door caught his eye. It was slightly ajar. He pushed the door open slowly and slid through the doorway without a sound. He saw no-one. He heard a groan coming from the end of the passage. His courage did not desert him. He held fast and moved forward ready for any intruder he might find. In a flash he took in the picture. What he saw was not what he expected. A very pregnant young white woman sat hunched over on the toilet. The shock immobilised the warrior for a brief moment. Marg was the first to speak.

'It's okay. My husband has gone to get the nurse,' she explained.

'Sorry miss,' he said. 'The front door was open. I will go outside and keep watch until he comes back.'

The courageous warrior slipped out of the house faster than he came in. I burst into the house not long after, pleased with my efforts. I called out, 'The midwife will be here any minute with a car to take you to the clinic. Leanne is on her way to be here with Rachel.'

The contractions were stronger now. Marg was readying herself for the challenge ahead.

As she slowly moved to the car for the 250-metre ride to the clinic she added, 'You'd better make sure you close the front door.'

Later that morning at 5am a healthy Heidi Ruth was born and was received with much joy. The labour and delivery had gone well. An hour or so afterwards Marg began to haemorrhage. The doctor was summonsed from the Sunday morning service. A drip line to a bag of saline was inserted while a nurse was dispatched to pick up some compatible blood for Marg from the Kainantu Hospital some eight kilometres away. With her blood replenished the danger passed. By late afternoon, less than 12 hours after Heidi was born, Marg and baby were back home to a very excited *big* sister. The Ukarumpa community swung into action. Teenagers came to look after Rachel, meals were delivered, and the nurses continued diligently in their home care. People cared for Marg at a level that would have been impossible in the hurly burly of city life. Over the following weeks she steadily regained her strength.

Two weeks after Heidi's birth, the sight and smells that greeted us at the Wideman's home on Christmas Day lit up our eyes and stirred our digestive juices. Every variation of Christmas delights lay beautifully presented upon the white table cloth. The smell of freshly baked bread filled the air. Our traditional favourites of roast veggies browned to perfection were served along with roast chicken. All was readied for our Christmas celebration. It was time to thank Jesus for his provision, to eat and be merry.

Alas for me, there was no joy in the eating. I laboured with every mouthful, forcing each morsel down out of politeness. The coffee was bitter and the conversations whirled around me in a fog. The short walk back home was tiring. I used the last of my strength to put Rachel to bed while Marg attended to Heidi. I fell down on the bed exhausted. Marg lay down next to me ready for recapping the day's events.

'I'm too tired to talk Marg,' I said. 'I'll need to see the doctor in the morning.'

The doctor ordered a blood test. The diagnosis was confirmed: Hepatitis A. The doctor explained, 'Hepatitis is highly contagious. The virus is transmitted by contaminated food or water, or if you have had direct contact with an infectious person. We need to locate the source of this infection if we can. Have you been anywhere different in the last month?'

My memory immediately took me back to a local village feast. I could see the *mumu* we had eaten from with its delicious slabs of pork, sweet potato, corn and bush greens all dripping with fat. The food was taken from the ground oven, placed onto banana leaves and brought to the welcomed guests. I remembered the privilege I felt to be part of this great crowd farewelling a missionary Lutheran family. Their daughter Katja was one of my students, yes the reader of *Watership Downs* in German and English. Rachel and her friend Joanna, as usual were the centre of attention and were whisked away by the young ladies. It left us free to enjoy the occasion, to eat freely and relish each flavour.

'Yes I know where and when I picked it up,' I replied.

'Good. We will need a list of people you have had contact with since then. For now go home and rest. There is no treatment. The liver is affected but it will heal itself within six months. Just rest and you will make a full recovery'.

I found that hepatitis has a rhythm of its own. It is not subject to the mind or the will. It cannot be rushed nor can it be spoken away. It gives you only as much energy as it allows, not a step more. I was not the first in my family to be acquainted with hepatitis. I was not yet school age when it struck Joe. At almost the same age we shared a common story. With my body in shut down, all activity stopped. The only free agent that remained was the mind of the Dreamer, and it was a mind of its own!

After a week a book found its way into the Dreamer's hands. It was the story of an Aboriginal pastor and leader of his people who lived his early years near the banks of the Murray River, not unlike the Dreamer himself. His ancient tongue called the Murray River, *Tongala*. He was the same joyful man the Dreamer remembered as an eleven year-old, sauntering out to the school oval with the grade six boys to show them how to throw a boomerang. It was his autograph that he had requested that day that was treasured above all others.

The book was not large but it felt heavy in the Dreamer's hands. It took all his effort to hold the book up to read. After just a few pages, *The Boy from Cumeroogunga – The story of Sir Douglas Ralph Nicholls, Aboriginal Leader* slipped from his grasp. He could hold it no longer. He lay exhausted, spreadeagled on the bed, but the story remained lodged in his mind and it began to do its work.

The book told the story of a baby boy born in 1906 on the banks of *Tongala*. He had a joyous spirit that matched that of his mother Florence. Florence was the daughter of Aaron Atkinson who had roamed the bush with his mother Kitty. Kitty saw the very first white man who intruded onto their sacred river country.

The story was about Kitty Atkinson's great grandson, Doug Nicholls. Doug's story itself was a story of dreams, hopes, close-knit family and significant friendships with *outsiders*. It was a Christian white man who purchased land and provided education for dislocated Aboriginal people at Echuca in the 1880s when governments did not care. It was a Christian Indian teacher, Shadrach James, who continued the work, found love and married into the tribe.

For almost 30 years Doug Nicholls' mother's generation embraced the dream and lived an independent and fruitful life. Douglas was born into this thriving Aboriginal community. It was at this time that the NSW government decided they knew what was best for Aboriginal people. With it came policies of separation and containment in the name of government Aboriginal welfare. Douglas was instilled with the character and strength of his mother and father. He followed his dreams; not the stunted expectations being imposed on him. He embarked on a journey starting as a bullock dray driver as a 14-year-old, followed by a VFL footballer, professional runner, boxer, ordained pastor, cricket club greenkeeper, Aboriginal rights campaigner, 1962 Victorian Father of the Year and eventually the Governor General of South Australia. At every step it was his close-knit family and a significant white friend who supported his dreams.

When I finally finished reading the book some weeks later and my energy levels began to rise, a clarity of thought emerged. Ben Mason and Pastor

Doug Nicholls, whose lives collided just momentarily with mine, drew me towards a different future. The Dreamer, now dreamed of something else. I said to Marg, 'I am thinking our next step is working alongside Aboriginal people whose languages are still strong. Where and how I don't know.'

Marg's face showed a mixture of surprise and simultaneously, delight. Once again the Dreamer had made a sudden announcement of an idea that had swirled around in the privacy of his own mind for days, or even weeks. The announcement however, was only a shock in its timing, not in its content. Marg had waited for this moment for a long time.

Marg knew this was for real. It was not an idea that would fade or be replaced by the next bolt of inspiration. Since her visit to Alice Springs around the time of our engagement, she had dreamed of introducing her husband to the Australian outback with its red dust and the people who attracted her. Just when it looked like they had taken a different course, and when the responsibilities of motherhood were consuming her energy, the time she had hoped for suddenly arrived. Her dream was becoming his dream. She had not forced it and didn't see it coming. Life had simply been full enough. Then hepatitis changed all that. Life stopped still. God immobilised her husband leaving no energy for a man who rarely sat still. It took all that so the Dreamer could dream of a different future. A future that she had set her heart on from when she committed her life to mission when she was fifteen years old.

27

Further Up And Further In

Location: Nompia, EHP
Date: 1982
Event: The Battle to get to 'The Last Battle'

It was mid-morning when we headed out of Ukarumpa for the forty-five minute drive to Nompia village. It was a perfect dry season day. The weather was mild and the sky a subdued blue with wafts of white clouds in the distance. Marg sat in the front of our borrowed Land Rover with her baby snuggled in her arms. She looked very content. It was aided by the beauty of the kunai grass swaying gently across the rolling hills and the promise of a few quiet days away on our own with different scenery. Rachel at two and half sat up proudly on the bench seat between her Mum and Dad. She liked to play *adults*.

I carried no map but it did not worry me. Des Oatridge, the owner of the Land Rover and 25-year veteran in this part of the world, had given his instructions, 'Just follow the road. You can't miss it. The Swiss Mission is at Nompia village. It's the last village at the end of the road.' Des's advice was gold. It was all we needed.

We made good progress as there were no other vehicles on the road. However, we were not without company. The road was a thoroughfare for people coming and going, walking in single file carrying their produce to and from market. Coming to a fork in the road I hesitated. I wasn't sure which road to take. I called out to an old man sitting on an upturned flour drum, observing his world, 'Rot bilong Nompia, i stap we?'

A toothless smile spread across his face. He pointed his chin towards the fork that I could now clearly see was the main road once it was confirmed. I nodded and waved as I drove on. The road narrowed and the grass between the dirt tracks that formed the road grew longer.

'It can't be too much further,' I said to Marg. She didn't need my reassurance. She was enjoying the scenery and our family adventure.

We passed around the outskirts of a village. It was unusually quiet. There were no children running around laughing or amusing themselves by greeting white strangers passing by. We turned a corner leading further on from the village. It was then that I brought the Land Rover to a sudden stop. Propped up against a star picket on the edge of the road was a sign on a square metre of old three-ply. In large black letters, there was no mistaking the message.

TAMBU, ROT I BILONG SATANI
Stay out. Road belongs to Satan

Somewhere not too far in the distance was the retreat house of the Swiss Mission: the refuge we were so much looking forward to. In front of us was a sign suggesting that it would be better if we stopped and turned around and went home. If we didn't stop and go back the sign suggested something bad could happen. My eyes diverted from the sign to my beautiful young family. A decision needed to be made.

My first reaction was steeped in habits long formed. I was not going to be told what to do. I could listen to reason but not to a threat. I wasn't turning back. An accompanying thought was just as strong. It came from my simple acceptance that the cosmic and earthly Jesus rose from the dead. He was alive now and loved a situation like this. The two thoughts ran parallel. I was up for the fight but without any surety of winning. Jesus on the other hand had already had the fight with Satan, and won. Satan was no threat to him. I turned to Marg and said, 'I am going ahead.'

Marg nodded her approval. I had no time to ask how she came to that decision. I felt my adrenalin running. My eyes scanned the terrain. The Land Rover moved forward only slower than before. Looking through my side mirror the back of the sign faded into the distance. It was nothing but a piece of discarded wood.

We turned a bend and the road narrowed some more. It was a road less travelled. The kunai grass came up to the edge of a shallow drain that ran beside the road. Turning around required going off road. That was a risky option. Looking forward, a hundred metres up the road, my eye caught movement that was far more menacing. Spread either side of the track was a party of warriors with their body paint glistening in the sun. Some carried large shields with long spears on the ready. Others carried the more agile bow and arrow. A quick estimate numbered a war party of about forty.

I gently put on the brake and pulled to a stop. I took a quick glance across at Marg and the children. Marg looked calm. No panic there. She held her baby a little tighter.

■ **Marg recalls**

I could sense that Barry was calm but very alert to the situation. It

assured me, and I was happy to leave it with him.

My brain computed the various scenarios within seconds. If they were hostile, and they looked it, I concluded that hostility was not likely to be directed towards us. This was no regular group of *rascals*. They were spread out across the hill as a show of force. They had a score to settle and it was unlikely to be with outsiders just passing through. I edged the vehicle along the track, wound down my window and hung my elbow out as if we were on a Sunday drive. When we were within earshot of a group of warriors gathered beside the road, I waved towards them and pulled up twenty metres short.

'Rot bilong Nompia i stap we?' I called out. A big grin crossed the face of the nearest warrior.

'We are from Nompia village. You keep going.' He beckoned us forward and waved us on.

We passed through our very own guard of honour. Warriors standing tall, holding spears, grand shields and bows and arrows waved and greeted us. We smiled, waved and drove on. We had provided a pleasant momentary distraction from the retribution and harm that they were seeking towards their enemies.

The lady from the Swiss Mission pointed us in the direction of a small round house with traditional woven walls and a thatched roof at the far end of the property. A rambling pink bougainvillea grew up the wall and onto the roof. The house sat in a spacious lawn with a cornfield running up to the perimeter of our oasis. Not more than five minutes' drive away we had passed through a field earmarked for tribal war. A small collection of Swiss chocolates laid aside for visitors added to our warm welcome. This was a place for blessing and we immediately felt it. The Holy Spirit was already restoring me out of a spiritual sameness that had crept into my life.

The next morning the village church bell rang out calling the villagers to worship. We entered the thatched roofed building with dirt floor and narrow wooden benches on both sides: the left side for women and the right side for men. Marg, Rachel and baby Heidi, strapped to Marg's front, took their seats to the left. Rachel was immediately whisked up into the arms of a young lady and planted on her hip. We had learnt not to be concerned for Rachel. She always seemed at home in a sea of black faces. My side of the church was conspicuously bare. An old man with a withered leg and stick sat nearby. My mind immediately went back to the strapping and impressive warriors of the previous day. None of the old men present were capable of fighting. If they could they would not be at church. The only exception was a strong handsome man in his late twenties. He sat alone on the front bench. He wore long trousers, casual short sleeve shirt and bare feet. He carried a conspicuous New Testament with a red jacket.

When time came for the sermon, the young man rose and walked to the pulpit. He opened his Bible and read in his own language. To illustrate the Scripture passage, he drew on a chalkboard a man with a spear killing another man. He then drew a second picture of a man killing another man in retaliation. The preacher spoke passionately for a few minutes then put a cross through both actions. I understood not a word he was saying but felt the power of his message. This was no theoretical sermon. Almost every young man in the village was out seeking revenge: caught up in cultural expectation and bound together by the unique shared experiences of war. This one man stood alone. He would follow Jesus and his commands to forgive. I sat not noticing the hardness of the wooden seat, my eyes locked on this young man. When we dispersed after church I sought a little more information from the Swiss missionary.

'What can you tell me about the young preacher?' I asked.

'His younger brother was killed by warriors from the village down below. The village expects him to pay back for his brother's death. But he is a strong Christian and he is choosing a different way – the way of forgiveness and love.'

I looked across at this strong muscular warrior for Jesus. Tears filled my eyes. I felt an amazing privilege to be his brother and to join him in worship.

Nompia village was the perfect holiday spot for us. Nowhere to go, nothing to do, except nibble on Swiss Lindt chocolate, relax, and read and dream. Two years previously we had bought ourselves a set of C S Lewis' *The*

Chronicles of Narnia to celebrate our fourth wedding anniversary. They came with us to Papua New Guinea unread. It was now time to complete my education and read the *fifth gospel* of the evangelical elite.

The Lion, the Witch and the Wardrobe made its appearance from left stage. By the time it exited right stage the Dreamer found himself in a world familiar to him. The Professor's words to Peter now on the bedroom side of the wardrobe summed up the mystery, that is God.

> *Once a King in Narnia, always a King in Narnia. But don't go trying to use the same route twice. Indeed don't go trying to get there at all. It'll happen when you are not looking for it.*

Each *Chronicle* brought a new adventure, always undergirded by the all-powerful and mysterious Aslan and his sure but unexpected arrival. Lucy summed it up with heart-breaking agony. Her adventure in Narnia had come to an end. It had spoiled her. The life of the soil, of the ordinary, of the here and now that awaited her offered no joy. Lucy pleaded with Aslan,

> *'It isn't Narnia you know,' she sobbed. 'It's you. How can we live, never meeting you?'*
>
> *'But you shall meet me, dear one,' said Aslan.*
>
> *'Are you there too, Sir?' said Edmund.*
>
> *'I am,' said Aslan. 'But there I have another name.'*

I was reading a fantasy story for children. I wasn't expecting to meet Aslan but then he showed up. Just as the last battle for Narnia was lost and all hope gone, Peter and his friends come bursting into the story exerting their authority over the evil one in the name of Aslan. Then he appears. Aslan freezes over the old world and invites all who have faith in him to join him in Aslan's world of beauty and wonder. '*Further up and further in,*' Aslan commands.

I begin to run with Peter. I am now not a reader but I am in the story. Delight fills me as the community of faith grows as different ones appear. My heart melts in awe of Aslan when I see he has a place in his world for Emeth the unwitting follower of Tash. Beauty abounds: waterfalls flow. Then for a brief moment a tragedy is revealed. Back in England Peter and his family have been killed in a train accident. They have left the life of the soil behind them, albeit in tragic circumstances. There is no going back, indeed no desire to go back. The world of Aslan promises more than they could have ever dreamed. Aslan assured them this real world is created by the Giver of Dreams.

> 'It goes on for ever, and in which every chapter is better than the one before.'

I stay sitting in my chair with the afternoon sun beginning to fade, and with no desire to move. Jesus' promise of eternal life feels so real. I could almost touch it. Jesus changes everything. He is the door. He exudes true life. And he chose me. The Dreamer had found time to dream again.

A few days later, Marg and I drove back from our retreat down the same track and passed the sign warning us that this road belongs to Satan. It was still there but it held no sting. The enthusiasm for the task had returned as we got ready for our final six months teaching in Papua New Guinea.

Three weeks later Nompia village was raided. The school, their gardens and the cornfield were burnt and destroyed. The villagers retreated into the mountains for safety. I wondered about the local preacher who dreamed of a better future. A world punctuated with suspicion and hate was winning. I prayed for this warrior of warriors and hoped that Aslan would soon show up. Together they could change everything.

28

Back To The Books

Location: Melbourne
Date: 1983-84
Event: La Trobe University, SIL School

The Evans' house was next door to ours at Ukarumpa. There was nothing special in that, except for what happened as a consequence of a casual Saturday morning conversation between neighbours. Peter and Bev returned from their furlough in Melbourne six months before we were to leave. I told Marg previously that if we were in Melbourne I'd like to study. Now Peter was telling me of a course he had just completed at La Trobe University. It piqued my interest when he said, 'This course was the best one I have ever done. The subjects on how people learn to read was so helpful I will be applying what I learnt directly to the literacy program we are running in the Barai village.'

Peter's endorsement, combined with my sudden heightened sense of intuition turned a casual conversation into a pivotal moment. The world of the here and now stopped in that brief moment and the Dreamer took centre stage. 'I'll be taking this course next year,' I thought to myself.

Marg was hanging out the washing and well occupied with the children. She was not thinking about next year or any grand plans. Saturday morning was time for chores. Without any preliminary introduction I blurted out my intentions. 'Marg, I know what course I'll do next year, if we're in Melbourne. It's a Bachelor of Education at La Trobe.' Marg was again in familiar territory.

Marg was by nature cautious about declaring the future. Dreams could be dashed and the agony of dealing with the disappointment followed. The Dreamer preferred to declare his dreams and then see what happens. By the time they crashed he would hardly notice because he was already dreaming of another future. Marg could not move on so quickly. Her practice was to seek confirmation from Scripture, ask for a sign from God and test the decision. Being led by the Spirit was not impulsive as it almost always was for the Dreamer. He knew it only when the moment arrived and not a second before. Once he saw the future, it was enough. Confirmation came in the doing, not in the waiting.

Marg brought a reality check. 'You know university applications for next year are probably closed by now.'

She was right. I had not thought of that.

Her reply was not meant to dash the Dreamer's hopes. She continued, 'If they receive your application in time, and the university offers you a position, then it will be a sign that it's the right thing to do.' Marg suggested the Dreamer not limit his options to La Trobe but to apply to Monash University as well. She liked having a backup.

I quickly dispatched a hand-written letter to La Trobe University enquiring and applying for the course and giving my background. The Dreamer complied and wrote a similar application to Monash for similar subjects. Three weeks later a letter with La Trobe University's imprimatur arrived in our mail box.

> *Dear Mr Borneman,*
>
> *We have received your letter enquiring about enrolling in a Bachelor of Education for next year. Your letter arrived as applications closed. However, given your circumstances, we have decided to make an exception and treat your personal letter as an official application. You are accepted into the Bachelor of Education starting March 1983. Please fill out the enclosed application and return it to us as soon as possible.*

The response from Monash came soon after. It read: *Applications closed. Apply for the following year*. Marg had her confirmation in neon lights!

Peter asked us if we would like to rent their house in the Melbourne suburb of Heathmont. It was a 30 minute drive to the university and similar to the

Wycliffe National Centre at Kangaroo Ground. The reduced rent included sharing the house with their 18 and 20 year-old sons who would sleep in the bungalow. We agreed.

On moving back to Melbourne my budgeting instincts became a dance between the man of the soil and the Dreamer. I was always on the look out for paid work we could do to make ends meet, while still trusting God to meet our needs in unexpected ways. I confided in Marg, 'Our savings will last three months. We are going to need to find some extra income.' It was a statement of fact, rather than undue concern. A solution would come from somewhere. We just did not know where.

Soon after I was asked if I would do relief driving over the summer holidays for St Vincent de Paul. It involved picking up and delivering furniture for their secondhand stores. When I saw that the contract finished on Monday 7th March I marvelled at God's timing. It was the day before my first class at uni! The money earned for this short contract was not enough to cover course fees or living costs for the year, but for the Dreamer the end date was God speaking. He would provide for our needs.

The course required me to attend classes three nights per week over one year. My previous Diploma of Teaching, plus teaching experience earned me two years credit of the three year degree. The study was stimulating and my results near the top of the class. With the classes at night, I was free to do a couple of days of relief teaching each week with the Education Department. The principal at one of the schools called me to his office. 'Our grade five teacher will be away all of second term on long service leave' He then asked, 'Would you be willing to be her replacement teacher?'

'Absolutely,' I replied, not giving much thought to the workload but seeing it as God's provision. The three month's pay at relief rates would be substantial. It was only after the semester that I read in the course fine print that a student should only do one unit per semester when teaching full-time. In my enthusiasm for study and rejoicing in the Lord's provision I missed that small matter. I can only assume the Holy Spirit also missed reading the fine print.

As the Bachelor of Education finished, the SIL (Summer Institute of Linguistics) Introductory Course to Linguistics and Language Learning began. It was a prerequisite to Wycliffe membership and recommended by the Northern Territory Education Department for teacher linguists. The course fitted well with the two options we had settled on for our future work. We would either join the Northern Territory Bilingual Schools Program or join Wycliffe and work with the SIL Australian Aborigines Branch. We were comfortable with either option. SIL linguists worked hand-in-hand with the NT Bilingual Program. They were colleagues, not protagonists. To help with our decision I wrote to both organisations asking, 'Why should we work for you and not the other organisation?'

Within a few weeks the two replies came back. One typed and the other hand written. The typed one came from the Education Department. The head of the NT Bilingual Program, Dr Stephen Harris had worked as a volunteer with SIL in PNG for two years. He met and married his American wife there. Dr Harris' typed letter highlighted the excitement of being part of a new initiative, its educational relevance, the progress already made. It was compelling reading. In the final sentence he added the starting salary. My eyes settled on the figure. It was not the amount that worried me. It was the simple fact that it was included. I was suspicious that perhaps he was trying to persuade me by the salary. If so it was to no avail. Finances would not drive this decision.

The hand-written letter from the SIL Literacy Coordinator highlighted the strength of SIL's approach. SIL gives you ample time to build relationships with the local community and to learn the language. This was non-negotiable. Understanding language and culture were key to all long-term work. The second advantage was to do with money. SIL programs did not rely on government funding priorities that constantly changed. You will have less funding with SIL but you will be more flexible, have more time to connect with people, and plan long term.

The stated SIL advantages were also compelling. It ticked the boxes. From an educational philosophy perspective, I was attracted to grass roots informal community literacy programs. From my own personal story I saw the translation of the Scriptures in the local language as akin to my own experience as a seventeen-year-old when I was given a New Testament in everyday English. We would join Wycliffe Bible Translators if our application was accepted.

29

Coming In From The Cold

Location: Wycliffe, Kangaroo Ground
Date: 1964-5
Event: Trusting God as provider

I was both bemused and warmed by the assessment of my written doctrinal statement on the fundamental truths of evangelical Christianity. It was a requirement for joining Wycliffe Bible Translators. The doctrinal checker was generous in his approval. His summary read,

Theologically very sound with a clear and refreshing account in his own words of the reformed evangelical Protestant position.

I could define the attributes of God, describe the person and work of Jesus and the Holy Spirit, and summarise Paul's thoughts in his letters to the early church according to sound evangelical reformed orthodoxy. Yet I was as an outsider and a stranger when Jesus first interrupted my life and invited me to follow him. What it meant at the time I had little idea. I simply accepted the invitation. He allowed me to take stumbling steps without fear of me falling. I did not know enough to predict him so he was able to come at unexpected moments and in mysterious ways. He taught me to seek rather than to know, to look for the way before knowing the way. I liked being an outsider seeking after God who was my Saviour and friend, yet still a mystery.

I wondered what would change now that I had come in from the cold. What did it mean for the Dreamer to be *a respectable child of the church, a better theologian,* and *an acceptable Wycliffe missionary*? Was there still room to wonder and wait for God to turn up, not knowing what might happen, or what someone else might think? Did coming in from the cold threaten the Dreamer's very existence?

On the other hand, joining Wycliffe presented one great advantage. It gave the Dreamer an opportunity to come alongside the poorest and most forgotten people of the earth. He was sure it was the giver of dreams who was giving him this opportunity. Surely it promised even bigger dreams and new discoveries of who Jesus is, not fewer. There was no turning back.

One aspect of joining Wycliffe demanded risk-taking. Wycliffe paid no salary and nor did it pay superannuation. Members had to trust God for their provision both for today, tomorrow and into old age. I had of course known this from our two years serving in Papua New Guinea. However, I then had a logical backup, a safety net. We only had to survive for two years.

This time it would be different. In joining Wycliffe as a career, we were forfeiting our most productive income-generating years in exchange for low income. The very thought was attractive to the Dreamer on two counts. Here was an opportunity to discover what it actually meant in everyday life to look to God to provide for their most basic needs. It was also an opportunity to learn what it meant to be content in all circumstances. Jesus taught that the satisfied life is not about having material things but about being led by the Spirit. This would be one way to find out what this really meant. Before the adventure began, I needed a private conversation with God to lay down some ground rules.

Long walks alone and praying in the Spirit remained my connecting point with God. It was where dreams were welcome and where they touched earth. It was where the things of the soil might be given an unexpected spiritual interpretation. The conversation went on for several weeks.

The Dreamer:

'As a man my first responsibility is always to provide for my family. My wife has done all the hard yards having our children and caring for them. She should not have to worry about food and shelter for her family. That is my job. You understand that. So this is between you and me. The only way I can fulfil my responsibility is by trusting you to be our provider. I am counting on you. I don't want to be fickle and say I have faith in you for this and that and then take it back tomorrow or the first time we appear to lack something. Give me the faith to believe. Once we have settled this, we won't need to talk about this again.'

Jesus' response:

'It is time we did a recap. Haven't I been looking after you from when you were born? Do you think the journey you have been on has been of your own making? Do you think the jobs that you have had came by accident, or your clever planning? I have provided you houses to live in, opportunities to study, places to go and you have not starved. Remember when your funds were running low and a friend out of the blue repaid you the $1000 you had loaned him ten years before. Who do you think reminded him? So here we are. For five years you have not had a regular salary and you have never been without food on the table or a roof over your head. Five years or twenty years is the same to me. I can provide for your family. I am also your father, and fathers have a responsibility to provide for their children. You can trust me.'

As that matter was settled God's provision immediately followed in an unexpected way. Marg was relaxed and in no hurry as the first contractions alerted her that the time had come for our third baby to arrive.

'Give the hospital a ring and let them know we are coming in,' she said.

I rang the Maternity Ward and forewarned them. Marg already had her bag packed and ready to go. I let the two young men living with us know we were on our way to hospital. They would take care of Rachel and Heidi should they wake up.

'There's no need to rush,' Marg said. 'Both Rachel and Heidi took their time. I'm sure it will be a few hours before the baby comes.'

Marg's assurance calmed me. The short 20 minute drive to hospital began smoothly and unhurried. Being the middle of the night the traffic was light. We did not say anything but both knew it was the lull before the storm when Marg would garnish all her maternal power to bring forth the life that was in her. Her previous deliveries had not been easy. Her strength and resolve on both occasions amazed me. It was time for another battle.

Marg suddenly broke the silence,

'The contractions are getting quite strong now and coming more quickly. I think the baby is on the way.'

Suddenly every bump felt in the road was doubly hard and each red light doubly long.

Our relief was enormous as two nurses met us at the door. They summed up the situation immediately. 'Come with us,' they said.

I parked the car and a few minutes later was in the maternity waiting room waiting for a call. I introduced myself to another expectant father. After a brief exchange he asked,

'Have you chosen a name for your baby?'

'Yes. If it's a boy we'll call him Andrew Mark.'

'Are you a Christian?' My new friend enquired.

I was surprised by his question.

'Yes I am.'

As I answered a nurse came in and called out with some urgency, 'Mr Borneman'.

I stood and walked towards her.

'Come! The baby is on its way.'

Ten minutes later Andrew Mark left the protection of the womb and made his entrance into his new world and the security of his mother's arms.

■ Marg recalls

Having had such a good experience at the clinic in Ukarumpa I was not in a hurry to get to the hospital early. We did however cut it fine. I was grateful there were no complications for bub or me. A few days later when I met Kaylene (wife of Barry's waiting room friend) we were surprised to recognise each other. We had met briefly in the Wycliffe Foyer a few months earlier when Kaylene was volunteering on the switchboard. We now shared the joy of us each having a son.

We were delighted that our two girls now had a brother. Another wonderful gift to our family. Unbeknown to us the Lord was already providing for our future needs. Stephen and Kaylene became one of our most generous financial and prayer supporters over the next 30 years.

The Wycliffe Personnel Manager stated what we already knew, 'Your financial support is only at 65% of what you need to live in Darwin. We need you to have 80% of your income promised by churches and friends before we release you to the field.'

I had already formulated my response. 'We have already been accepted for field training. We are willing to go with less. We can trust God for the difference.'

The resigned look on the manager's face suggested this was the direction he thought the conversation would go. He explained, 'We accept 80% for two reasons. SIL, who you will be seconded to on the field, is predominately an American organisation. We have found most Australians can live on 80% of what Americans think they need. The other reason is to receive supplementary income from Wycliffe USA you have to have 80% before you go. Should your income fall below 80% when on the field they will make up the difference.'

I replied, 'In that case we will opt out of receiving money from the supplementary fund. We are happy to live on whatever finances we receive from churches and friends here in Australia and whatever other ways God provides.'

The manager was a man of integrity. He had reasoned well on behalf of Wycliffe and for our sake. He had our best interests at heart. He also did not doubt that God provided in different ways for different people.

'Okay if you voluntarily remove yourself from receiving Emergency Funding, I will release you to go to the field.'

The journey with God as our provider was now the new experiment. One that would be with us day by day, year by year, one decade into the next. It suited the Dreamer's picture of *The Old Man Up Top*. He was the mysterious generous provider who was still to be fully discovered. My trust had nothing to do with the fact that I could attest to a sound evangelical reformed protestant position. It had everything to do with experiencing God who surprised me with his kindness, and an expectation that he would do that again.

30

Is The Devil Real?

Location: Melbourne
Date: 1985, 2024
Event: Church youth camp

Twenty or so teenagers from the Outer East suburbs of Melbourne gathered for a weekend camp by the Yarra River. On the Saturday evening the camp leader asked the question, 'Do you think the devil is real?'

The responses split evenly between *no* and *yes* with a smattering of *not sure*. A young lady doing catering at the camp interjected. She was a year or two older than the campers and part of the young adults group at the church. She began, 'I once attended a seance...' The camp leader gently interrupted, 'Let's talk about that later.'

Half an hour later the teenagers gathered outside around a fire to enjoy the remainder of the evening. Inside the camp hall the young lady joined the other two leaders and myself. The leader asked, 'Tell us about what happened.'

She was in safe company. They were all friends.

The young lady recounted her experience:

> When I was in Grade 5 at Primary School I went home from school with some friends and we decided to have a seance. I knew it was not right, but also I didn't believe anything would happen. At one stage after a question was asked of the spirits, I was the only one with my finger left on the glass and it moved and it was like my finger was

glued to the glass and it took some effort to break the connection. We finished up soon after that and I ran home feeling unsettled but also not understanding what had just happened nor did I feel there was anyone I could talk to about it. Then about 6 months ago, after attending church and as I was going to sleep, I had a half awake dream where part of me was calling out to worship God and the other half was calling out to Satan.[1]

There was a pause. The leader did not ask any questions of clarification. He simply offered, 'Can we pray for you?' The young lady nodded. At 32, I was the oldest person in this small gathering but I was not the leader. The youth leader was in charge and I was glad he was. He placed a hand on her shoulder. I appreciated his confidence and quiet authority. He prayed, 'Jesus remove whatever may have taken advantage of our sister during that seance and her act of disobedience.'

The prayer was quietly spoken but the reaction coming out of the young lady was anything but quiet. A scream pierced the room. It was not her voice but something else. It was guttural and hideous, cold, and loud. I felt its coldness as it went by me and out of the building. It passed by the group singing around the campfire. As it left, the young lady was thrown from her feet to the floor.

In the midst of the chaos, I was surprised by a calmness that enveloped me despite the chaotic scene. I was sure the same calmness was present with the other two men. Jesus was in charge. The three of us knelt down beside her, now lying on the ground. It seemed her whole breath was taken from her when the evil tormentor left.

'Breathe in,' the other leader instructed her. She took a small breath. 'Keep breathing in.' With each breath the colour began to return to her face and her facial muscles relaxed. It was all about the young lady being set free, and it was Jesus who was doing what he does best. She was in good hands.

Soon she had enough strength and peace of mind to stand. I needed to be alone with God and my thoughts. I excused myself and went for a walk. I walked by the teenagers gathered around the fire and wondered what impact this event had on them.

---

1. This retelling was provided by the young lady and used with permission

I asked Jesus, 'Jesus, what is this about? This is something I could expect in Papua New Guinea, but not with a church girl from middle class Melbourne.'

Jesus' answer came gently. 'I have been wanting her to be free for a long time. I love her. That is the reason for all this.'

The theology of what happened could be worked out later. When I had walked long enough in silence I returned to the room. The two young men and the young lady were still standing where I had left them, praying quietly and seeking Jesus. I joined them. There was a joy in her face and an evident hunger for more of Jesus. She was being transformed.

The following night at the church Sunday service, the young lady led the worship She was radiant and full of joy as she sang. People noticed the change in her and wondered what had happened.

The next Sunday following the morning service, we said our goodbyes to friends from the church and others who had driven across town to see us on our way. Our destination was Cairns, 3,000 kilometres north, and then a flight to Papua New Guinea for three months of survival training in preparation for our Wycliffe assignment in the Northern Territory. I had not seen the young lady or the youth leader during the week nor did I see them that morning. With no debrief on what had taken place, my understanding was limited. I wondered what it meant for her. I concluded I did not need to know.

Over the following thirty-nine years this story re-entered the Dreamer's thoughts from time to time but was not spoken about to others. It was the young lady's story of deliverance and freedom, not the Dreamer's story. Jesus had simply allowed him to be a privileged observer.

The church was overflowing, just as it often had in the early '80s. Chairs were gathered from every room to allow seating for an extra one hundred plus people in the foyer.

It was 2023 and we had returned to the same church for a funeral of a friend's father. Following the service across the room I saw a familiar face.

She was talking with a friend from that same era. Was it her? I made my way through the crowd to find out.

She recognised me. Yes it was! I asked about her life and what she had done since we had seen her. She and her husband had become ordained ministers. They had pastored a church for many years and were now hospital chaplains in the city and loving their roles. These were not the questions I really wanted her to answer. My mind had gone back to a young lady being set free of something very ugly in her life. I wondered if that event still had any relevance to her now and if she was aware that I was the unwitting observer.

When a pause came in our conversation I simply asked, 'Do you remember a camp?'

Without any further explanation she exclaimed, 'Do I remember a camp! It was life changing for me!'

'Tell me what happened.'

For the next fifteen minutes she recounted the event step-by-step. It was vivid in her memory. She described how the youth leader offered to pray for her. She agreed to it not expecting anything in particular.

Then she recalled being thrown to the ground with all her breath sucked out of her. She did not remember the demonic scream but she remembered fighting for breath and being told to breathe in. While this was happening, she said she was taken outside her body and saw herself being split right down the middle and then lying on the ground. She was somehow an observer of her own deliverance.

As she began to breathe, she stopped being an onlooker of the event and returned to her body. A calmness came over her and eventually she was able to stand.

She then added, 'It was then you did the strangest thing.'

'What was that?' I asked, hoping it was not something needing an apology four decades later.

'You just said, "I'm going for a walk." And off you went.'

She then added. 'While you were off walking we were praying and I was saying to God that I just wanted to love and worship him. Just then you came back in, looked at me, and said, "You shall love the Lord your God with all your heart, and all your strength". It was exactly what I was praying. Something happened right then. I was set free to worship God and suddenly I felt absolutely loved by God. Knowing I am loved by God has never left me since that day.'

I was dumbfounded. I could not recall that prayer for her nor did I know its impact. What I could say was that a short prayer like that was in character. I rarely said long prayers. After I returned home from the funeral, a long walk with God was needed. 'Why did you let me know about this after all these years?'

My mind went to the prayer. In its timing and content it seemed like a declaration from God for my sister. Perhaps this was a reason I did not remember it. It was not my prayer. It was his. I wondered if there were other times in my life when God spoke through me that I was unaware of. I also wondered if my reluctance to get too involved in people's lives meant I was also missing in action when the Holy Spirit had work for me to do. I was sure that was true.

Then came the final thought from God. 'You know that book you are writing. Well this story needs to go in your book. It is a story of me letting someone know they are loved by me. Everyone needs to know that.'

31

Stranded Again

Location: Coonabarabran
Date: 1985
Event: Hospitality at its best

We drove out of Melbourne in our grey long-wheel-based Toyota Troop Carrier without a concern in the world. We were a family on an adventure, heading for Cairns, and on a mission with God.

The rolling hills of the Newell Highway which replaced the plains country north of the Murray River, surprised us. It was beautiful to the eyes and made driving an extra joy. As we passed through Coonabarabran late on the second afternoon the thought of stopping the night crossed our mind. Marg noticed a motel on the north side of town with separate well spread-out units. *A perfect place to stay with young kids*, she thought to herself. But her husband was keen to make the most of the remaining daylight. Every kilometre covered today was one less kilometre to travel tomorrow.

About ten kilometres on from Coonabarabran, where the road through rolling hills is lined with cypress pines, a hidden danger lurked. At the bottom of each slope where the rain water flowed, the road surface was uneven. It was of little consequence for the Troop Carrier. The same could not be said for the trailer. As it hit another pot hole we heard a tyre blow. The jolt vibrated through the trailer. It now became a lead weight for the Troop Carrier which eventually drew to a halt a further 100 metres up the next slope.

I got out and inspected the damage. The skid marks along the verge showed the left wheel had completely locked up by the time we stopped. It did not take a mechanic to see what was wrong. The axle was severely bent but not yet broken. Fortunately it had stayed directly behind the Troop Carrier and not catapulted itself to one side.

The set of circumstances sounded familiar. Here we were starting on God's mission and we are again stranded in a place where we knew nobody. It was not Sydney this time, but outback New South Wales.

Marg calmly stated, 'I know where we are staying tonight. There's a motel on this side of town that will be just perfect.'

I unhitched the trailer, grateful that there was space to tow it off the road. We headed back into Coonabarabran as the sun started to set. We booked the very unit that had caught Marg's eye half an hour earlier. With our children settled into their new home without a worry in the world we voiced the next question, 'What do we do now?'

Marg suggested, 'Let's ring a local church for help.'

After a brief prayer the thought came, 'Ring the Assembly of God pastor.' Why *Assembly of Go*d we did not know. We had not been to an Assembly of God church before.

We looked up the White Pages. Yes, there was an Assembly of God church in town, and dialled the pastor's number.

'Hello, I'm Barry. We're missionaries with Wycliffe Bible Translators on our way to Cairns. Our trailer has a broken axle about 10km north of here. I'm wondering if you can help us?'

My new *mate* just laughed and said, 'You've broken down in the best place in Australia.' Twenty minutes later he arrived pulling a long trailer with a winch.

'Jump in,' he called, 'Let's get this trailer off the road before it's dark. It's not safe to leave it there overnight.'

On the way he explained, 'When your phone call came, I already had the trailer hitched up. I knew straight away I was meant to help you.'

STRANDED AGAIN

Forty-five minutes later the trailer sat on the lawn in front of our unit at the *Castlereagh Village*. As my new mate was about to leave us, he said, 'I'm busy tomorrow so I will send my assistant around to give whatever help you need.'

The assistant pastor was an older man, gentle in nature. He knew the town well. He looked at the trailer and offered, 'I know a Christian who works just across the road at the engineering works. He can fix this. If it's okay by you I will go ask him.'

After making arrangements for the trailer, he took Marg shopping. In our hour of need we experienced the body of Christ at its practical best. The trailer was returned two days later with a re-fabricated axle, free of charge. It was re-engineered for the toughest of roads in Australia. Coonabarabran was indeed the best place in Australia to break down.

While we were waiting for the trailer I began asking myself why I had so much stuff with me. The one thing that struck at my core was the question

of why was I carrying my collection of theological books and biblical commentaries with me and the new bike that I rode to and from college. Why hold onto them? Why not share them? I'm sure what followed was the most significant sale of theological and church history books in Coonabarabran. For our generous pastors it was an unexpected delight. For the man of the soil it was a comfort to know we carried less weight, and for the Dreamer it was how he wanted to live – freely sharing the good things that matter to him and not letting those good things get between him and God.

We drove out of Coonabarabran rejoicing in Jesus and the hospitality of country people in welcoming strangers. We took it as no coincidence that the start of our first missionary journey and our second missionary journey found us as strangers needing the kindness of Jesus people. It is something a stranger never forgets. It is a beautiful thing to experience. Just maybe it is what God has made us for.

32

Embracing Limitations

> Location: PNG and Darwin
> Date: 1985
> Event: Malaria

Village living near Madang in PNG was part of SIL's orientation training to make us more resilient, to prepare us for living in remote places, and wean us off the comforts of western life. However, for me it was more akin to a holiday camp amongst friends than a case of culture shock. Living without electricity and by the pressure lamp at night took me back to my earliest memories. The stillness of the evening and the stars suspended in a clear, dark sky garnished no fear. We found Papua New Guineans the easiest of company and they always loved a story. It also gave us plenty of time to read. Rachel delighted in mastering her first reader and I read *Poland*, an historical saga by James A. Michener. It was a perfect home for the man of the soil and the Dreamer.

One thing dampened our village living experience. First Marg and then Rachel and Heidi experienced the high temperatures, chills and lethargy so easily identified with malaria. It was a particular problem in the village as a nearby tidal swamp was a breeding ground for malaria-carrying mosquitoes. Marg administered some additional anti-malarial tablets, and by keeping themselves hydrated, the symptoms subsided and good health returned.

Just as they recovered, malaria became my companion but the symptoms seemed more severe. I took additional chloroquine tablets and in the evenings retired to our bamboo bed. The cool incoming sea breezes beckoned relief that my body craved for but did not come. In the middle of the night, the terror began. My mind could not be stilled. It was as if it was ruled by another force. It raced around and around in my head on a course of its own, swirling into a vortex. The centre of its attention was singularly focused on Michener's description of the brutal treatment of the imprisoned Poles by the Nazi German occupying force. All the imagined blood and gore, the horror and cruelty was replayed and replayed. In my mind I was witnessing firsthand the worst of human behaviour. It went on and on throughout the night. By morning I was exhausted but my temperature subsided and a better day came.

I prided myself in my ability to sleep, to dispel anxiety and live on the positive side of life. I could count the number of sleepless nights on one hand. It was a gift I had from birth and I assumed it was everyone's gift for the taking. I now treasured a sane mind in a way I did not before. We are finely tuned. I asked God to safeguard my mind for the long haul. The sheer anguish I experienced of human evil towards another stayed with me. I hoped I would never see that day in the flesh. War brutalises people, even good people, even my grandfather.

We put my reaction to malaria down to an old adage that men are indestructible when they are healthy but always dying when they are sick. With just one week left of village living Marg wasn't sure that my symptoms of malaria should cause us to leave early. We would stay until the end. Her only concern was for Andrew (one year old). She had asked God to protect him and as yet he had not contracted malaria. Her husband would be fine.

I was fine until the last full day in the village. The small octopus at my feet in the dugout canoe was making my head swirl. The heat of the sun bearing down and the temperature gauge in my body rising, turned the inside of my head into a pounding drum. With all my effort I fought off the pain hoping that this fishing expedition would soon be over. I hoped I had the energy to last the day.

Our host family prepared the evening farewell feast of bone fish and other staple food along with what remained in our pantry. As guest of honour, the family placed good portions of the local cuisine before me. I persevered eating what I could but without joy. The rhythmic thumping inside my head went on unabated. It was almost time to go, mission completed, when our host insisted on one final expression of hospitality. Placed before me was a plate of delicately fried calamari. All I saw was the swirling octopus at my feet in the dugout canoe. I gingerly took the calamari in my fingers and ate slowly. The joy on the face of our hosts invited a response.

'This is delicious. Thank you so much.' It was a total lie. Our friendship required it.

With the formal obligations finished we said our farewells and headed back to our high set village home. I climbed the wooden stairs, leaned out the back window and heaved and vomited for the next fifteen minutes. The village pigs that roamed free suddenly congregated under our house and feasted as I had done earlier in the night. Mercifully I slept well enough that night. Next day we packed up our belongings, dispersed our gifts and crossed the lagoon in a dugout canoe for the last time.

The malaria symptoms followed me from Madang, resurfacing during our short visit to Ukarumpa, and again as we drove the 4000 km from Cairns across Queensland to Darwin. At Mataranka, a half day's drive south of Darwin I barely made it to our room for the night after a full day of driving. I immediately put the air conditioner on and crashed on the bed exhausted. Marg took the children down to enjoy the hot springs. The next day was my good day. We safely drove the remaining 400km to Darwin.

The lethargy that engulfed me at the doctor's reception room was now familiar. I did not have the energy to stand. I cared little that I was lying face down on the floor in the waiting room with my head resting on my folded arms. Sitting up was too tiring. My name was called. I crawled into the doctor's room on my hands and knees. I could see by the doctor's look that my entry was a little unusual. I gathered all my energy and pulled myself up onto the chair. I didn't wait for introductions. There was little time to waste. 'I have malaria,' I offered.

The doctor was not impressed. 'We don't self-diagnose here,' came his curt response. I had no energy to argue.

Malaria had been eradicated in Darwin in the 1960s when DDT was the fix-all for mosquito infected swamps. It was very rare to have a case in Darwin. The doctor had reason not to rush a diagnosis. He made some rudimentary observations, took a blood sample, and sent me home.

Less than an hour later a phone call came to the SIL centre where we were living. The message carried a tone of urgency. 'Get the young man to the emergency ward at the Royal Darwin Hospital as quickly as possible.'

A nurse was waiting for me when I arrived. She ushered me into the intensive care unit. A saline drip was ready next to my designated bed. The nurse tried to insert the IV drip into my arm. She tried once then twice. The vein collapsed each time. I was too dehydrated for the vein to hold the drip. She tried the other arm and was relieved that it held. With the drip inserted, the restoration process back to equilibrium slowly began.

The doctor pulled himself up alongside my bed. He had the authoritative bearing of a person who is a carrier of important knowledge. 'The blood tests show you have malaria.' I didn't say I could have told him that along with every villager on Malapau Island. I was grateful that he now had scientific evidence so he could treat me. He then took on the reassuring posture required once the hard facts are digested.

'I am afraid you will be here for some time. You are badly dehydrated and will need to be on a drip for a number of days. You also have two types of malaria. One is Vivax and the other Falciparum.' Vivax I expected. Falciparum malaria was new to me. The doctor was now entitled to his bearing as the dispenser of knowledge.

The villagers in PNG could have explained it to me had I asked. Vivax symptoms were one bad day followed by a good day, as it had been for Marg and the girls. It is manageable when treated properly. Falciparum on the other hand melts the brain and kills the body. It was the deadliest parasite found in humans.

The doctor outlined the proposed course of action. 'We are immediately starting a heavy course of anti-malarial drugs. Falciparum is resistant to chloroquine which is what you have been taking. We will be prescribing quinine and another drug as well. You won't be going home until we have eradicated it from your system.'

The diagnosis was comforting. I had reason to feel sick. So I was not the characteristic male who, when he gets sick, thinks he is dying. At least not this time!

I became an instant celebrity. Two nurses gathered around and explained their problem. The protocols for treating malaria required me to be kept in bed under a mosquito net. The old Darwin Hospital was typical of a tropical army hospital with fans and open windows. It made sense then since the anopheles mosquito that carries malaria was found in Darwin. The old protocols had not been rewritten for the newly built, four storey, air-conditioned Royal Darwin Hospital where I was now a patient. It seemed that I was their first malaria patient in the new hospital. The nurses laughed. 'There are no mosquito nets in the hospital. I will have to go home and get one of my own. Protocols are protocols!'

The recovery was initially slow but after a few days it began to pick up speed. Ten days later they released me from hospital. By then Heidi had a reoccurrence of Vivax malaria and joined me in hospital. They had to find another mosquito net for her.

Our first two weeks on the mission field were not what we expected. I was thankful for the medical care and that the family was well. I was thankful for Marg's prayer for our son and his protection. I never thought to ask God why I was the one who got really sick. My theology did not expect God to protect me from the consequences of being human. If a female anopheles mosquito bit me then there was an even chance I would get the malaria parasite and have to deal with the consequences. That is what is meant to be human, to be a person of the soil. It has limitations. Better to embrace those limitations and not see them as contradictory to God's Spirit. I was comfortable with the paradox.

God did not need to answer my *Why?* All I needed was to know Jesus was with me and I was in his hands. It was ironic My confidence in the goodness and love of God towards me was at its greatest when I was in my weakest state. I was a man of the soil but it did not define me. In the pain and limitations brought on by malaria, that mischievous joy and eternal hope that comes from him remained.

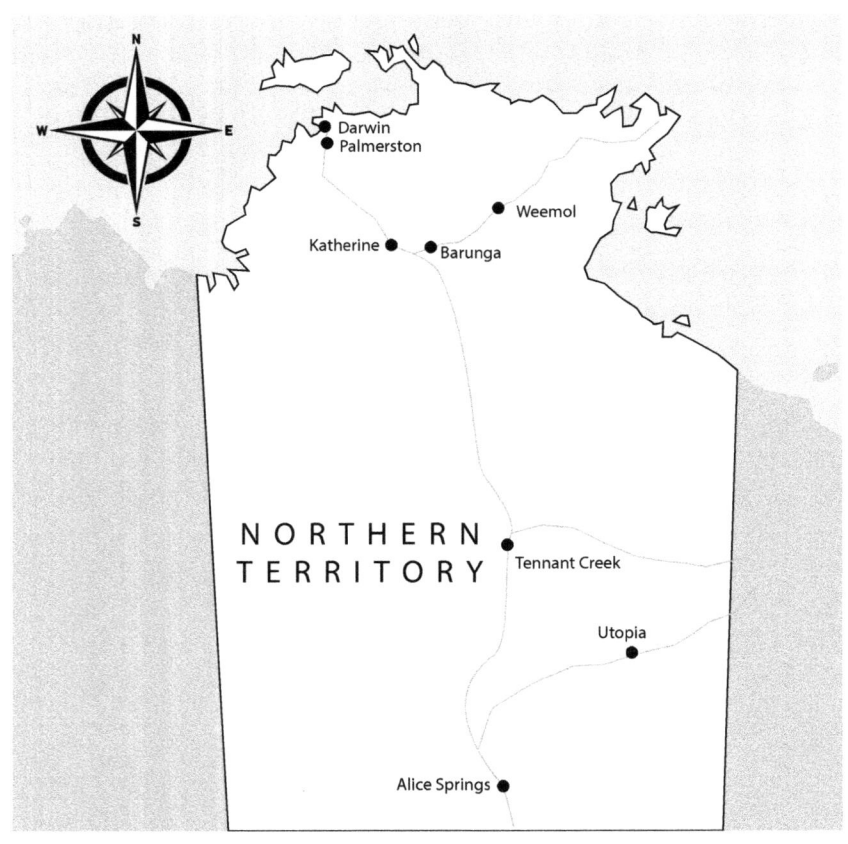

33

The Parable Of The Good Samaritan

Location:	Barunga
Date:	1936
Event:	An 300km round trip to Darwin Hospital

It was Sunday morning and our third day staying in the Aboriginal community of Barunga on the Central Arnhem Highway, 400 kilometres south-east of Darwin. It was a short two-week *taste and see* for us and the local Kriol speaking church and community. If it worked out for everyone we would move there when housing became available.

Unlike Marg, I did not have the practice of reading the Bible every morning. However, when I woke this Sunday morning I was drawn to read the story of the stranger who generously took care of the Jew who had been beaten and robbed on the road to Jericho. Those who passed by and were expected to help were too pre-occupied with other matters. It was the stranger who helped. I put my Bible down. God was telling me something. I was puzzled. At breakfast I mentioned it to Marg.

'I think I am going to find out what the parable of the Good Samaritan means today.'

An hour before the morning church service I noticed Jimmy sitting under a tree about 30 metres from the mission house where we were staying while the missionaries were on holiday. The sun was already hot. I sat down crosslegged a metre or two from Jimmy. Silence filled the gap for a while and when the time seemed right I opened up the question. Looking at the ground in front of me, I asked, 'How is your son doing, Jimmy?' I knew that Jimmy's eighteen-year-old son (nephew) was in intensive care at the Royal Darwin Hospital on a dialysis machine.

'They reckon he gonna die. He proper sick one.' Jimmy's words were followed by more silence. I waited, holding back the white man's tendency to provide an answer.

'What do you want to do old man?' I asked. Jimmy quietly replied, 'I'd like to go and see him.'

More silence.

I asked, 'Has your family got a motor car, Jimmy?'

Jimmy again replied quietly, 'No motor car.' I had only seen three private cars in the community of 1100 so I was half expecting that answer. I hunted for a solution.

'What about that council mob? They got a new toyota.'

'I can't have that one. Not my family.'

We sat in silence for a little while longer. Jimmy seemed satisfied in just having the conversation. However, the morning's Bible reading was going through my head. I broke the silence. Looking away into the distance I asked Jimmy, 'Old man, if you had a motor car what would you do?'

Jimmy replied in the same quiet pensive voice, 'I'd go now.'

'Okay, you now have a toyota. I will take you and your family to Darwin.'

Jimmy's face lit up at the offer. He was not expecting it.

'When do we leave, Jimmy?' I asked.

'Half an hour,' he replied.

'Half an hour,' I replied in affirmation.

We parted company. Jimmy headed back towards his camp and I headed back up the stairs to the mission house. Marg was already prepared for something unexpected.

'I'm taking Jimmy and his family to the Darwin Hospital. It's about 5 hours' drive so we should make it to the hospital by mid-afternoon.'

Marg took it in her stride. She would go to church as was expected of us in the morning. In the late afternoon when it was cooler she might do some visiting around the camp.

I arrived at Jimmy's camp just as the church bell rang out across the community. About fifteen men, women and children climbed silently into the back of our long wheel-based Toyota troop carrier. They put a mattress on the floor for the children. The adults sat along the bench seats on either side. Jimmy climbed in the front with me. Jimmy had a request. We need to go to Beswick to pick up his mother.

I had not counted on that. It would slow us down. Beswick was the next community a further 30 kilometres along the Central Arnhem Highway. It would add at least another hour to our trip. I did not object. I had put myself in Jimmy's hands and he knew culturally what was required. I did not. Another dozen men, women and children climbed aboard at Beswick. I asked no question. In silence we began the long drive to Darwin.

As we passed through Katherine heading north, I now had time to reflect. I knew how this might be judged by my colleagues. The warning was ringing in my ear. 'The first lesson you need to learn is not to be taken advantage of because you have a vehicle. You will just become a taxi service and that is not what you are there for.'

I reasoned that this advice was given for good reason. I also assumed that advice and convention sometimes needed to be broken. Breaking it on my third day in the community was earlier than I was expecting.

The trip to Darwin went smoothly. Not a complaint or word out of place came from anyone. The children sat quietly or slept on the mattress. We stopped for a ten-minute toilet break and to stretch our legs at Coomalie Creek. It was midafternoon when we arrived at the Royal Darwin Hospital.

Ten of us squeezed into the lift. I pressed floor four ICU. Stepping out we followed the signs to ICU. Jimmy, the mother and a brother walked beside me. The others followed along behind filling the width of the corridor. I sensed that Jimmy was feeling uneasy. Hospitals can be daunting for strangers. The hospital that cared so well for me when I had malaria suddenly felt like a very foreign and frightening place through other eyes. A nurse walked down the corridor towards us from a distance. I could see a bothered look on her face. She meant business. She is probably at the end of a long shift I thought. When she got within a couple of metres of us she stopped and asked, 'What do you want?'

I answered for everyone.

'We have come to see a patient who has not long to live. I have his mother and father with me.'

She immediately ignored me and looked straight at Jimmy. 'Are you the father? Are you husband and wife?' We can only allow his actual father and mother to visit.'

I was shocked by her abruptness. It was no excuse but I could see the tiredness in her eyes. The thought of finding gowns for everyone in order to go into ICU was too much for her. Jimmy and the brother immediately picked up that they were not welcome. 'We will come back tomorrow,' Jimmy quietly said.

Jimmy, the mother and the brother turned and headed back down the corridor to the lift. I joined them in silence. The nurse turned back up the corridor. We had come five hours drive and could not cross the last hurdle. No protest came from Jimmy. It was the way life was. I felt sick.

I had not planned to stay the night in Darwin. When I offered to bring Jimmy and his family to Darwin I calculated that we would arrive by 2pm, visit the hospital for an hour, and then drive back to Barunga, getting home about 9pm. With Jimmy's comment that he would come back to the hospital tomorrow we now needed a place to stay. Once back in the troop carrier I asked Jimmy, 'Where can you stay, Jimmy?'

He answered with some assurance, 'Bagot. I have family there.'

I knew Bagot. It was a large Aboriginal community in Darwin. It was known to be fairly noisy when money was around. Tonight would be quieter. It was *milo*[1] week so both food and alcohol would be in short supply.

---

1. *Milo week* referred to the week when there was no government payment and money was short. It stemmed back to the drink *Milo* (chocolate drink) that filled a hungry stomach when on a cattle station or mission.

I drove into Bagot community confident that there would be a place here. Jimmy directed me by the signal of his hand. After passing several houses he indicated for me to stop in front of a large house. 'We can stay here tonight,' he said.

Jimmy and three others got out and went into the house. The rest of us remained in the vehicle.

Five minutes later Jimmy came out. He had a disappointed look on his face. He climbed back into the front seat and said to me, 'We can't stay here. We have too many people. No food.'

I felt numb. How much disappointment and rejection can Jimmy handle. The hospital and now here.

As upbeat as I could I asked again, 'Okay Jimmy. Where do we try next?'

'Maybe that old mission place, Rita Dixon. We could try there. They will let us stay the night.'

I also knew *Rita Dixon*. It had once been a children's home but was now shut down. It still had the old mission house but all the other buildings had become derelict or had been pulled down. I also knew the two single missionary ladies living there. I would do the talking this time.

It was just down the road from Bagot. I drove in feeling confident. There were no buildings that I could see where we could obviously stay but the old cement slabs were still there on the ground. I would ask for a couple of cement slabs. The two ladies had worked at Barunga in the past. They would know the family. They were also soft hearted. Everyone stayed in the vehicle and I went alone to the door and knocked.

I was greeted warmly. I quickly told them the background story and asked, 'I just need a couple of cement slabs to put our swags down for the night.'

My optimism was quickly shattered. They explained, 'We are not allowed to let anyone stay here. The mission and government policy won't let us. It no longer has the amenities for that. I am sorry we can't help you.'

This time I had the silent walk back to the car. Jimmy already knew my answer. 'Sorry Jimmy. We can't stay here.'

I started the engine and drove out of the compound in silence. The sun was displaying the last glimpses of an amazing sunset over the waters that woo tourists and locals alike. Darkness was setting in.

I was living the parable just as I had told Marg that morning. Those whom I had expected to help had not. The council car was not available, the hospital not welcoming, Bagot family thwarted by 25 extra mouths to feed, a mission bound by council rules and mission policy. What next?

The question came to my mind as if directly coming from Jesus himself. 'Are you going to help?'

It was a question best suited to the Dreamer where convention can be overlooked for a better future. As soon as the question was asked, I knew the answer. I needed to put a few things in place first. I assured my friends everything would be okay. I had a place for them.

We pulled into the carpark at Karama Shopping Centre.

'It is time to eat, Jimmy,' I said.

We had gone all day without food and no one had complained. I got out of the car and headed into the shopping centre. Only a couple of people followed me, Jimmy among them.

'Why isn't everyone coming to get something to eat Jimmy?'

Jimmy told me what I should have known. 'They don't have any money. Pay week is not til next week.'

I had ten dollars in my wallet. I abandoned all those cautionary instructions of being taken advantage of. These people were now family. I couldn't let them go hungry.

I told Jimmy quietly, 'Don't worry, I'll get the tucker.'

I bought the largest packet of sausages and a loaf of bread with my ten dollars. First, however, I needed to make a phone call. I rang the SIL Centre after hours number. I let it ring for two or three times and put the receiver down. I did not want to know what their policies were on people staying at the Centre. I suspected that if I asked for permission it may be denied. At least I could now say, 'I rang but no one answered the phone.'

We drove into the SIL Centre on McMillans Road and parked in the driveway of the second house on the right. It was the house allotted to the Bornemans.

'We are staying here tonight,' I said to Jimmy. 'Tell everyone they can make themselves comfortable. There is plenty of room for swags outside on the driveway or on the floor in the lounge.'

I headed across to the BBQ next to the meeting house. I poked my head around the corner and saw my colleagues standing and singing a hymn. The Sunday evening service was just starting. I ignored the music and checked the wood pile. The fire was soon alight and the hot plate sizzling with the evening meal. No-one clamoured for the food despite their hunger pains. There was a subdued relaxed atmosphere as different ones gathered in small groups sitting cross-legged eating their sausage and bread. Families soon settled down to sleep on blankets laid out on the ground. It was hot and humid but no rain in the air. A number migrated inside to sleep under the fan.

I sat down with Jimmy and a small group of men. I pulled out our photo album from our time living in the village in Papua New Guinea. It was a source of great interest. The story telling began.

An hour later I lay down in my own bed. I pondered the day. I had a couple of questions which I was not expecting answers to. 'Why Jesus did you tell me what was going to happen before it happened? Was that just to show me that today was your idea and not my idea? Also when I hear from you, you always seem to ask me to do the unexpected. Is that how it is always going to be?'

With my questions asked I lay contented in my bed with one last thought, 'I am happy for more days like this Jesus. I almost missed it. I am so thankful I haven't.'

Next morning we tidied up the house, loaded everyone into the troop carrier and headed again to the Royal Darwin Hospital. Before we left, an elder SIL stateswoman came walking by. I strolled over to her and asked the question I did not want to ask on the phone the previous night. 'Does SIL have a policy on who can stay at this Centre?'

She gave a smile and said, 'I am sure there is a policy.'

Whatever that policy was, her whimsical look suggested it was best ignored. Having 25 people in one house is probably one of them. Providing overnight accommodation for Aboriginal people not associated with our work was probably another one.

I stepped out of the lift to the ICU floor feeling apprehensive. This time, at Jimmy's suggestion, it was just himself, the mother and brother, along with me making our way along the corridor. Perhaps he saw how overwhelmed the nurse was the previous day. We arrived at the nurse's station at ICU and received the warmest of welcomes. They were delighted that family were visiting. I retreated outside. An hour later Jimmy came out of the hospital. 'We can go home now,' he said. 'We had a good visit.'

34

Labelled

Location:	Barunga and Katherine
Date:	1986
Event:	Fitting in

Our two-week stay in the mission house at Barunga was fuller than we expected. After the trip to Darwin with Jimmy we took another two-hour drive. This time we went fishing 'just a little way' along *the track*, officially labelled *Central Arnhem Highway* on the map, to Flying Fox Creek, though we didn't know that was our destination! Our Aboriginal friends were hoping to catch a barramundi. Marg and my objective was to build relationships, hear stories and learn. I was no fisherman. What we did know was that the community knew more about us than we knew about them.

Perhaps impressions had already formed. The principal of the school offered us a vacant Education Department house once it was repaired. It came with a request that I be available as a relief teacher when regular classroom teachers were away. We jumped at the opportunity. Two months later we drove out of Darwin and back to Barunga for a longer stay.

We were not sure what label best described us. All the white people living in communities had labels defined by their job: teacher, nurse, store keeper, pastor. Though I was registered as a relief teacher I was not part of the school fraternity. Though we associated with the church mob we were not leaders in the church nor were we the missionaries. We were not university academic researchers though we studied linguistics and learnt Kriol, which was the everyday language of the community. While we weren't sure what our label was, the community was observing these newcomers and making their own assessments.

Marg started a Kriol Bible reading class at the request of Daisybell. Half a dozen ladies joined her most days in the late afternoon shade. Some were employed in the bilingual program and could read well. Others could hardly read at all. Daisybell never missed a reading class and her perseverance was rewarded. Our children opened up friendships at church and school. Rachel joined the grade one class and Heidi the preschool class. Andrew at nearly two years of age was simply everyone's friend. We found a natural connection with the teacher-linguist supporting the Kriol program.

Our house was located in the far corner of the schoolyard and became a popular place for children to play after school. People observed us, categorised us and named us. I heard I was described by the nickname *Emu*. Like the male emu I looked after our kids while Marg was at reading class and I could be seen bringing clothes in from the line and pushing Andrew in his stroller. Rachel came home from school and informed us

that she was called *Ngarritjan*. She had a label on her desk telling her so. We found out that I had been given the name *Bangardi* and Marg *Wamutjan* based on who we related to. We had brothers and sisters, mothers and fathers throughout the community whom we did not yet know.

Marg's borders continued to naturally expand into the community as a mother and through her community reading sessions. The Christian mob were mainly women. My world became more static as I related to a few remarkable old men who happily sat and told stories of earliest contact with white people and experiences in the cattle industry. It was difficult to break the ice with the young men. As I walked by the lush football oval I noticed an increase in activity. A group of footballers were in training for the inaugural Barunga Festival. I wandered across the oval and joined the young men kicking the ball back and forth. It was not difficult to join in. The sporting field was where I felt most comfortable. Without a word spoken I was treated as one of the team. By the end of the training session their curiosity needed to be satisfied. Two of the men casually spoke to me, 'You missionary eh?'

'Is that what you call me, *missionary*,' I replied a little surprised.

'Yeah you missionary,' they confirmed with a smile. I had heard the term *missionary* used often in the community. What was unexpected was that the word *missionary* was used for white people they admired. The reasons given were consistent. The missionary helps us, the missionary lives with us, the missionary knows us. The missionary learns our language. These positive qualities had definitely not filtered through to my anthropology lecturer at university, or perhaps they had been filtered out.

My new friend then said, 'But missionaries don't play football.'

I replied with a laugh, 'This missionary plays football. I just want to train with you. Is that okay?'

'Yuwai,' came the affirmative answer with a broad grin.

I learned quickly that football was an opportunity to experiment with the impossible. Calculated game plans were non-existent. Flare and daring ruled supreme. The more flare and the more daring the better the game. A sensational leap hanging off the shoulders of an opponent was attempted with the remotest chance of it being successful. A scintillating zigzagging run out of the backline was encouraged even if it risked a turnover. If the scoreline mattered it did not show. Delight was not in the final score but how the game was played. For the Dreamer, it was not only the perfect way to approach football but the perfect way to approach the spiritual life. It was the playing with flare and daring and occasionally trying the impossible that mattered. The results would take care of themselves.

35

Bottom Camp

Location:	Barunga
Date:	1986
Event:	A walk in the cool of the evening

It was time to begin the evening routine. Dinner, story time and children's bedtime. Life is determined by habits and habits are hard to break. One night I was feeling uneasy. My intuition was interfering with life's practice. I told Marg my thoughts.

'I feel I need to go for a walk around the camp for some reason. I think it's a God thing.'

Marg knew how unusual this was. Her husband was not a person to stroll around the camp looking for company for no apparent reason. She was more the extrovert.

'If you think you should go then by all means go.'

I wandered down towards bottom[1] camp. I then swung off at ninety degrees along a dirt road that headed out towards the back of the camp. I had not walked to the end of this track before. The community itself was unusually quiet. I wondered where the people were. I did not have to wait long. A further 250 metres down the track I saw a large gathering in an open area. I could see cars parked with their lights on and people sitting on blankets. Together they formed a large U shape. It was about 50

---

1. Different sections of Barunga carried a local description. Bottom camp was housing furtherest from the store and council offices.

metres across and 100 metres deep. Campfires were scattered around the perimeter providing warmth against the freshness of the dry season night. I was drawn towards the gathering. I recognised some of the Christian mob sitting some distance away. Across the other side of the field, within the field itself was a single small fire. I recognised my friend Jimmy sitting alone on a rug. On a plastic chair in the middle of the field was his wife, Queenie. A lone large-framed man with an equally large cowboy hat stood next to Queenie. There was no one else close by. Everyone else was distant onlookers. I leisurely walked the 50 metres across the field towards Jimmy. I was aware that all eyes were on this white man intruding into *blackfella* business. No one was expecting this, me included. My mind was racing. I was in unknown territory.

I sat down on the rug next to Jimmy. I now had some cover as I observed all that was around me. The stillness was eerie. I struggled to put a finger on it then realised the constant sound of squabbling and barking dogs was absent. I asked, 'What's happening, Jimmy?'

'It's Queenie,' he said quietly. 'She is proper sick. She has gone *longlong* you know *crazy*,' he said pointing to his head.

I knew Queenie. She was a quiet and gracious lady who sat on the fringe of the church group.

'We got the *klebabalamen* to come and fix her up,' Jimmy offered. The English word sometimes used for *klebabalamen* was *witch doctor*. I suddenly felt conspicuous. The teaching of the church was clear. There were two choices in life. You either take the good road or the bad road. A true Christian doesn't keep company with the devil. A true Christian would not be here. God had corralled me into a place that was against the teaching of the community church.

Questions swirled around in my head. 'Jesus, by sitting here, am I saying it's okay to mix light and darkness?' As quickly as I asked the question a counter thought came. 'It was God who brought me here and Jimmy is not asking me to go. So stay!' The Dreamer warmed to the latter statement. The best adventures with Jesus were those that started with not knowing the answers or how it would finish.

All attention swung to the *Klebabalamen*. He strode back and forth passing Queenie who was sitting forlornly on the old plastic chair. His strides were strong and deliberate, his back straight. Once he was 10-15 metres past Queenie, he turned abruptly, then strode back toward the chair with real purpose. He wrapped his strong hands on either side of her head, looked intently at her, before striding away again. It was a masterful performance. A billy can of water lay on the grass next to the chair. He picked it up and took a mouthful of water. He held her head in both his hands, placing his mouth up against her forehead. He turned and spat the water out with a huge spray. He repeated this dramatic movement several times. His showmanship was exquisite. His actions conveyed authority and assurance.

I could not take my eyes off him. The more I looked, the more I saw a fellow human. The persona did not define him. I wondered about his motivation. Was this the only way he thought that he could help her? Was he performing a ritual handed down from generation to generation for desperate times like this? Some may see him as a tool of Satan bringing deception, but right now it was not for me to decide. I sat observing like everyone else.

One last spray of water and he wound back the performance. Jimmy rose from the blanket and walked over to the *Klebabalaman*. They spoke. Jimmy returned and sat next to me. He explained, 'A spirit entered her head when she was down at the waterhole last week. He could see small holes in her head where it entered. It has been swirling around in her head sending her crazy.'

'Is she going to get better Jimmy?' I asked.

'He doesn't know. He didn't think he was able to make it go.'

A number of men were now standing with the *klebabalaman*. He walked towards me. I stood up. We shook hands politely acknowledging each other. Two *klebabalaman* in our own way I thought to myself. I knew our meeting was breaking convention, but I was not writing the script.

I said to him, 'I will pray for Queenie.'

He nodded in approval.

His task was done. He was rewarded with $400 for his services and a carton of beer. His performance was worth every cent.

Queenie moved from the chair and sat on the blanket next to me beside the fire. I sat silently weighing up the situation from her perspective. I concluded, the *klebabalaman* has left her in a worse position than she was before. He has identified the problem but not solved it.

'Can I pray for you,' I asked.

'Yuwai', she replied. I knew I was to pray but had no idea what to pray. Should I pray based on the prognosis of the *klebabalaman*? The picture of me boldly casting out an evil spirit that was not present amused me. It would be a performance in Jesus' name to match the *klebabalaman*. It would be equally ineffective. I thought about the safe option. Why not simply pray peace and comfort over Queenie. I scolded myself. It was too tame and too lame given the circumstances. Praying with the mind was becoming complicated. I was out of my depth. I looked at Queenie and was struck by her forlorn figure. I felt Jesus' love for her. It was time to pray. I moved alongside Queenie and said,

'I am going to pray for you in another language that God has given me. The Holy Spirit will be talking to your spirit. Is that okay with you?'

Queenie nodded her head.

I began to pray for her very quietly and gently in tongues, not raising my voice or making any grand gestures. The words that came were soothing and rhythmic with each syllable fully articulated. Queenie was the only one who could hear it. The words were just between us. I sensed a peace coming over Queenie and was grateful for that. I was not looking for a public fight between the forces of light and the forces of darkness. I concluded my prayer with a blessing in Kriol and the liturgical safety net, 'I ask this in Jesus' name. Amen.'

The dogs were now barking and fighting, people talking and walking back to camp. Queenie looked up at me and thanked me with a smile. I sidled up to Jimmy who was sitting just a few metres away. We agreed we should catch up again soon.

I walked back home along the dirt road alone. I wondered what it all meant. What I did know was that with Jesus it was neither about me nor the *klebabalaman*. It was about Jesus' love for Queenie.'

A week later we met again under the tree where Marg held her Kriol Bible reading sessions. Jimmy's son (nephew) had been transferred to the Royal Adelaide Hospital renal unit. Jimmy told me he was homesick for his family and country. I suggested they record a message for him on my cassette recorder and send it to him. Queenie was no longer the lethargic figure of the previous week. She was alert and ready to share her story. I placed the microphone in front of her and she began to talk in Kriol. The speed of the language made it difficult for me to follow. Queenie's storytelling was in full swing. I then heard her talk about being really sick. I listened intently. In the flow of Kriol, a single sentence caught my attention. I heard her say, 'Dijan misionari iya bin pray bla mi en streidawei det siknes bin gowei na.'

Had I heard her right? I didn't know. When she finished recording we sat quietly for some time. My curiosity needed to be satisfied. I asked her, 'Did I hear you say the sickness went away when I prayed for you?' Queenie was puzzled by my uncertainty.

'When you prayed for me I got better. The sickness went away. Jesus healed me.' She was adamant.

My hesitancy to believe God had restored Queenie through my prayer, was not a product of humility. I had a deeper struggle with the idea of God using me for the miraculous. I was more attracted to a personal and private spiritual life than to public performance. If I did not have that deeper struggle, I would have immediately known from Queenie's smile that farewelled me that night that God had intervened. Whatever was said when I prayed in tongues would remain a mystery to me, but one thing was certain, it communicated very clearly to whatever or whoever was causing the problem.

I turned to Jimmy and asked, 'How do you think Queenie was healed from her sickness?'

He replied with a sense of relief on his face, 'I don't know. I am just happy she is better.'

36

'This Sit-Down Money Is Going To Kill Us!'

Location: Barunga
Date: 1986
Event: An old man's observation

The old man was thought to be over 80 years old. No one was sure. That would take his early days back to the turn of the century when white men were a novelty in his part of the world. Old Hickey enjoyed sitting in the shade and telling his stories. I had the time to listen. He spoke eight languages to varying degrees. He never went to school himself but he took it as his duty to round up any child who remained in the camp when they should be at school. He carried an authority of a lawman and one who had lived life fully. In more recent years he became a stalwart amongst the Christian mob. His stories clearly suggested this was not always the case.

He told me about his father's first meeting with a white man and what a scary proposition the white man was. He told me about his days working in the cattle industry and poisoned waterholes. He told his stories always with good humour. He was a tough resilient character. He was an observer of life. We sat in the shade of a tree not far from the community church as he observed the world around him. In the distance he saw a young man who had recently come out of prison. The young man was sitting around not doing anything in particular. The old man directed his question to no-one in particular though I was his only company. There was no humour this time.

'What for that white man give him *sit down money*?' He looked at me with a concern for his people. He added, 'That *sit down money* is going to kill us.'

I was not expected to answer. But I had no answer for him anyway. White man's answers usually didn't make sense. Unemployment benefit was a very new thing in the community and he did not like what he saw. I couldn't tell him that some white people thought Aboriginal people receiving unemployment benefit was a great step forward. I couldn't tell him for some white people it was an issue of justice and equality. I wondered if the government policy makers would listen and take notice of an old Aboriginal man who knew his own people and the risks they faced. For him this *sit down money* was like poisoning the waterhole. For the old man this was not justice.

I also could not tell him that many white people blame the Aboriginal man for being lazy, for drinking too much, and taking unemployment benefits. The old man saw it more clearly. It was the white man, the government who were giving young people this *sit-down money*. The cause of this problem was the government of the white man. Aboriginal people were not lazy, but this *sit down money* is going to make him lazy, and it will kill him. The old man had worked all his life as a hunter of kangaroo, emu and occasional cattle. He was a warrior, and later a cattleman, and did well at whatever he put his hand to. The stereotype of a lazy Aboriginal was one he could not identify with. He despised the thought and feared it. That was 1986 and his words still ring in my ears.

37

White Man Always Pushing

> Location: Barunga
> Date: 1985
> Event: The art of listening and negotiating

Scene One – Coronation Hill Negotiations

I entered the Barunga Council Office for purposes I don't now recall. The receptionist gave me that reassuring look that said I will be with you in a minute when I have finished the task I have at hand. The office was particularly busy that morning but then it had been for the last few weeks. A constant stream of visitors were making their way to Barunga. Meetings were called, deadlines set, and decisions made. The future, or otherwise, of the uranium and gold mine at Coronation Hill was dependent on it. Most of the visitors either vehemently opposed the venture or supported it. They all understood that the position of the Jawoyn community would be a compelling factor in the final decision of the Commonwealth Government. These strangers would befriend, cajole, and offer incentives on the one hand but equally use the media to pressure, threaten, and marginalise anyone with opposing views. It was called the art of doing the deal. It was the *munanga* (white man) way of negotiating.

The phone rang on the desk over to the side. A distinguished Jawoyn man with whom I had a personal acquaintance answered the phone. The conversation did not last long. He turned to me and commented forlornly, 'Another newspaper reporter.'

I immediately imagined the headlines the next day. *Jawoyn Supports Mining*, or equally it could read *Coronation Hill Backflip: Jawoyn Says No to*

Mining. The reporter would have satisfied himself that he had his sources, but the headline would be his own for a different audience. The Jawoyn called it *humbug*. Annoying chatter and demands without listening.

I left the council office sobered by what I observed. My own culture riding roughshod over Aboriginal decision making. Conservationists opposed the mine because it may set a precedence for mining in Kakadu National Park. Miners argued that existing mining leases should be honoured. Not to do so was a missed economic benefit and presented sovereign risk. Political parties were influenced by public opinion in Sydney and Melbourne, or the northern suburbs of Darwin with an eye to the next election. They all seemed to be tarred with the same brush. They did not come to listen. They came for a result that suited them.

The distinguished Mr Silas Roberts (OBE), first Chairman of the Northern Lands Council, Justice of the Peace, Roper River (Ngukurr) mission educated and lay preacher, was highly regarded. Silas had interacted with white men, politicians and mining companies more than most on behalf of his people. He had no axe to grind but he was a smart observer of human behaviour.

Nine years earlier in 1977 he had described to the Fox Commission the difficulties Aboriginal people faced when dealing with white men. He put it this way,

> *We see white men as always pushing. We know white men think differently from us, and they are not all bad. But even this Commission is pushing in its own way ... Our people are not as free to make decisions and give evidence as white men seem to be ... We have got to make decisions in respect to land our own way. It is a long hard road to the final answer.*
>
> *Sometimes a person or group will say 'yes' then talk a little bit more time and then say 'no'. Then more talk might take place after a few months and still no final answer. Then all the people who really belong to that country will go over it again until everyone is sure of his answer and then the answer is given. That may be years after the first talks if the question is a hard one. p47*

There was no doubt the decision around Guratba (Coronation Hill) was a hard one. It was complex. In the course of informal conversation mainly with younger men I heard that the employment opportunities were important. I heard that the recognised traditional elders needed to be respected, and I heard varying weight given to the reality of the Bula Spirit and the likelihood that disturbing Bula would lead to natural disasters. There were also some who didn't hold any position. Like any community, each Jawoyn weighed the factors differently according to their perspectives, personality, family loyalty, and individual circumstances. It was for situations like this that their highly developed art of establishing a consensus existed. A process required patience and an undetermined amount of time.

The outsiders preferred deadlines that forced premature decisions. Swarms of strangers never tiring of pushing. Always presenting their case according to their own logic. As a white man living in Barunga I was not impartial to holding my own white man's analysis of the ensuing drama being played out under the national spotlight. My summary was that the whitefella outsiders acted with the underlying assumption that they simply knew better than the Jawoyn, and more hideously that they also knew what was best for the Jawoyn. Left to their own devices the Jawoyn could not make the decision. These outsiders carrying their own agenda were the modern day superintendent of the reserve. They were men of the soil frustrated with the apparent indecision of the Dreamers.

Scene Two – Negotiating a funeral

A much respected and well-loved old lady passed away. Everyone in her community recognised her as a Christian. For years she never missed attending Christian fellowship meetings or church when it was held in her community. She abstained from alcohol, she prayed, she quietly shared the good news of Jesus, and she gave her time and money doing good for her family and community. She had chosen God's way as a young person and lived it for a lifetime. She was fully Aboriginal and fully Christian. For her family her funeral represented a common dilemma. How would they balance their desire for it to be a Christian funeral along with other family and cultural obligations? They could not make this decision alone.

I was on my regular mid-morning wanderings looking out for someone to chat to and practise my Kriol. It was then I just happened to run into an old man with whom I always enjoyed a conversation. He was lean with the frame of a stockman on which the cattle industry in Northern Australia was built. He was another great storyteller and an upright man associated with the Christian mob from time to time. We meandered along in no hurry or to any destination that I was aware of. Eventually he sauntered over to a group of men sitting randomly in the semi shade, facing different directions. He indicated that I should join them. I followed his lead and sat cross-legged in the dirt in the fashion of most of the men. A few older men had plastic chairs or an upturned flour can to sit on. Not a word was said to me. I didn't feel like an intruder.

The purpose for the meeting soon became clear. A man stood up and told a story that related to the old lady who had died. No one looked directly at the man speaking, but it was clear everyone was intently listening in silence. When he finished saying what he wanted to say he sat down. No questions were asked of him. After a pause of a few minutes, another man stood and told a story that related in some way to the old lady. When he had finished saying what he wanted to say he sat down. No questions were asked of him. A period of silence followed then another man spoke until around a dozen men had told their story. Some remained sitting when they spoke and some stood. I assumed there was an unspoken order but I did not know it. I assumed the content of each person's speech and its authority was influenced by their relationship to the old lady, and their position in the community, but I didn't know that either.

Each story told of some aspect of her place in the community, her family and place amongst the Christian mob. The final man then spoke. He did not tell a story of his own. Instead he indicated that he had weighed up all that was said. It was obvious even to me that he carried the authority to do so. The conversation was in Kriol, and while I could follow the general meaning, the nuances were not clear to me. One statement however stood out to me,

> 'Dijan olgamen im brabli Kristjan. Im nomo hafwei. Im garra abum Kristjan fyunral na.'

This old woman was a proper Christian not halfway. She will have a Christian funeral.

I did not recognise the spokesman as a man associated with the Christian mob. He was speaking on behalf of the family and community.

When the meeting took as long as it needed to take, it quietly broke up and the men wandered off in different directions. I was an observer the whole time and did not speak a word nor was I asked to speak. I thought I had stumbled into the meeting, but now realised this could not have been the case. For some of the men it was important for me to be there. They had arranged it. My mind went back to that first trip to the Darwin hospital more than six months before. She was one of the old ladies in the back of our troop carrier. Then there was Marg's connection with so many of the older ladies. We were somehow integrated into the community in a way I did not understand. For this reason I was invited into the conversation. This was decision making their way. No-one is excluded.

Scene Three – Scene One Reimagined

The Dreamer in me was seeing a different future. It was a similar meeting with a gathering of different participants. Sitting randomly cross-legged on the ground, some on chairs and some on flour drums were representatives from conservationists, miners, politicians, the Northern Land Council, and leaders in the Jawoyn community. Each was given the opportunity to tell their story about Coronation Hill without ridicule of anyone else or making any disparaging comments. Each person respectfully listened without any rolling of the eyes or heckling. When all was said that needed to be said, they all sat and waited in silence. The group of Jawoyn elders then summarised a concluding position. No action plan was made nor their summary expected to be acted upon.

The group agrees to reconvene again at some time in the future for another conversation. Some new participants are added to the meeting. More stories are told. Again, when all that needs to be said is said, the elders articulate their position. Once articulated everyone disperses in their different directions. No more humbug, no more pushing, no more manipulation through the media for their own agenda. Each person leaves satisfied that all sides of a complex issue have been heard and that the best decision possible has been made by the people traditionally responsible for the land.

They agree to meet again for a third time, only a more distant time into the future. The stories and the summary by the elders have time to percolate and bubble and settle. A consensus that respects the traditional custodians of the land and ceremony leaders, that recognises the economic advantages for the young people, and identifies the negative impact on the land is starting to emerge. Time does not weary them. They wait, they talk, and when all have been heard, a decision will be made by the custodians of the land – and it will be for the good.

38

Morrow's Farm
– More Than A Place To Stay

Location:	Katherine: Morrow's Farm
Date:	1987-1990
Event:	Gojok

When the NT Education Department needed their house back at Barunga we no longer had a place to live. We packed our belongings into our trailer and drove to Morrow's Farm on the outskirts of Katherine on the banks of the Katherine River. Bruce Morrow, a Christian farmer had agreed to store our trailer in his shed while we went to Victoria for Christmas holidays. When we arrived at the farm I noticed a partly completed high-set house on the property. I asked Bruce, 'Who is that house for?'

Bruce was a man of few words and he simply smiled and said, 'Perhaps it is for you.' Our move to Morrow's Farm would wait a further five months. Before the move we had other business to attend to.

Marg was expecting our fourth child. Our supervisor suggested we extend our annual holiday in Melbourne and have our baby there. With three young children we needed a place to stay for this extended time. On hearing of our need, a friend from our Melbourne church immediately offered us her home for as long as we needed it. She would simply move back in with her mum! Marg booked into the remaining ante-natal classes at Box Hill Hospital that was now a familiar place.

This time round, when contractions started increasing their strong rhythm late one night, we decided it was time to go. As soon as our friend Ruth arrived to stay with our children, I rang the hospital and we headed off. To Marg's surprise and delight she was reunited with the same midwives who remembered Andrew's speedy arrival two and a half years before. The old team was back together again. What an amazing provision that we suspected included some intervention from a fun loving, life giving Heavenly Father. With great joy, Naomi came into the world without a hiccup, and in a much more leisurely way than her brother. Again the birth came at no cost to us due to the Australian public health system.

Baby Naomi was three months old when we moved into our three-bedroom high-set house on Morrow's Farm with the Katherine River and bush on one side and paddocks with cattle grazing on the other. It was the ideal setting for our young family. It was also an ideal place for our Aboriginal friends to camp, fish and relax away from the noise of community. In hindsight it seemed like all roads led to Morrow's Farm. A place where creativity, academic application, spirituality, the joy of simple living intersected and fed off each other. I was in my mid-thirties and I had arrived at a place of contentment and purpose. Over the course of the next few years creativity flowed as I put flesh and bones to a Kriol Reading Book, songwriting and recording workshops for Aboriginal Christians in 1987 and 1988, checking the natural flow of the Kriol translation, and running a Kriol story writing competition that received UNESCO recognition in the 1990 International Year of Literacy. Initially however the slightly removed and comfortable environment brought its own risks.

The pull to slowly merge back into the white world was ever present. The pull to undertake further academic study and the time required always lingered. Solo time was the Dreamer's sweet spot and the farm provided that in abundance. I could see the dangers. The personal relationships built with Aboriginal families would slide down the priority list. Instead of walking alongside friends I could find myself walking and viewing my friends from a distance. Soon they would be objects for my work. My skin name *Bangardi*, and Marg's *Wamutjan* would be token reminders that we were once family. But there was one remedy to all this. Marg was not about to let it happen. She specifically put out a prayer request for her husband to find a close Aboriginal friend in Katherine.

Marg arrived home full of enthusiasm from one of her regular visits with a family at *Corroboree Hostel*. She exclaimed, 'Irene asked if you would go and visit her husband at Katherine East.'

I looked at Marg blankly. I was not ready for a *cold* visit to someone whose wife thought it was a good idea for someone else's husband to visit him. I could see both him and I unenthused by the whole idea. Seeing my resistance to the idea Marg added, 'Just go around and say hello. It can't be that difficult a thing to do.'

It was not with any personal conviction that I made the visit. The house was easily identified with its fire pit in the front yard. Two plastic chairs and an over-turned flour drum lay under a shady tree. Tufts of grass made their intermittent appearance in contrast to the bare ground. It was a familiar sight and one I felt comfortable in. I slowly made my way to the front door which was wide open. I called out and waited. A man in his mid-twenties with a black beard came slowly to the door. He had a limp and an easy smile. The meeting should have been awkward but it was not. We greeted each other and *Gojok* invited me to join him in the front yard away from the kids playing inside. We each took a chair and moved to the shade. It seemed like he was expecting me. Conversation was unforced and relaxed in either English or Kriol. It was the beginning of many such times together. His home became the home that I felt most relaxed in other than my own. It was where I went for company, not as a missionary fulfilling his felt need to be about the Lord's work, but as a friend.

Gojok read *The Australian* newspaper whenever he came across a copy. He liked to talk about issues broader than his own community. He was a gentleman, a scholar, brother and a friend. Six months after we first met, the health service employed him to run education programs to reduce substance abuse in the camp communities around Katherine. We translated 'The 12 Steps of Alcoholics Anonymous' into Kriol and published it in booklet form. We checked the draft translation of the Kriol New Testament together.

Gojok and his family became part of ours. He called Naomi his baby girl. She would jump from Marg's arms into his whenever he and his beaming smile came into our presence. I awoke one morning and looked down at the small campfire that glowed a few metres below our bedroom. Gojok and his family were camping the weekend, fishing in the river during the day and sleeping by our house at night. They were still asleep, snug and comfortable under their blankets near the embers of their campfire from the night before. Then I noticed a familiar shape snuggled under the blanket. It was our *baby* daughter. I was not surprised. I didn't know when in the night or morning she decided that being snuggled up by the campfire was a better place than her own bed. I didn't ask. It looked so normal because it was.

Gojok and his family, along with some other guests, celebrated Christmas Day '89 with us. After our roast dinner the children all dressed up as the characters in the Christmas story: Mary, Joseph, a shepherd, angels and wise men with their gifts. Laughter and parental pride filled the occasion. The perfect Christmas.

My fear of not being able to connect in a genuine way with Indigenous life in town did not eventuate. Gojok and his family had a lot to do with that. Marg also had a lot to do with it. So it was that our home at Morrow's Farm on the banks of the Katherine River became more than a place to stay. It was an oasis for our family, as well as a place to dream, to work, and be hospitable.

Postscript: 35 years later 2022

Gojok and I have stayed in intermittent contact over the years. In 2022 we drove into Katherine after visiting a friend on a cattle station three hours to the south-west. As we pulled into a service station for fuel I said to our daughter Rachel, 'It doesn't feel right to be in Gojok's country and not see him.' Rachel agreed. She called him *Daddy John* and from time to time would make the 8 hour trip from her home in Darwin to visit his family in Weemol along the Central Arnhem Highway to the east of Katherine. We simply didn't have sufficient time to make that trip in our three week visit with Rachel.

As we were talking, Gojok and Irene pulled into the same servo. None of us could believe it! His beaming smile was still as bright as we remembered it. We greeted each other with a hug, found some shade by the roadside, and continued our conversation as if we never had been apart. After asking about our family in English he then switched to Kriol and said,

'Bangardi ai garram kwesjin fo yu.'

Bangardi, I got a question for you.

'Yuwai, wanim det kwesjin na?'

Yes, what's the question?

'Wat wi garra du bla det mununga praolem?'

What can we do about the white man problem?

'Wanim det prablem?' I asked.

What's the problem?

'Wal im nomo lisin. Wen det mununga kam la miting, wal im reken im alredi sabi ebrijing. Im nomo sabi bla lisin.'

They don't listen. When they come to a meeting they already think they know what is best. They don't know how to listen.

We laughed together as he shared stories about white men in air-conditioned rooms making decisions without talking to traditional owners. He said they don't learn the language and listen like that old missionary mob. He said it is getting worse, not better. I told him a story about a conservationist from the city who assumed my father knew nothing about the native grasses that were growing on his land. The conservationist could have learnt a lot about how to graze cattle and maintain native grasses at the same time from my father, but he never asked.

Gojok laughed, 'That's just the same for us. They don't ask and they don't listen. They think they know better.'

His question appealed to my sense of humour, 'What are we going to do about the white man problem?'

We laughed some more as we walked back to his vehicle. It was friends like Gojok who saved me from becoming a *white man problem* and believing I had the answers.

I also believed that the Giver of Dreams had warped time and heard our cry so Gojok and I could rendezvous and laugh together one more time at the service station. Friendship is important to Jesus. After all Jesus did say he called us 'friends'. He knows what it means to be a friend.

39

The Legacy Of Pastor Bill And Madge Rosas

Location:	Katherine
Date:	1987-1990
Event:	Church and a miracle

At Ridley College I was introduced to the English translation of Swedish Catholic Theologian Hans Kung's classic *The Church*. It was one of the few theological books that remained in my care. Kung put eloquently into words what the Dreamer experienced.

> *The believing and baptised Christian therefore needs, in this ultimate sense, no human mediator at all in order to find and maintain fellowship with God in Christ. Every believer ... has a direct relationship with God, which no human being in the fellowship can take away from him, and no human, nor ecclesiastical authority can disrupt. It is this most intimate personal sphere that ultimate decisions between the individual and God are taken ... This is where God's grace makes direct contact with man, God's Spirit guides him. This is where he finds his ultimate freedom and his ultimate responsibility. No one can judge, control or command the decisions that are made in this sphere of direct contact between God and man.*

Kung 1968:373

For the Dreamer maintaining a relationship with Jesus was his personal responsibility. No one else nor any ecclesiastic authority could add to it or disrupt it. This gave the Dreamer a freedom to appreciate different churches while not being bound to one. It also meant choosing a church to belong to was not straightforward.

The logical church for us to attend in Katherine was the Anglican church but when we prayed, we sensed a different answer. The church that came to mind was a Pentecostal church. This was not without risk. Their enthusiasm did not concern me. What I was cautious about was what I perceived as an unhealthy elevation of the pastor and the assumed personal control over people's lives. As we packed the kids into the car and headed to their Sunday morning service, I did not go with great confidence. I soon found I had no reason for concern.

Bill and Madge Rosas exuded a gentleness and patience birthed by a life of hardship, thankfulness, and God's Spirit. The church members called him Pastor Bill. I called him Bill, but occasionally I would find the words 'Pastor Bill' on my lips, not as a title but as an honourable description of the man.

Bill was a slight man in his early 60s with a beaming smile and warm disarming personality. Madge was amongst the most elegant and hospitable ladies you could imagine. Bill relished a good story interspersed with an infectious laugh. He encapsulated a rich cultural heritage as a Yidinji man from North Queensland and descendant of black-birders from Tanna Island in Vanuatu. They both lived all their formative years in Queensland subject to the draconian government restrictions imposed by *The Act* and yet they carried no malice. While the white man's system sought to curtail their freedom and determine their future the Giver of Dreams set them free and invited them to set sail and catch the wind to wherever he would lead them.

The first breeze that caught young Bill Rosas' attention was a miracle. His bedridden grandmother was seriously ill and on the verge of death. Christian relatives visited her smoke-filled bush hut made of sheets of bark and prayed for her. The next morning she got out of her bed, healed and transformed. Bill remembers her going from a devil worshipper to living only for God. Granny Rosas became a prayer powerhouse. These were no ordinary times. It was in the midst of the Pinnacle Pocket Revival that began in the 1930s when God chose to lavishly pour out his love and grace on Aboriginal and South Sea Islander families. This was at a time when the white man system in Queensland could not trust them to have a full education or a vote.

Bill loved to tell the story of an old man at Pinnacle Pocket who had never been to school, was totally illiterate but when the Spirit of God touched him he could read his Bible in church and preach powerfully. Then there was the story of a hundred-year-old lady getting out of a wheelchair, and even someone being raised from the dead. Every story was told with a laugh and a fond memory of what God can do. Bill's stories always pointed to a greater truth. Pastor Bill would say that the easiest thing in the world to do was to become a Christian. Jesus had done it all. You only have to believe. He would laugh as he said it. Apparently in some cases it was also easy to heal the cripple, raise the dead, and for illiterate men to read. It was easier if you came from the Aboriginal and South Seas Islander community at Pinnacle Pocket in North Queensland with its rich Holy Spirit history.

Several months later at the end of the morning service Bill reminded everyone, 'Don't forget our service tonight. We have a special guest with a healing ministry coming. He has a gift for praying for people with back problems and for people who have one leg shorter than the other. So please come.'

I pricked up my ears. The casual comment about a *leg lengthener* reminded me of a previous conversation I had with God six years before. When I found out that my left leg was slightly shorter than my right leg I told God that it did not worry me and that he did not have to heal it. As a throwaway line I added that if I ever came across one of those *leg lengtheners* who pray in Jesus' name then I would get my leg sorted. I wasn't expecting it to happen. Now I was confronted with a dilemma. Do I go or not go?

I walked in late and sat down at the back. I was determined to keep my emotional engagement to a minimum. Pastor Bill introduced his guest in his usual informal and enthusiastic way. The guest told of one healing event after another. I was too preoccupied with my own dilemma to appreciate the miracles. I wanted to get it over and done with. I would keep my word to God, but not caring if it would mean healing or not. Eventually the stories stopped and the offer was given.

'If anyone would like prayer for healing please come forward.'

I walked to the front. I understood that the problem was likely a slight misalignment of the hip rather than one leg shorter than the other. I stuck to the cruder description. I stated, 'I have come to get my leg lengthened.'

The *leg lengthener* asked me to sit in a chair provided for that purpose and to stretch out my legs. He placed his hands on my ankles. He had hardly started praying when my left leg levelled up with my right leg. It was done. I stood up and said, 'Thanks mate, it is all good.'

I walked to the back of the room and headed home. The next time I did strenuous exercise the ache in my hip was gone. I marvelled at the mystery. I did not ask God to do it, nor did I expect him to do it because I deemed it insignificant to my faith. Yet he did it anyway. It was his decision to realign my hip, not mine.

Hans Kung wrote:

> *No one can judge, control or command the decisions that are made in this sphere of direct contact between God and man.*

Bill Rosas understood this and so did the Dreamer. The briefest connection with Jesus was enough to change everything. It was a mystery, a sacred space that we did not control.

The fellowship and friendship with Bill and Madge Rosas was a personal gift. For Bill life was never just about the church. It was always about Jesus and his love for people. I reasoned Jesus' love was as infectious as Bill's laugh. Bill experienced great sorrow when his beautiful wife Madge passed away three years later at the age of 61. But Bill's spiritual strength was deeply rooted in the prayers of Granny Rosas decades before. He continued to be Jesus' ambassador. We visited Bill at an old people's home in Katherine when he was 92 years old, the year before he went 'home to glory'. He interspersed his infectious laugh with stories of how good Jesus was, just as he had always done. Then he confided in me, indicating in the direction of Rachel, our daughter who arranged our visit. 'That one is a proper missionary' he said. 'She does not boss Aboriginal people around. She just loves them.' He followed it with his characteristic infectious laugh.

Tears welled up in my eyes. There could not be a higher commendation from a more noble person.

POSTSCRIPT

I rarely share my leg lengthening story publicly. It was personal. Three decades later I included it amongst my stories of unusual events in my life when speaking to a church congregation in Melbourne. My quandary of what to do when the leg lengthener came to town lent itself to a humorous retelling. After the service a lady came directly to the front of the church where I was standing. She got my attention and said 'My left leg is shorter than my right leg.'

I asked, 'Do you want me to pray for you?'

She replied, 'Yes.'

I prepared her for disappointment. I offered, 'Whether you are healed or not has no bearing on God's love for you. His love is shown by the cross and the forgiveness of sin.'

'I understand that,' she responded.

'I have never prayed for this before. I don't particularly have a healing ministry.'

She looked at me in a way that suggested she was fine with that too. I had lowered all expectations. Hers and mine. Just then a young church leader called out, 'Testimony just means do it again Lord!'

The words rang in my ear. 'Do it again Lord.' I called over another young man whose broken back had been healed a couple of years before. I needed re-enforcements. We asked her to sit on a chair. We straightened out her legs in front of us and held them in our hands. There was a notable difference. Then we both prayed.

Before our eyes her left leg lengthened and became level with her right leg. I was sure it had to be the faith of my friend.

As one happy young lady walked away I said to my friend, 'That was great mate. You are a real pro.'

'Never prayed for that before,' he replied. We were two novices together.

The next week we heard that young lady had been for a walk and her leg ached. She realised she was still wearing her slightly raised left shoe! She didn't need those shoes anymore. She was healed!

I was now a *leg lengthener*, not that I would be telling anyone. But how did it come about? The answer I reasoned was in the declaration, 'Testimony just means do it again Lord.'

In the Dreamer's world where heaven and earth intersected, it made sense. The young lady's healing was somehow directly connected to what happened to me 30 years previously back in Katherine. What happened to me in Katherine had a direct connection back 30 or 40 years previously to something God did at Pinnacle Pocket when Bill Rosas was a young man there. The Pinnacle Pocket Revival came through a man who attended the Welsh Revival as a young man in 1905. Perhaps he experienced a similar miracle. That would be four miracles spread over 110 years somehow connected to each other. For the Holy Spirit they may seem only moments apart. It is possible. I love the thought. I love the imagination of the Holy Spirit and how he crafts his story through his people.

40

One Country, Two Worlds

Location: Coles-Myer Philanthropy Trust, Melbourne
Date: 1983
Event: A Literacy project application

I was greeted with a handshake. The Bible Society corporate funding representative did not look out of place in the swank little coffee shop in Bourke Street Melbourne. His dress trousers, business shirt and tie were smart but conservative like others around us. I was suddenly aware of the comparison. I wore casual trousers, a long sleeve shirt rolled up halfway to my elbows, leather shoes on my feet and no tie. I hoped I passed the grade.

My new friend ordered a cappuccino for me and a flat white for himself. There was no billy tea on offer. Now it was time to get down to business. On the opposite side of Bourke Street were the offices of the Coles-Myer Trust: the reason for my briefing. The Bible Society fundraiser took control of the conversation, keen to ensure I had clear instructions.

'The appointment with Mr Robert Coles is in half an hour at 10.30am. His personal assistant has allocated 25 minutes for the meeting. The appointment is for you alone. I won't be coming with you.'

It was then I realised he was entrusting the relationship built between Bible Society and the Coles-Myer Trust and their Chairman Mr Robert Coles, to me. He took a sip of his coffee and went on making the most of the remaining time.

'Keep in mind these three things. One, build a personal connection. Two, thank him for the opportunity to present the proposal, and three, answer any questions he has about the proposal.'

I nodded affirming that I had taken note. I was impressed. He was focused in his presentation and engaging. However, through no fault of his own, it was far too smooth, though not suspiciously so, for someone with country roots. I could not be his substitute. We parted company. I crossed the street and took the lift to the floor of the Coles-Myer Ltd Trust. I recalled the time my mother took my brother and me with her on a shopping spree to Myers in Bourke Street. The highlight for us boys was having lunch at the cafeteria. It was an unforgettable luxury Phyllis indulged us in.

I stepped out of the lift and everything around me conveyed the sense that I had been transported into the world of the *old money* establishment. The wide double door entering into the office reached three metres from the floor right to the ceiling. It was sheer glass. If it was meant to impress, it achieved its purpose. Behind the glass door I could see clearly into the office which was superbly appointed in a minimalist style. A well-dressed, smart and confident middle-aged lady sat behind a single desk. On seeing me she immediately rose and moved to the door, opened it and invited me in.

'Welcome Mr Borneman. Take a seat. I will let Mr Coles know you are here.' She had that professional and personal manner that made everyone feel they were important.

As I waited, seated in a leather chair, my mind went back to three weeks prior. Marg and I and our 18-month-old Naomi were camping at Weemol 250 kilometres east of Katherine. We slept in a tent beside a waterhole. Roaming feral buffalo were our main concern at night. I wore old jeans, a threadbare cotton shirt, and no shoes. The language spoken was neither BBC English nor common Australian English. It was Kriol, the Aboriginal camp language that combined Aboriginal thought patterns and cattleman's English. We were very comfortable in this setting. During the day I drove off through the sparse bush, guided by the subtle hand movements of the traditional owner. He pointed out an old scrubby tree indistinguishable from any other in the nearby vicinity. It was a sacred tree. Sacredness stemmed not from natural beauty or grandeur but from the story associated with it. We arrived at a deserted outstation, lit a fire and enjoyed billy tea. The stillness and isolation were intoxicating.

The time machine warped and I was suddenly back in the here and now. 'Mr Borneman, Mr Coles is ready for you now. Please step this way.'

The door opened into one enormous office. I immediately estimated it to be about the size of half a tennis court. On the far side from the door, sitting behind a mahogany desk was the sole figure of Mr Robert Coles.

'Mr Borneman to see you, Mr Coles,' his assistant announced.

Mr Coles rose from his chair and walked towards me with an outstretched hand. 'Robert,' he said as we clasped hands. 'Please take a seat.' He directed me to a lounge setting consisting of two identical leather couches at right angles around a coffee table. As I sat down on one couch he sat on the other. I estimated he was probably about 20 years my senior, perhaps in his early to mid 50s. He was relaxed and at ease as he was in his territory. I trusted that I also appeared the same. 'Tell me about the project,' he said, sitting back on the couch.

I was now in my territory. I took from my bag a Kriol Bible and an introductory reading book based on the creation story in Genesis. I placed them on the coffee table. I explained a short history of the Kriol language, the key components of a successful literacy program that responded to the needs and motivation of the learner, and why the creation story with its repeated phrases, concrete objects and storyline in their own language increased the learner's likelihood of success. I advocated an *each-one teach-one* approach in which one family or community member who could read better than someone else, is encouraged to help others to learn

ONE COUNTRY... TWO WORLDS!

to read. The project required a small literacy team to visit communities and family groups to demonstrate how they could help each other to learn to read. The funds covered travel costs and the gift of a literacy kit.

Mr Coles seemed genuinely interested. I decided to take a risk, I opened the Bible to the first chapter of Genesis and suggested he have a go at reading it. I explained that it was written phonetically. 'Just read after me,' I said.

He was now not just Mr Coles head of the Coles-Myer Philanthropy Trust, he was a participant experiencing the same joy we were hoping to offer our Indigenous friends.

We were past the appointed time when Robert Coles said he would recommend the literacy project to his Board. He then asked a question I was not expecting.

'Could you comment on a couple of the other project applications we have received?' He went to his desk and picked up a manilla folder and opened it. He pulled out a project proposal and asked, 'What do you think of this?' It was an Aboriginal language retrieval project.

As I left, I took one last look at two large oil portraits that hung on the back wall either side of the mahogany desk. I had noticed them when I first stepped into the office and was aware of them staring down at me the whole time. I assumed one was Mr Robert Coles' father. I also assumed that while they were just an oil painting to me, they carried a degree of sacredness to the Coles family. Sacred not because the portraits were painted by an Archibald Prize winner, but because these paintings pointed back to the carriers of the values and vision of Coles Ltd. The world of a remote Aboriginal outstation and an ASX listed corporate boardroom had almost nothing in common. However, both relied on artefacts, whether it was a portrait or an old indistinguishable eucalyptus to maintain the stories that gave them meaning and direction.

A month later I was informed the application for funding from the Coles-Myer Philanthropy Trust for a Kriol Literacy Campaign was successful. For the next two years these two worlds were connected. Reports and photos came back to the Trust of Kriol speakers in remote communities helping each other to read Kriol, and in particular the book of their choice, the *Kriol Holi Baibul*.

41

Teach Me To Read

Location: Katherine
Date: 1988
Event: An old man learns to read

Nathaniel was in his fifties. He had been a hardworking stockman and was renowned as a bushman. His bush skills were not replicated in the schoolroom. Indeed he had not been to school. A mystical encounter with the living God when riding out bush one day changed him. He returned to his community and over time he became a natural leader of the Christian mob. There was just one impediment that Nathaniel felt deeply. He had a great desire to read his Bible, but he had never learnt to read.

Once while Nathaniel was visiting family in Katherine, word was conveyed that he would like to see me. I drove to his house, comfortable in the knowledge that simply visiting and sharing a story was probably all that was required. I reasoned he would know that a band from his community recorded Alawa and Kriol songs in our lounge room on Morrow's Farm. That cassette was in high demand. He would also know that I worked for the Kriol Bible translation mob.

I parked my car in front of the house and walked towards the front door. Nathaniel was already at the door to greet me. We exchanged greetings and Nathaniel quickly directed me to two chairs waiting in the shade.

Nathaniel asked directly, 'I want to learn to read the Bible. Can you teach me to read?'

An illiterate person in their fifties is rarely given much chance of learning to read. I was not going to tell Nathaniel that. I went to my car and got a copy of the recently published second edition of the Kriol Bible. It included Genesis and a collection of other Old and New Testament books. I opened the Bible to the creation story in Genesis and began to read.

'Longtaim nau wen God bin meigim ebrijing, no enijing bin sidan…'

That simple choice of creation story had only come after many months of research. My conversations with my Kriol speaking friends suggested that they were not motivated to learn to read per se, but they were motivated to read something, and that something was most often the Kriol Bible. Nathaniel was a case in point.

I read several verses from Genesis and then stopped. I went back to the start and asked Nathaniel to read along with me. I read slowly, pausing from time to time to let him take the lead. He couldn't do it. I continued reading on to the end of the section. His reading skills were negligible but not completely absent.

Undaunted I introduced Nathaniel to the next step that only the Dreamer really believed in. The man of the soil was far too pessimistic for what was to come. I asked Nathaniel who could read in his family.

'My granddaughter can read. She goes to school.'

'Can you ask her to come out and read with us?'

Nathaniel did not hesitate. He called her to come. She was about twelve years of age with a bright personality. I invited her to read from the Kriol Bible with me.

She stood next to me looking down at the page. As I read each line she had little trouble reading along with me though she read tentatively. She could obviously read English well and just needed time to adjust to the phonetic alphabet used in written Kriol. She was soon taking the lead when we came to repeated phrases. On the second read through only a few words halted her fluent reading.

She delighted in showing off her skills to her grandfather. I thanked her for reading for us and she went back into the house. Then I said, 'Old man you don't need me to teach you to read the Bible. Your granddaughter could teach you. You just need someone else who can read better than you. They can help you.'

The Dreamer saw a future where everyone got to play. Teaching belonged to anyone who knew a little more than the learner. As a specialist white educator I was a hindrance to creating such a scenario. As I drove away I wondered if I had let Nathaniel down. My suggestion was not what he was expecting.

Eighteen months later Nathaniel was again in Katherine staying with family. I drove around to the family house bringing two gifts for him. One was the still popular Alawa and Kriol song cassette, and the other was a Kriol calendar with Bible readings marked for each day.

Nathaniel invited me into the house and offered me a cup of tea. I was being welcomed into a longer conversation. I passed Nathaniel the calendar and pointed out the Bible reading for the day. I suggested that perhaps we could read the verses together. Nathaniel picked up a well-worn Kriol Bible sitting on the bench. He opened it and began to read. His reading was slow and careful but he was clearly reading with understanding. When he finished the short passage Nathaniel kept reading without a pause. I was in shock. The Dreamer had instructed him with the hope for such an outcome. The man of the soil doubted that I should have left so much to chance. He preferred intervention.

A little incredulously I asked, 'Nathaniel, how often do you read?'

In a matter-of-fact way, he replied, 'I read my Kriol Bible every day. God wakes me up in the middle of the night to read my Bible.'

This explained why the pages of the Bible were so worn. A new world had opened up for this old stockman. I reasoned that he was now perhaps amongst the most literate people in the world simply by what he read: the most significant literature known to mankind was now his companion, his daily bread. I had come expecting to be disappointed but I left rejoicing. Dreams of new possibilities do come true sometimes. Believing is worth the risk.

I made some enquiries about how the old man learnt to read. The answer came back: the community taught him to read. The Anglican Church had ordained him as a minister because he was a leader in the community and a leader among the Christian mob. He wanted to learn to read to fulfil his duties. Each morning he chose a passage of Scripture to read at the evening fellowship meeting. He read the passage and underlined every word that he did not know. He then asked those who could read what the underlined words said. He then erased the underline marking and read the whole passage again. Again he marked the words he did not know. And so the process went on until he was confident he could read the whole passage. At the fellowship meeting he had one of the younger men at his shoulder as he read the passage out loud for everyone to hear. If he had forgotten a word they whispered it in his ear and he continued to read. His family and community were proud of him. They said he was a bush man who learnt to read in his old age. I could see the Giver of Dreams smiling. He enjoyed surprises. He enjoyed doing the impossible.

42

Come Holy Spirit

Location: Melbourne
Date: 1989
Event: John Wimber Conference

Marg spoke with the excitement of someone who was the bearer of unexpected good news. 'Alison has written to say she would like to pay for us to go to the John Wimber Conference.'

'That's amazing,' I responded, 'I don't reckon she has much spare cash to splash around. She must really want us to go.'

'She would love to be there herself,' Marg added. 'She'd be excited about giving us the opportunity.'

'I wasn't thinking of going because we have a lot to do before we drive back to the Territory.'

'Well it looks like you are now. I'll stay home and look after the kids. I'll let Alison know that you will go.'

People's generosity toward us always seemed to come as a surprise and it invoked deep gratitude. The gratitude was not primarily for the money. It was for the fact that in the every day routine of life a friend would pause, consider our needs, and act on it. At its essence it was the Holy Spirit at work through the giver, and we never stopped being humbled by it.

The little I knew of John Wimber attracted me. He was a product of the Jesus Movement that brought the unchurched into the church. I wasn't a hippy, but I definitely came from the unchurched group. John was evangelical but with a twist. Wimber argued that when it comes to doing the stuff Jesus did, 'everyone gets to play.' I had no argument with that. In a few weeks we would return to the Northern Territory where conferences like this were rare.

I met up with Paul, a good friend from Ridley days. We took a seat not too far back and not too far forward. Inconspicuous was good. It had been a few years since I had attended a large Christian conference. I scanned the crowd. Five thousand people was my estimate. There was a buzz not dissimilar to the expectations that are in the air before a concert. I could feel the anticipation rising up in me.

After a time of singing, John Wimber strolled onto the stage. Stroll was the operative word. He was in no rush. He was a big man, overweight, relaxed and casually dressed. He spoke in the same manner that he moved. It was like having a casual conversation with you. I immediately liked his style. A high-octane charismatic performance from an American preacher was never going to sit well with me. Wimber's relaxed approach was not because he was a Californian, though that probably contributed. His rationale was that if anything happens it will be because the Holy Spirit does it. He was not about to force anything. Towards the end of his message a sentence he spoke rang out in my mind. 'Some people are particularly called to serve the poor.'

He had given it no extra emphasis yet the words moved from my head to my heart. I was being stirred.

Wimber stopped his message to observe what was happening. He calmly said, 'The Holy Spirit is doing something here. Come Holy Spirit.'

My emotions stirred deep down inside me. A raw emotion moved through my body. I tried to ignore it but it was a losing battle. My body doubled up in anguish and tears poured through my sealed eyelids as I entered an intimate moment with God.

John Wimber, sitting on his stool, said by way of explanation, 'The Holy Spirit is speaking to different ones about serving the poor. Don't worry if you are shaking or crying. That is the Holy Spirit.'

Wimber's casual voice then offered an invitation. 'Could those people whom the Holy Spirit is talking to please come to the aisle. I would like to have a word with you.'

I gingerly made my way to the aisle and towards the front. I joined about fifty other people. Wimber's words seemed directed at me. He said, 'For some of you this is confirmation that your ministry is to serve the poor. It also means staying in the organisation you are currently working in. If this is you, I want you to share what the Holy Spirit is saying to you with your immediate supervisor the next time you meet.'

I immediately knew that advice was for me. What astounded me was that I was meeting with my supervisor two days later. She lived and worked in Darwin 4000 kilometres away and rarely came to Melbourne. While in Melbourne she agreed to my invitation to meet with my lecturer at La Trobe University to discuss evaluating our Kriol reading project.

I met Eirlys thirty minutes before our appointment. I described to her my experience and the call to serve the poor through adult literacy and training of Aboriginal translators for Bible translation. She listened without comment. There was nothing I said that was new to her. She was a very experienced literacy worker, trainer, and advocate. I admired her. She too was motivated to serve the disenfranchised. With my speech finished, we went to our meeting. We did not talk about it again.

A little more than a year later, Eirlys asked me to fill the role of SIL Literacy Coordinator. I could still remain involved in the Kriol program but I would be available to help other language programs should they ask. It was what I joined Wycliffe to do. It also gave the Dreamer a bigger paddock to play in. I attended an SIL Literacy International Conference in Dallas, USA and engaged with literacy specialists from around the world. It was exhilarating. A keynote speaker challenged us to not only delight in a beautiful learning experience for a single person but to think about how to institutionalise a program to serve more people. His provocative statement was that a poorly run institutionalised literacy program will have more impact than the most successful of isolated one-on-one learning experiences. It gave the Dreamer food for thought. He loved the one, but what about the many?

I had not long settled into the role of Literacy Coordinator when Eirlys resigned from her position as Associate Director for Language Programs. She was moving back to live and work more closely with the community she had served for over two decades in The Kimberley. To my great surprise the Director asked me to take her position and be his deputy.

The Dreamer wondered how much the move of the Spirit at the Wimber Conference and validation of God's concern for the poor orchestrated what was to come. Each decision that took us from Katherine to Darwin and into this new role was logically made. They were decisions that every man of the soil would make based on the facts before him. But in the unseen world it appeared that God was pulling strings to lay the foundations for him to use the Dreamer for his purposes. Come Holy Spirit.

43

The Great Australian Dream

Location:	Palmerston
Date:	1989, 1992
Event:	Buying our first home

Fifteen years of married life and the Dreamer had not yet provided a roof over his family's head that they owned. The great Australian dream of home ownership was a distant mirage but that did not concern him nor Marg. When the time was right, God would give them the okay to buy a house. If he didn't, then the Dreamer assumed the *Aussie dream* to own your own home wasn't for them. What he was confident about was that God would always provide a roof over their head. That was enough.

A close friend with a family of three children confided in me that his finances were not in a good state. House mortgage rates were at 13.5% and credit card debt interest had risen to 23%. He said with tears welling up in his eyes,

'Barry, I can't meet our monthly loan repayments on my income. Every month I'm getting further and further into debt. My credit card is maxed out.'

He was desperate. He drew the only conclusion he could think of to save the situation,

'I'm going to have to sell our house. It's the only way out.'

I didn't respond to his emotional need. I was never good at that. My default response in emotionally-driven scenarios was to step back and logically assess the overall situation.

'You can't sell your home. The housing market is so depressed you will get less than what you paid for it.'

'I don't know what else to do.'

In situations like this many will want to pray. I didn't. I assumed none of this caught Jesus by surprise. What I needed were facts, cold hard facts.

'Tell me your full financial situation. Something might be possible other than selling your home.'

It is not often two good friends get to share so deeply over matters so important. I challenged his spending patterns including his tithing. The choices were his to make, but nothing was off limits. Despite his best efforts the debt could not be reduced. He was right. The interest rates were simply too high.

I could see only one solution. He needed an injection of cash to pay out and close his credit card account. He also needed to decrease his home loan with a lump sum payment. The thousands of dollars saved on interest rate payments would be adequate for him to keep his home and even improve their financial position.

The conversation between Marg and me did not take long. I put the question, 'Could the house deposit we have set aside not be for us, but for our friends?'

Marg immediately liked the idea. We were one in our decision when I called our friend and offered our solution.

We signed a loan agreement. The loan, adjusted to the consumer price index would be repaid to us whenever they sold their house. We would trust God with the timing. It was a glorious moment for each of us as friends and as brothers and sisters in Christ.

■ Marg recalls

> *I could see no reason not to do it as we were not about to buy our own house at that time. A significant friendship had grown between us right from our first Sunday in Darwin a couple of years earlier when they invited us back to their home for lunch. Hospitality is what they did well in a very relaxed manner. We had spent a lot of time in their home and*

we did not want them to lose it. If we could do something we would and we felt blessed to be able to help.

Six months after giving the loan I heard a small voice suggest to me, 'It is okay for you to buy your own home now.' For the Dreamer it made sense. With no house deposit, little in our savings account, and income below the Australian poverty line, God says, 'Go ahead.' Only God could say that, and only God could do it.

Our ears were now attuned to how this might happen. Through a set of unexpected provisions, the full amount of the loan we had extended to our friends was restored to our bank account over the next twelve months. My friend to whom we had given the loan told me of a cheap suburban block going for sale in Palmerston. We purchased it for 60% of the original price. We planned to build on it but soon realised we were too busy with our work to think about building. It was not God's solution for us. We sold it, making a substantial profit!

In 1991 we moved into a government supplied house in Palmerston for people on low income. It was perfect. The rent was moderate. It was close to school for our children, to St Luke's Anglican Church for worship, and the cricket oval where I now captained a local team. Our lounge quickly became a drop-in centre for the kids in our court. We were well settled and had no intention of moving. It was then that I confided in Marg, 'I think something is going to happen for us to buy a house. God is up to something.'

We didn't need to wait long. Two days later the Saturday morning ABC radio news caught my attention. It reported that the Northern Territory Government was offering a new scheme for low-income people to buy the housing commission home they were living in. The newsreader's voice came with such clarity that it was as if God was highlighting this portion of the news just for me. I relayed the news to Marg.

'I think we have our answer.'

No long discussion was required. We made our application as soon as the offer became available. The letter from the Department of Housing arrived. In anticipation I ripped it open and read it. It was not what we were expecting. Our application was refused. It stated that our income was too low to service the loan. The irony did not escape us. Our income was too low for a government initiative specifically set up to help people on low income to become home owners. Now that was *some* achievement.

I wrote to the Department of Housing requesting an interview. Permission was granted. I traded my shorts for long trousers, my sandals for shoes, my T-shirt for a dress shirt. I shaved, combed my hair and drove to meet my detractor. The choice of dress was deliberate. Our suburb had a reputation and it was not complimentary. For us it was a beautiful place to live. Our neighbours were open and straight to the point. They were rich in their acceptance of people without the judgement that can impoverish those from wealthier suburbs. First impressions were going to be important.

The air conditioner immediately cooled the sweat running down my back as I entered the office. The gentleman sitting behind the desk rose and walked around to greet me. He was warm and friendly. His rich Irish accent added to the warmth of the occasion.

'What can I do for you?' he asked, directing me to a chair in front of his desk. I passed the letter over to him.

'I want to talk about this letter turning down our application to buy our house.'

He read it silently. I asked, 'Is there anything we can do to change that decision?'

He looked up and said sympathetically, 'Unfortunately no. Your income is far too low.' His tone was one of friend, not bureaucrat. I went straight to the point giving my counter-argument.

'Sir, I don't drink, smoke or gamble. We have not missed paying our weekly rent since we moved in nine months ago. Isn't that proof enough?'

'By looking at you, I already know that you can do it.' My trousers, shoes and dressy shirt had done their job. 'It is just that you are not even close to having the income that the department guidelines say you have to have.'

There was a short silence then he offered a way forward.

'Is there any way we can increase your income?' he asked. The Irish accent never sounded more beautiful. The choice of the word *we* was an invitation for collaboration. We both instinctively knew that between an Irishman and a Dreamer, no bureaucratic set of rules could get in the way of sorting this matter out.

The income I had submitted was our real income. I couldn't change that and wouldn't change it. However, I asked, 'Can we project forward to what our income could be in the coming financial year knowing we need to increase it.'

'We could do that,' he replied with a twinkle in his eye.

'Then this is easy,' I said, 'My wife and I are both qualified school teachers. We could do relief teaching. Put us down for an extra $3,000 income from relief teaching.' The Irishman smiled. He took a few notes of his own but asked for no written commitment on my part.

I then added something I had completely forgotten,

'We also have a deposit.' A look of astonishment crossed his face. He exclaimed,

'No one I deal with has a deposit. This changes everything.'

He went back to his notebook and wrote down some quick calculations. He rose from his seat, shook my hand and offered these beautiful words,

'Your application is approved. You will soon receive a sale offer in the mail.'

The letter did come, and this time without any unexpected surprises except on one account. The purchase price of $78,000 was 15% under the sale price I had planned on. The loan repayment was the same amount as the rent we paid. We achieved the Great Australian Dream of home ownership simply by filling in a form and without moving house. I had said once to God that it was an insult in my eyes to ask him for a house of our own when I compared it with Jesus suffering on the cross. The forgiveness of sins and the freedom and joy he gives was enough. Material things were secondary.

In the end God did what he wanted irrespective of my theology. He ruled, not me. He obviously has earthly dreams for his children that they don't even know about.

Our friends repaid the loan when they sold their house a few years later, and then moved overseas to do mission work. That repayment allowed us to renovate the house by turning our carport into a large bedroom for the older girls. We sold our house in 2006 and put the money into a term deposit marked for a future house. When we moved to Melbourne in 2007 the banks would not give us a home loan because our personal income was still too low. The 2008 global financial crisis hit, the banks stopped offering customers home loans for a couple of weeks. It was then, when buyers were scarce, that we purchased our home in Croydon, a suburb of Melbourne, with the money in our house savings account. We did not need a bank loan anyway.

44

Compelled

Location: Darwin
Date: 1992-93
Event: Training Aboriginal translators

My colleagues had spent many years living in various regions across Northern and Central Australia, building relationships, learning a local Indigenous language, studying its grammar and developing an alphabet so it could be written down. Many had invested in bilingual education, published dictionaries, and formed local translation teams training Indigenous friends to translate the Bible into their own language. They were highly dedicated and educated people who had abandoned mainstream expectations for a life of service. I had nothing but respect for each of my colleagues. Yet despite all this, the direction of their discussions totally unsettled me. Tears welled up in my eyes, my stomach tightened and my spirit groaned deep within. I recognised it as that same force that had ambushed me at the Wimber Conference in Melbourne three years earlier. I moved to the back of the room while my colleagues continued their conversation.

'What is this about?' I asked God. His answer was reassuring.

'I am just letting you know I care about this too. How you feel is how I feel.'

The hot topic under discussion was, *What skills does an Aboriginal translator need to become a lead translator?*

As each skill and attribute required was added to the list I had the awful realisation that the list looked like us, only a better version. We were making our Aboriginal translators in our own image. It was not done out of bad intent but it was inevitable when we listed what was important to us. We needed to begin from a different starting point. We needed to build on the strengths that only they had.

Two days later the deep groaning within was replaced by an optimism and excitement with what God was doing. An ambitious motion was brought to the floor for a vote. It read:

> *Motion to approve the development of an accredited translation course for a minimum of five Aboriginal translators.*

As the Associate Director I was responsible for language programs and training. It was my job to answer any questions. I was expecting some difficult questions but I got none. One of my colleagues from Central Australia spoke up first.

'None of the translators I work with are ready for this. I can't see my translators doing it.'

'That's okay,' I responded. 'This motion is not requiring anyone to have to do this training. If your translation team is not ready, that's fine. The course is optional. It is meant to be an opportunity, not a requirement.'

Another asked, 'Why five participants and not ten or twenty?'

I answered, 'It will take a lot of effort to develop this course.' So I asked myself the question, "What is the least number of translators we would be willing to put this work in for?" The number I came up with was five. If we can find five interested participants then we will give it a go.'

When the talking was done it was time to vote on the motion. It was unanimously approved.

My tears from earlier in the week turned to joy. I was so proud of my colleagues. But even more I was amazed at my God. He was letting me know that the Holy Spirit was also a player in what was to come. He was equally at home in curriculum development and meeting the requirements of educational bureaucracy as taking me to a third heaven. He was the God of the man of the soil and the Dreamer.

Dr Christine Kilham, a linguist, translator and educator, was the leader of the pack ready for implementing this new program. Chris had already written the textbook *Translation Time* for this purpose. She was brilliant, she was impatient, and a passionate believer in the abilities of Aboriginal translators. She referred to Topsy, her friend and fellow translator in the Wik Mungkan language of North Queensland, as equivalent to Shakespeare in her grasp and use of her own language.

Chris came into my office ready for a fight. 'Can't we just forget the Education Department requirements and go it alone.'

I sat silently not committing one way or the other. By organisational structure I may have been Chris' boss, but based on experience, academic achievement and drive, Dr Christine Kilham AO was my boss. Taking my silence as an invitation to put her case further, Chris went on, 'They won't accept my *Translation Times* textbook as evidence that we can teach this course. We have to rewrite the whole course into their template following their criteria. Not only that, it could take 12 months to get through the government accreditation process and even then they may not approve it.'

Chris' frustration at what she considered Educational Department bureaucracy moved to a plea. 'Let's just put the training course in the budget and start ourselves. We know how to teach this stuff and there are translators ready to start.'

I knew she would not like my answer. I replied calmly 'The answer to that question is *No!* It is not because we can't teach the course, but because outside recognition of their skills and commitment is important. We need it to be a government accredited course.'

I was now firmly the man of the soil and walking arm in arm with bureaucracy crushing the woman of dreams. Chris looked at me with a face that was not convinced. But she was a warrior for Aboriginal translators. Chris headed back down the corridor to her office, shut the door, and got back to work.

Chris' urgency may have come deep from within her, as one who intuitively knew her clock was ticking. Not long afterwards Chris received news that devastated her and us, and threw our plans into turmoil. Her body was ravaged by an aggressive cancer. She would soon begin chemotherapy.

Dr Christine Kilham died on 11 August 1993. She was 54 years of age. She had a grandstand seat when the first group of eleven students began their *Certificate III in Translating (Indigenous)*. She was looking on again when a Larrakia Christian elder extended the *welcome to country* at their graduation. She was on her feet cheering as the graduates led into their graduation ceremony with the traditional Djambarrpuyngu water dance. And again as the Northern Territory Minister for Education presented the certificates. And yes, she was smiling as she *overheard* the same minister say to me as we walked back to his car,

'I won't forget this night. It has been one of my best experiences as the Minister for Education.'

It was people like Christine Kilham, and other colleagues like her, who planted the seed for the systematic training of Aboriginal translators. Some never saw the fruit in their lifetime but it was from their tears and disappointments that life came. It is in dreaming that the seed is planted. Then one day, when we are least expecting it, or we are weary by the delay, the Spirit moves and the resurrection comes.

Other trainers took up the mantle from Chris Kilham with compassion and distinction. Over the following seven years more than fifty Aboriginal translators from remote communities completed the course. The completion rate of 90% demonstrated their competence, their dedication, and thankfulness to be given an opportunity. It compared at the time with an 18% completion rate for students from remote communities studying in an equivalent government training institution. As important as the academic training and skills development was, of equal significance was the connection made between translators from different language communities. Their world simply became bigger and richer for it.

Ten years later the federal government decided it was too difficult for its bureaucracy to monitor registered private providers offering a single course with a limited number of students. Regional officers were authorised to find a way to close them down to save the cost of oversight. When the last group of students completed their certificate, we handed our registration back as a Registered Training Organisation. It was the end of an era. A golden era of creating fresh opportunities for the disadvantaged remote communities of Australia. For me, the dream realised was more than just the result of the efforts of some of my gifted colleagues, both students and trainers. It was a move of the Spirit.

45

Leave Me Alone God

Location: Waxhaw, North Carolina
Date: 1993
Event: Wycliffe and SIL International Conference

I had a skip in my step. I could feel the adrenalin running through my veins. I took in every new sensation, every new face. I knew the feeling well. I felt alive and mischievous. I made my way to the large wooden doors leading into the conference room. A cheerful older man playing the role of security, checked my lanyard hanging around my neck. All was in order.

Name: Barry Borneman
Organisation: SIL – Australian Aborigines and Islander Branch
Code: Voting Delegate

He opened the door allowing me to enter my first SIL and Wycliffe International Conference. The year was 1993. The location, the SIL Jungle Aviation and Radio Services (JAARS) headquarters in Waxhaw, North Carolina. I looked forward to hearing stories from among the 400 plus delegates attending from the far corners of the world. At forty, I was one of the younger attendees. I was a new kid on the block with only seven years of field experience. Many of those present had twenty, thirty, forty years of experience serving among minority language communities of the world.

As I stepped into the auditorium I scanned the gathering. The back third of the hall was open space leaving room for people to move around. There were a few small groups standing and chatting. Others were moving to seats set out in rows in the front half of the auditorium.

'Where do I sit?' I asked another friendly security man stationed inside the door. He saw the colour code of my lanyard and said, 'In the middle aisle, Sir. That section is reserved for voting delegates.'

I took a couple of steps towards the middle aisle. Then just as quickly I came to a sudden halt. My stomach began to churn almost buckling me over. I resisted, straightened my body, and took a few deep breaths. The churning deep inside intensified. I was losing the battle. Under my breath I demanded my way, 'Leave me alone God. I want to behave. I did not come to make a spectacle of myself.'

The answer that flashed into my mind was not threatening but it was non-negotiable.

'What you see, is what I see. Now do what I am asking you to do.' Resistance was not an option. I knew where I was to sit.

The Chairman of the Conference sat on the stage behind a long table with other assorted dignitaries. He cleared his throat and spoke into the microphone.

'Could everyone please take your allotted seats. We are ready to start.'

I knew it was the Holy Spirit who corralled me to sit with my colleagues without a vote. Instead of walking straight ahead I walked to the right towards a row of seats for non-voting delegates and invited guests. I took a seat not far from David Gela, the Director of the Papua New Guinea Bible Translation Association (BTA). We nodded acknowledgment to each other. I remembered David and his wife Sineina from when I taught at Ukarumpa over a decade earlier when BTA was just forming. My new companions were younger and small in number, dwarfed by the 300+ voting delegates. They were more black than white. The vibrant African dress colours contrasted against the casual dress of the middle section. My absence from the voting section went by unnoticed.

I sat silent along with my non-voting invited delegates as a major agenda item came up for discussion. *Should National Bible Translation Organisations be able to become full members of SIL International?*

The voting delegates discussed the topic with passion in the style of Robert's Rules. Arguments for and against were taken up with enthusiasm in a robust discussion. Some voiced their doubts. Their arguments were based on what was different. The National Bible Translation Organisations were not structured like us. They didn't have the same capacity. They were not financially sustainable. Some argued there was nothing gained for them to have a vote on legislation that impacted SIL and Wycliffe missionaries. Having them present at the Conference as brothers and sisters was enough. Others vehemently pleaded that the organisational constraints needed to be loosened so they could find a way in. I felt the irony of the voting delegates with voice answering on behalf of the very people who sat around the perimeter. If I was in the middle aisle, I am sure I would have stood and given an impassioned plea for inclusion. Having voice would have made me feel better but it would not have helped me to understand. It was only in sitting and being the topic of conversation without voice that I could experience a fraction of the hurt, the exclusion, the frustration that it can bring.

As the discussion intensified, an exasperated African leader was given voice by the Chair. He stood to his feet. He was not a tall man but he was powerfully built. He thanked the Chair for the right to speak and faced the voting delegates. His face was earnest. With a commanding voice he both challenged and pleaded with his hearers. 'You gave us birth,' he began. 'You raised us and taught us all that we know. Now we just want to move into adulthood. Can't you let us take our place beside you in the work. Is that too hard?'

His raw emotion stilled the auditorium. His words reverberated in my head. Others had been talking about how a decision like this affected our governing rules and legislation, or how we had traditionally done business. It was an abstract argument. The African leader had pulled the conversation back to its core. We were talking about family, about relationships, about shared inheritance. That was what was at stake.

The motion was finally put, then amended, the amendment approved, and then finally it came to a vote. I sat with the outsiders looking in as our future was determined by others. A resounding vote was cast in favour of inclusion. The anguish I had felt heightened the pride I now had for the collective wisdom of my colleagues with vote. The delegates knew that the way things were could not continue. However, the discussion also revealed that sharing control and forgoing the inherited role of gatekeeper of the Bible Translation movement would be a painful transition and for some an impossible one. Humanly speaking that is always difficult to do. Perhaps this is why the early Church celebrated Jesus:

> *Who, being in very nature God, did not consider equality with God something to be used to his own advantage; rather, he made himself nothing.*   Philippians 2:6-7 NIV

He gave us an example of what is near impossible even for those who follow him. I knew it was this same Jesus who had stopped me at the door.

Over the next twenty-five years Wycliffe transformed into a network of over 100 organisations from all parts of the world. English was no longer the first language of the majority. Women were present in larger numbers, and the white male became a clear minority. Robert's Rules gave way to round table discussions, fellowship and consensus. The Wycliffe Board was elected based on the vote of all in attendance.

What I do know is that this did not happen because of my efforts. It happened because people in power made decisions to share power. It also happened because there was a move of the Spirit working in far more people than me. I just had the privilege and the uncomfortable experience of getting a small glimpse of Jesus' heart. He is for the dispossessed, the voiceless, the weak, the unnoticed, the forgotten.

46

Betrayal

Location:	Darwin
Date:	1934-5
Event:	Betrayal

My eyes were transfixed on the letter in front of me, the unstamped envelope with my name neatly written on it lying to one side on my desk. It was not what I was expecting in my first weeks as the newly appointed Director for the SIL Branch. The letter had nothing to do with the strength of Indigenous languages, literacy campaigns, translation, or training programs that were our core activities. It had everything to do with personal choices that I knew would send shock waves through our close community. The letter plainly outlined the choice that my colleague had made.

I read it over several times collecting my thoughts and endeavouring to control my emotions. It was a well-crafted letter not written in haste. It made fleeting attempts to show thoughtfulness but this did not hide the cold and calculated reasoning of someone self-absorbed in his own insular world. In short, he was leaving his spouse of many years, resigning from the organisation, and moving to an undisclosed location elsewhere in Darwin. He wrote that it was his personal decision and that no-one else was involved. He then pointed out an organisational policy that required couples with marriage breakdowns to return to their sending country and organisation. He noted that since he had resigned this did not apply to him. However, it would apply to his wife. She would have to return to the USA. He wrote that he did not think that was fair. The irony of comment did not escape me. His wife was away overseas, encouraged to take a long-planned holiday with her family. In the meantime, he plotted his escape and abrogated his responsibilities. Who was he to decide what was fair?

I could feel a growing anger brewing inside me. It was fully directed at the letter writer who had until this letter arrived, been my close working colleague. If there was a call to act with compassion and forgiveness, I did not hear it. My anger and my disappointment controlled me. I shouted out into the air, 'He didn't even have the guts to tell her. Now he was leaving me to do his dirty work.'

My thoughts were man to man. It could have been Joe talking. Like Joe, I had no sympathy for skullduggery. I wondered what I would do if he walked into my office. 'It could be ugly,' I thought. I had no idea what *forgiveness* looked like in the heat of this battle, and I was unsure if I was ready to ask Jesus what it might look like. My anger though had to give way to another immediate reality. I was the leader that my colleagues would rely on to chart a way forward. This devastating news needed to be handled calmly and rationally for the sake of everyone. I let my spirit pray. I listened to each unintelligible word that rolled off my tongue. It gently stilled me.

A group of about twenty people sat in a circle chatting amongst themselves as the last stragglers arrived. It was unusual to have a special members meeting called with such short notice, but then they had just voted in a new leader. He may do some things differently.

I thanked everyone for coming. That part was easy. There was a pause for a few seconds and then I went straight to the point.

'The reason I called this meeting is because this morning I received a letter from our colleague telling me he has left his wife.'

I opened up the floor for people to comment. The words were subdued as were the people. Some spoke of unusual behaviour they had seen in recent days from our former colleague. My news made sense of these actions. This was not a spontaneous decision.

I then asked something that I knew was impossible without God's help. 'I ask one thing of you. When you leave this room I want you to choose not to gossip, or to speak against anyone. I know this will be difficult because many of you will be hurting and angry. However, we can't make our feelings the main game. Our primary focus is to support his wife and family.'

I looked around the group and saw small signs of affirmation. She was a much-respected colleague who worked tirelessly as part of our team developing the accredited course for Aboriginal translators. She was a friend to our family as well as to a number of others in the room. We were united as best we could be.

My calmness on the outside and firm direction helped keep the ship afloat in stormy seas. On the inside the events continued to hit a raw nerve in me. I took a long walk alone with God, full of questions. 'Jesus, isn't being a follower of you and being faithful to your wife one and the same thing? You taught me that gold standard, so what do I make of this situation?'

'Did this person just feign faith in you without actually having a relationship with you? Why would someone bother to do that?'

'Can someone slice into a Christian vocation for the adventure, the prestige, or academic pursuit without knowing you?'

In my talking with Jesus I took one hope. 'At least my colleague is closer to salvation than he was before. He is no longer pretending.'

My mind turned to his wife. She would soon be arriving back from her family holiday. I had to meet her with the news. I could not pass that off to someone else. What complicated things was that I made it a practice of avoiding any strong emotional connection with any one of the opposite sex. If I found myself connecting well with a female colleague or friend I would deliberately put a distance between myself and that person to avoid any dependency developing. It was not something Marg required of me but it was my own unspoken strategy to remain a *one-woman man*. Deep down it hinted at something else. My formative years had not equipped me to share at a deep emotional level. I took that with me into adulthood. This time I could not avoid it or leave it to someone else. It was my responsibility.

Ann, my Associate Director, and I sat silently in the airport arrival lounge. I had no idea what I would say but suspected it would come out without any sugar-coating. Before I gathered my scattered thoughts, she came out through the exit door some ten metres away. We immediately caught each other's eyes from a distance. Her face whitened. When she got to me she said, 'He has left me, hasn't he?' I did not need to say a word other than 'Yes'. I did not know that God had already prepared her. It was 27 years later that I read her memoirs that reflected on this pivotal time in her life.

> *I have been re-reading a novel by Peter Carey, Oscar and Lucinda, and was again taken by the description of the glass structure Lucinda had made and was showing Oscar, a strong sense of beauty and joy: He saw a tiny church with dust dancing around it like microscopic angels. It was clean and pure and free from vanity ... The light shone through its transparent, unadorned skin and cast colours ... as glorious as the stained-glass windows of cathedrals.*
>
> *After reading that, I had what I can only describe as a kind of vision, a picture of myself in a dark and cold room in which I shiver, unable to get warm, with nothing to give me comfort. But gradually dawn comes: at first a distant beauty of colours in the sky, moving and inspiring but distant, unfelt, with no warmth. Gradually, the sunlight grows, reaching first only a little spot of my dark cold. I have to squeeze myself to fit into that little patch of warmth. But it grows ever bigger and then it reaches every crook and cranny of the room, filling it with warm light. I can move, I can leap about and still be in that warmth – and I can see a door leading out into a warm and spacious outdoors.*
>
> *... The vision I had of being in a dark, cold room, that's exactly how I felt in the transit hotel in Singapore airport on the way back from the U.S. I couldn't get warm and couldn't sleep; the room was pitch black and very cold (I couldn't get the air conditioner to work right!) And I had such a feeling of dread of what I would find when I got back to Darwin. Can I believe that the rest of that vision will prove true, the coming of the light and warmth? Only through God. From my own readings and the thoughts and words from others, I know the Lord has been preparing me.*

We headed from the airport to talk briefly with her church minister and to pray together. Late in the evening we arrived back at her empty house. I asked if I could pray briefly in tongues for her as I did not know how to pray. She nodded assent. As a few incomprehensible words quietly came from my mouth I had an immediate conviction of what was to come. I saw it clearly. She was embarking on a very long and dark road while being strengthened by God's steadfast love. Just when a way forward begins to emerge, the pain and disappointment would be felt again. There would be no short and easy solution. Her husband was not coming back. His mind was made up. So was God's. He would sustain her through a terrible time. The message for me as a leader was to trust her to God as much as it was for her. I communicated something of this prayer with her. I am not sure what she heard or how well I conveyed it. She got out of the car, entered the house and closed the door to contemplate a very different future to what she had before she had gone on her holiday with her siblings. The Associate Director and I went our separate ways with our own thoughts. I determined to be there for her for the difficult long haul, whatever that might entail.

What does one do with a dream? My first thought was to ask, 'Was it from you God or was it just a way of sorting out my mixed emotions?' I decided it was from God, or at least tentatively from God. In the dream I saw my colleague with another lady other than his wife. The interpretation of the dream was unambiguous. I weighed this up with his claim in his letter that no-one else was involved. If it was from God the obvious question was, 'What was I to do with this dream?'

The next day I called the lady in the dream into my office. I asked directly, 'Do you know where he is staying?'

A perplexed look came over her face. 'Of course not,' she replied. I then asked even more bluntly without any cautionary introduction.

'Are you having an affair with him?'

The shock of the question quietened her for a moment. She then raised her voice angrily, 'How could you even suggest that. I am mad about what he has done. How could he just leave his wife like that?'

'Okay, I am sorry I asked the question,' I lied.

She calmed down. There was no more for us to discuss. She turned and walked out. As she did I intuitively knew the dream was true. Eventually it would all come out. In the meantime, I steeled myself to provide all the support I could for the abandoned spouse and speak not one word against the lady I had just spoken to.

I rarely read organisational procedures. Most times I simply act on my own good judgement. This was one time I needed to read the stipulated procedures in full. The letter from international headquarters had already pointed me in this direction. I didn't like what I read. The instructions were clear. If a married member experiences divorce or separation, their assignment is cancelled. They then return as soon as is reasonable to their sending organisation. In this case it was Wycliffe USA. The reasons given sounded fair and reasonable. The home organisation was best placed to provide emotional and practical support for the person that the field could not provide. The consequences though were starker. That support would be provided for six months to assist with a transition out of the organisation. It was time for me and Jesus to walk the oval again to get some perspective.

'This is how I see it, Jesus. The organisation is going to ditch her in the same way that her husband has ditched her. He has kicked her in the guts and now the organisation expects me to do the same thing on its behalf. Well, I am sure you don't want me to do that. She matters more to you than she does to anyone else. So what do you want?'

The answer was simple. 'What I want is for her to decide of her own free choice about her future, not anyone else, not you, or any organisational procedure. She is mine. We can work it out together.'

The representative from Wycliffe USA came to assess the situation. He was a good man, compassionate but with a military background bound by the rules. We sat together over coffee. He delivered his verdict. Her membership with SIL would cease and she would have to return to the USA. Next morning I handed him my formal reply in a letter outlining seven reasons why the suggested course of action was inappropriate. I would not be complying. He took the letter with a resigned look on his face and commented, 'I thought this is where you would finish up.'

We shook hands as brothers in Christ, and he departed for the plane back to the US. I was buying as much time for her as I could. I now waited to hear the organisational response. My letter contained a bomb with a long fuse. In the letter I reasoned that Jesus was on my side. He cared for the vulnerable and so should we. I also reasoned that the local church and organisation in Australia were in the best position to provide the support and care required. I also knew that for an American organisation it was hard for them to believe anyone else could do it as well as they could for their own. I needed something original that focused an American mind. I then placed the fuse.

I pointed out that the local organisation was incorporated in Australia and operated under Australian law. These superseded Wycliffe USA regulations. In Australia to dismiss someone because of the actions of her spouse was illegal. Therefore, they would not be getting my signature to suspend her on two grounds. First, because I couldn't show that she had acted in a way to put at risk the good name of the organisation, and second because it was illegal in Australia.

The response was inevitable. There were letters and phone calls from important people all trying to persuade this new and inexperienced director to comply with their request. But there was also genuine sympathy and encouragement from other leaders who had faced the same terrible dilemma. Everyone was hurting in their own way. I was calm, friendly but non-compliant. The procedure for her to return to the USA could not happen without my signature. On each occasion I explained to whoever would listen something that Joe had taught me. 'I will choose where I put my signature. It belongs to me!'

Three months went by without my signature, then six months and still no signature, and then a year. My colleague and friend remained in Darwin loved and supported by those around her. Her home organisation was doing some deep soul searching of its own.

Internally the balance between advocating for my sister while not becoming emotionally connected was difficult. I found myself agitated when circumstances were stacked up against her. I was consumed by a sense of injustice which wore me down. My teeth were far more firmly locked and sleepless nights more common. I found it easier to leave things in my own life with Jesus than I did trusting God with someone else's struggles. I found it easier to forgive someone else's sin against me than to forgive someone else's sin against another. It was hard for the Dreamer to rise above the situation. It was complicated. I cared deeply but in silence.

Two years later Wycliffe USA changed their policy. Individual circumstances could now be considered. A spouse who is betrayed would not have to automatically return home and resign. I joked at the time that I was expecting a letter of thanks from the Wycliffe USA President for helping them to have the courage to change. The letter of thanks never came. In reality our sister's freedom to choose her own direction was all the thanks I wanted. In her own time she could dream again.

Many years later a letter arrived with familiar neat handwriting on it. Memories came back that had lain dormant, overshadowed by immediate demands and the passage of life itself. I read slowly,

> *Dear Barry,*
> *I am writing to ask for your forgiveness…*

The writer expressed his regret for the pain he caused. He had recently encountered Jesus in a deep way that contrasted with his self-centred life. He asked Jesus for forgiveness and was now doing the same to me. I processed the letter with the same filter that I read his first letter more than 20 years before. If all he wrote was true, then I trusted his new faith in Jesus would help him understand my reply. I wrote,

> *Dear …,*
> *Thank you for your letter. Concerning your request for forgiveness for the pain you caused me, I want you to know I am not the priority. The pain you may have caused me is minuscule to the pain you have caused your wife and two sons. I am peripheral when it comes to asking for forgiveness. The only thing that matters to me is that you have written to each of them and asked for their forgiveness.*
>
> *Regards, Barry*

It was short and to the point. Deep down I sensed his letter spoke of a new or renewed encounter and faith in Jesus. But I found myself still an advocate for his former wife, which overpowered the possibility of offering personal forgiveness and joy. In my head questions whirled. Was my response what Jesus wanted? Was it too hard? Could I have said the same thing with much more grace?'

Jesus did not answer my questions. He simply said, 'Trust him to me. His relationship with me is not dependent on whether your answer was appropriate or not.'

A number of years later my former colleague died. The service was live-streamed. I listened as his sons shared with grace and maturity on the life of their father. They acknowledged the pain but still spoke of hope and forgiveness. They too had received a letter asking for forgiveness.

I confided in Jesus. 'Jesus, they have shown me a better way. The grace to forgive is your gold standard.'

I again reflected on my own response to the letter. I had not given the Dreamer a chance to embrace the moment. Instead, I was locked in as the advocate, stuck in the soil, demanding that justice be done for another. An unspoken residual pain blinded me to a better way. If the Dreamer had his way he would have rejoiced in the redeemed life. It may have taken him to a new place of joy and thankfulness, somewhere between heaven and earth. I was never to know.

47

Thoughts Fulfilled

Location: Singapore
Date: 1995
Event A wrist watch

The tropical city of Darwin sits on the doorstep of Asia. Its substantial population of Timorese and Filipinos, reflected this. When I heard that the Asia SIL Linguistic School held in Singapore was facing financial and accommodation constraints I joined the dots. I offered our facilities in Darwin as an alternative training centre should they want it. Set on 12 hectares it was ideal for young families. Existing library and lecture rooms added to the attraction. The cream on the cake was the possibility of an agreement with the University of the Northern Territory (now Charles Darwin University) to credit the SIL course towards a Masters of Applied Linguistics. It was this proposal that saw me on the plane flying from Darwin to Manila, overnighting in Singapore. The Directors of Wycliffe and SIL Asia wanted to discuss the proposal face-to-face.

As the plane neared Singapore, I was aware that this was new ground for me. My mind went back to my rural upbringing where I seldom saw the face of an Asian person, let alone have a friendship. Those rural roots in many ways still defined me. I couldn't and wouldn't change that. I wondered about how a laid-back Aussie country boy might go in connecting with more sophisticated Singaporean or other Asian leaders.

My attention was drawn to an expensive-looking watch on the wrist of the gentleman seated next to me. I looked down at my own wrist. I did not wear a watch and had not for many years. I was accustomed to estimating time across the day within 10-15 minutes of real time. It served me well enough. My bare wrist however, became more conspicuous as my eyes were drawn to other passengers. Without exception they wore a watch, not just to tell the time, but they seemed to also make a fashion statement.

'It would be good to have a watch,' I thought.

The thought lingered and then faded. It was time to prepare for landing.

I was impressed by the efficiency of Changi International Airport. With only carry-on luggage, I was at the taxi ramp within 15 minutes of landing. I pulled out a home address that Wycliffe Singapore had sent me and handed it to the taxi driver. In another fifteen minutes I was knocking on the door of a double story private home. It was about 5:30pm. The mother and her daughter greeted me warmly. They were of Tamil ethnicity. My host quickly explained, 'I am sorry my husband is working tonight. He will join you for breakfast tomorrow morning.'

At 7am next morning, according to the bedside clock, I came down the stairs to be greeted by the smell and sight of a full English breakfast. A tall distinguished looking man was already seated at the table. He immediately rose and greeted me.

'How was the flight?' he asked.

'Great,' I said, 'but what was even better was Changi Airport. It is amazing. I was through customs and out in no time.'

His eyes lit up at my unsolicited comment on Changi Airport. 'Glad to hear it,' he said, before asking me about my family and then Bible translation work in Australia.

As we finished breakfast he said, 'I notice you don't have a watch.'

'No,' I replied, 'I don't own a watch.' As I answered he rose and opened the top drawer of a nearby English oak dresser. He reached in, took out a flat rectangular box containing a dozen wrist watches. He placed the box in front of me.

'Choose one,' he said.

He saw my hesitancy, so he added, 'It is okay. They are lost watches left at the airport that no one has claimed. You are free to take one.'

I selected a watch with a silver band and clear numbers on the face. I put it on my wrist. Perfect fit.

'So you work at the airport?' I enquired.

'Yes,' he replied with a smile. I am the General Manager.

An hour later the General Manager of the airport delivered me personally back at the departure lounge. For the Dreamer there was much to contemplate on the flight to Manila. A man of the soil whose eyes were dimmed to the God factor would describe the thought about the watch and the subsequent gift of a watch as random luck. The Dreamer, though, filtered everything with the thought that the unpredictable Giver of Dreams was more often a hidden player in his life. He was more than just the God who provides. Was it God who planted the thought in his mind, *It would be good to have a watch.* The thought itself would have faded from all memory but for one factor. The watch appeared. The thought was fulfilled. Did the thought come from within or did it come from without? If the thought of the wrist-watch came from God then maybe the thought to invite SIL Asia to come to Darwin also came from God. It was indeed a mystery. The Dreamer pondered, *When are my thoughts, his thoughts, or his thoughts, my thoughts?* It was possibly only when they were fulfilled that he would know.

48

Judgement In The Public Square

Location: Northern Territory University
Date: 1996
Event: Opposition

Darwin, the capital city of the Northern Territory, had a population of just under 100,000 in 1996. It was more a large provincial town than a city. People across a range of occupations, professions and ethnic groups mixed easily. The community became even smaller for those involved with Indigenous languages. A small collegiate group met occasionally under the banner of the *Top End Linguistic Circle* to hear a paper presented by one of their cohort. Linguists and educationalists easily mingled from the Northern Territory University (NTU), Batchelor College, SIL and the wider missionary fraternity. It was not surprising that in meeting we saw opportunities to cooperate together.

Dr Paul Black, the head linguist at the university, scrutinised each of the Asia SIL School applied linguistics units. He compared the content with the course content of the Masters in Applied Linguistics that the university offered. We waited with bated breath as he made his assessment. He concluded, 'In each overlapping unit the Asia SIL School course actually goes much deeper than ours. I think we can give credit for up to 50% of our course units.'

It was a generous offer reflecting the quality of the SIL course and the goodwill that existed. Three months later an agreement between SIL and NTU was signed. The mandatory photos were taken in the university office. The first batch of students from Asia was ready to come the following year. We were all well pleased with ourselves. Our SIL students and future linguists and Bible translators now had a pathway to a Masters in Linguistics and the University's Linguistics Department would have a steady stream of students. The ink had hardly dried on the agreement when accusations began to fly.

A lecturer at the university took aim at the agreement. Her accusation against SIL was made to anyone who would listen. Her position was unequivocal. 'NTU should not be making an agreement with a fundamentalist American Christian organisation that was a puppet of the CIA.' We were persona non grata. She found some allies who did not know us. A public meeting was called at the NTU. The topic: The appropriateness of NTU having an agreement with SIL.

I felt obliged to let SIL International know of the accusation and proposed debate. A fifty-page document was faxed through detailing any accusation that could be made against SIL with a fact sheet in response. Most of the examples were international. They also offered to send a representative to Australia to speak on our behalf. I turned down the offer. We would stand or fall on the reputation we had built locally. The intricate connection between language and identity and the emotional response that language arouses also meant our spokesperson had to be someone with Australian English. Australian *Strine* was the best unstated counter to the accusation that we were an American organisation. I was ready to be our spokesperson.

The university set the date for the public debate and invited us to attend. My lack of eye for detail did not at first pick up an obvious clash. When it did I was stopped in my tracks. The public debate was on the same day that I had set aside for prayer with my two Associate Directors, Paul and Ann. We were leaving the office to be alone and undisturbed for the first time in two years. What was I to do? As the Director I was expected to put the SIL case. My colleagues in the university would also be expecting it. I couldn't let them down. I was also looking forward to the showdown with some eagerness. I enjoyed a public debate.

The easiest thing to do was to reschedule the day of prayer. I immediately felt uneasy about it. Intuitively I knew where it was taking me. A series of questions slipped into my mind.

'Wouldn't God also be expecting you to turn up at your duly appointed meeting?'

'Which was more important, keeping an appointment with God or keeping one with men?'

'Do you think your words of persuasion are more influential than a simple request for God to intervene?'

I knew I was often glib in my affirmation of the importance of prayer. God now had my attention on the matter. The timing dilemma was no accident. He was forcing the issue. What do you most trust: your actions or prayer? The date for the day of prayer remained unchanged.

As the day of reckoning approached, I wrote up a history of SIL's involvement in the earliest stages of the bilingual education, and in establishing orthographies for Indigenous languages. I cited linguistic research, dictionaries, Bible translation and training programs. I noted partnerships with government agencies and the church. I handed my speech to David Crawford, our head of the *Certificate in Translating for Indigenous Translators*. Like me, he came from dairy farming stock in Northern Victoria.

As I drove away on that day to our place of prayer, David headed into the public square to defend our integrity. He was a gentle man not prone to provocation. He would deliver the information without any offence or undue sturdy defence. I suspected he was a far better representative for our cause than I was. Perhaps this was also God's intention. He had forced me to value prayer above direct participation. He also perhaps needed to replace me with a more suitable representative to defend the reputation of SIL.

The day of prayer was focused for good reason. As our time of prayer drew to a close, the great debate was already finished. The implications would already be reverberating around the university and amongst SIL staff. When we arrived back at SIL the post mortem had already begun amongst people crammed into the tea room. David took centre stage. He humoured us with his retelling. The smile on his face suggested a positive outcome. He told the story with us hanging on every word.

When he arrived at the university, he found out that he was one of nine people slated to speak. He was fifth in line with the lady who organised the petition against us a slot or two after him. What struck David immediately was the impressive list of people gathered to speak. Head amongst them was the highly respected Indigenous academic and activist Professor Marcia Langton. She was slotted to speak first. David recalled the moment. The atmosphere was electric. Whatever view she espoused of SIL would determine the whole course of the debate. David summarised her speech with some flare.

She noted that SIL in Australia has been around a long time. They were not newcomers. 'We know them and the work they have done advocating for Indigenous languages and serving communities through their research, literacy and translation work.' She then went to the core of the accusation, 'We also know they are a Christian organisation.' She then added her emphasis, '*a real Christian organisation*.' She then turned her attention to the position she held at the university, sitting in the Ranger

Chair in Aboriginal Studies. With some irony she pointed out the position was sponsored by a uranium mining company. She concluded, surely then we can partner with a real Christian organisation that serves our communities. She gave SIL her full endorsement.

Professor Langton was followed by a senior linguist from the University of New South Wales who happened to be visiting the university at the time. He told those listening that his research was only possible because of the data shared with him by an SIL linguist who had become a friend and colleague. He lauded the way SIL made its research available to others and serves the communities in which it works. SIL also had his endorsement.

David had us eating out of his hand. 'Wait. The best was still to come.' With a toss of his head and laugh, savouring the moment he went on. The third speaker was Stephen Harris an Australian who formerly headed the Northern Territory Bilingual Program. It was Stephen Harris who twelve years earlier wrote to me explaining why I should join the NT Bilingual Schools Program and not SIL. He was now a lecturer at the university but also married to a former SIL literacy worker from the USA. Stephen said, 'For years I hoped it was true that SIL was made up of CIA agents. In my old age the idea of sleeping with a CIA agent all these years really appeals to me. Disappointedly the evidence doesn't stack up. I am not sleeping with a CIA agent.'

His humour squashed the accusation flat. In all, seven people spoke in favour of a partnership between the university and SIL and two against. Game over. David summarised the day. 'A great victory was had,' he said.

The agreement between the university and SIL was now stronger than before the opposition arose. Those who previously had no reason to speak on our behalf had taken to the public square and defended us. They did it with more eloquence and humour than we could have mustered ourselves.

As I reflected on the events it seemed not dissimilar to an Old Testament victory over the enemy. How much our prayer contributed to the victory we would never know. But at the very minimum it placed God in the middle of the event. Without the time of prayer, we could have boasted in our victory as if it was our reputation and connections that earned it. With prayer we were humbled by the result. I also understood that God had forced my hand. It was a struggle for me to choose prayer and not action. God still had much to teach the Dreamer about prayer, and how the world of the Spirit intersected with the soil. It would be twenty years later before prayer totally refashioned my daily practice in leading an organisation. But that is another story for another day.

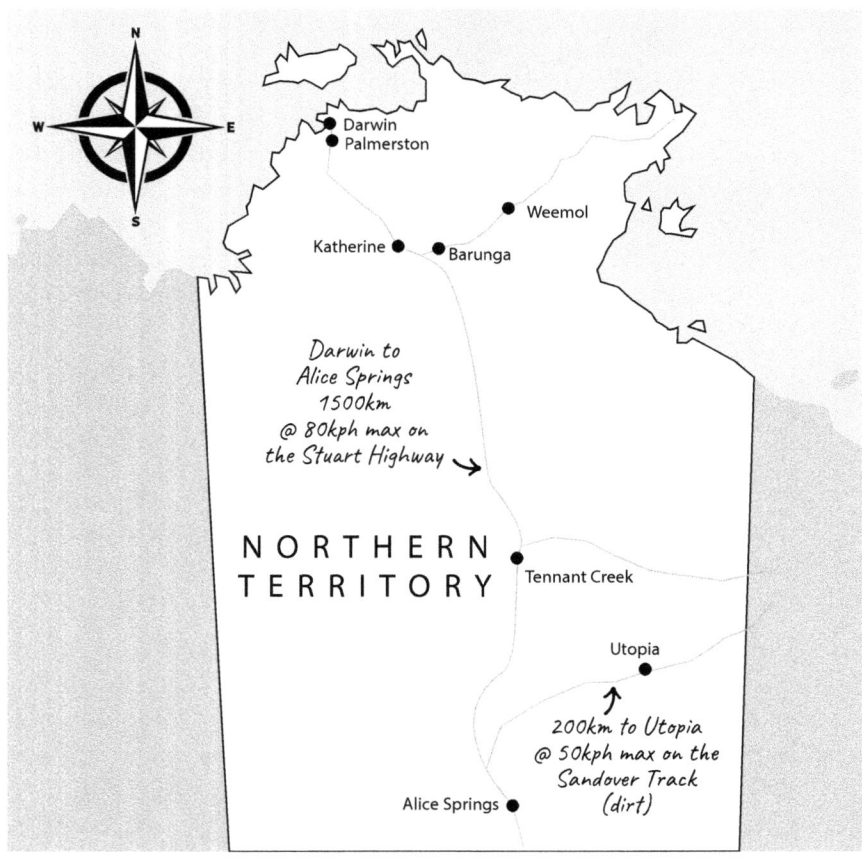

49

There Is No Precedent

Location:	Utopia
Date:	1997
Event:	Embracing the unexpected

The cattle station of Utopia gave its name to the region where sixteen separate Alyawarr and Anmatyerr speaking communities scattered themselves along the Sandover Highway approximately 300km northeast of Alice Springs. This was *country* for the Alyawarr and Anmatyerr over many generations, only interrupted by the arrival of pastoralists in the 1920s. David Strickland, an SIL linguist, translator and colleague was poised to relocate from his original allocation at Epenarra to Utopia. David would continue learning the Alyawarr language, and in conjunction with two other translators, work on the translation of the Alyawarr Scriptures. David's new home was a small out-station where the Urapuntja Health Service (Utopia Clinic) was located just two kilometres off the Sandover Highway. The only buildings were a medical clinic, an administration office, a few houses for a doctor, nurses, an administrator, and some very basic temporary accommodation. Some distance out in the scrub, half a dozen shade shelters provided temporary relief from the harsh sun. The place went by the local name, meaning *Spearing of Flies*.

It was early morning when Brian, our builder, and I rendezvoused with Bruce, our outback truckie, and his teenage son to travel the 1,700km from Darwin to Utopia. Bruce generously offered to tow and deliver for us a large second-hand caravan, aptly named *The Sherator* for David Strickland to live in. In doing so he would add over a 1000km to his planned trip to reach his next rendezvous point on the Queensland border, where he would escort a large oversized truck and its cargo back to Darwin.

The tray of our Toyota Dyna tip truck was weighed down with building supplies. A 44-gallon drum of diesel stood in the front right corner of the tray ready for refuelling. Petrol stations were few and far between where we were heading. It was still dark when we departed as we were keen to make the most of our first day on the road. With a top speed of 80km per hour, it would be three days before we arrived at our destination. I soaked up the quiet and anticipated the coming sunrise to welcome the new day. The open spaces restored my soul. I was leaving behind an office and a very heavy work schedule.

People tire me out, yet my job as director of SIL inescapably revolved around people. SIL Directors' meetings in the Solomon Islands, teaching workshops in Darwin and Board meetings all preceded this trip. In addition to these involvements, we had welcomed our first group of fifteen students from Korea, Japan, Malaysia and Taiwan for the year-long Asia SIL linguistics school. Each event was stimulating, the pragmatic outworking of previous dreams. I would not have it any other way. The pattern was set as far back as I could remember: to embrace life to the full and then retreat into the silence of my own world. For a time I was a man fully of the soil. Then came the dreaming. One day I was the entertainer but the next day the hermit. The internal contradiction was never resolved. Few of my colleagues were aware of this tension. My wife did her very best to live with it and to understand it. Out of love she gave me room, but she could only understand in part. Her eyes were filtered by a life that was enlivened by people.

This road trip was not work for me. It was an escape. We were only half an hour on the road when the powerful beams of Bruce's four-wheel drive lit up a bread delivery van parked just off the highway. Bruce put his lefthand indicator on, pulled over, and got out to see what the problem was. The vehicle's lights were dead. Daybreak was still an hour away putting the driver way behind his schedule. Bruce was the master of outback solutions. The problem was easily solved. The delivery truck driver sandwiched his truck neatly in between Bruce in the lead providing the headlights, and us in the rear providing the tail lights. We rolled into Adelaide River as day broke with his first delivery not too far behind schedule. It was the first of several stops that day. Every time we saw a hint of someone in need on the road, the left-hand blinker went on, Bruce pulled over, and with the minimum of fuss asked, 'You need some help mate?'

Thirteen hours expanded to fourteen and then fifteen hours on the road. It was a practical outworking of *love your neighbour*. Bruce lived as a child in a remote Aboriginal community of Lajamanu where his parents began translating the Bible into the Warlpiri language. His father died young and was buried there. Bruce was similarly attached to the land. The whole countryside was his home. As the day progressed, the further we lagged behind our intended time schedule. But nothing changed. Our schedule was never an excuse not to be available for the unexpected. Bruce lived in the present and without fuss or hurry.

I reflected on what my daily routine had become running from one meeting to another. The protocols and responsibilities of being Director set the agenda and the expectations of my colleagues filled in whatever spare time I had. There was little room for the stranger beside the road. I could not afford the distraction.

It took two days to reach the junction of the Plenty Highway and the Stuart Highway. We refuelled the Toyota and Bruce took the outback gravel highway north-east to *Spearing of Flies*. There he unhitched the caravan and continued along the dusty Sandover Highway to the Queensland border.

Brian and I continued with our truck south to Alice Springs to deliver supplies and meet up with David Strickland. The next day, with David leading the way in his four-wheel drive we drove back up the Stuart Highway, turned east onto the Plenty Highway then veered north-east along the gravel Sandover Highway. Late in the afternoon we arrived at the *Spearing of Flies*. It was a long, long drive to arrive at a place with few comforts. The nearest police station was 130 kilometres away down a bush track. Linguistically it was also isolated as those living there spoke limited English. Few had been to white man's school, and apart from purchasing goods from the store, they had no need to communicate in English. Alyawarr and Anmatyerr were still the languages that filled the air making it an ideal place for David to learn language. There was one direct link with the outside world. On the verandah of the administration office was a single public telephone.

The caravan was already parked and placed on blocks, thanks to Bruce's careful placement from the previous day. Our job was to construct a floor adjacent and level with the caravan and build a solid wall annex on top of it. It would become a second room for David and give additional protection from the hot wind and dust that roared across the plains. We immediately unloaded our truck that carried the building supplies. As the sun disappeared below the western horizon our work for the day ended. The cool evening breeze soon replaced the hot air. It was the outback at its glorious best. The stars in their thousands shone brighter and brighter penetrating the darkness. Thirty metres away a fluorescent light lit up the outside telephone. Hordes of moths and bugs delighted in the unexpected light. Everything else was dark and still and silent. It was a beautiful place to be.

Next day we made good progress. Brian was a first-class tradesman. David and I were his *third-class* apprentices. It was late mid-afternoon when the phone rang. This was not unusual. It had rung repeatedly throughout the day. Someone walking by would answer it and a series of shouts would ring out across the community to locate the intended receiver. What was unusual this time was that the shouts were for David Strickland. He answered then called me over. It was the SIL office in Darwin. I took the phone.

'News has just come from Pam in England that her husband John, has fallen into a coma. The doctors have given him only a couple of days to live. We thought you should know.' I put the phone back on the hook and walked slowly back towards the caravan where David was now sitting. I told him the news. The cancer John had battled had run its destructive course.

I was pondering something that I could not let go of. The same thought had crossed my mind two weeks before. At the time I had gently raised it with a colleague I trusted and the answer I got back was what I expected. There was no precedent for this. I agreed at the time, but now, on receiving the phone call the thought came back with added conviction. I could not hold it in. 'David' I said, 'I am thinking that I should go and see John before he dies. What do you think?' In many ways it was an unfair question but David replied without hesitation, 'I would love it if you could go. You would be honouring John and Pam and the work they did in a foreign land by going.'

'You know some people will see it as a misuse of funds. You know there is no precedent for a director to fly halfway around the world to see a dying colleague.'

The silence of the outback engulfed us for a few moment then David responded. 'Let me tell you why I think you should go. My brother was a diplomat with the Australian Foreign Service. He died in Vanuatu. The Australian Government sent a Hercules plane to pick up his body. They also arranged a memorial service in both Vanuatu and Canberra. No expense was spared because he died while in service for his country. It meant so much to my family. This is no different.'

David left me with much to ponder. He had confirmed my random thought. Alone under the sky of the great expanse of the Australian Outback the answer was clear. I would go Deep down I believed I would see John before he died. This was despite the fact that he only had a couple of days to live and it would be another five days before we could finish the job and complete the long drive back to Darwin. My thoughts did not equate with reason. They were the thoughts of a Dreamer.

I had plenty to ponder and time to do it. I needed more confirmation to be sure it was God's prompting. I scribbled the list of people on a note pad who would have to agree with my decision before I booked my flight to England. They were:

1. Pam
2. Marg
3. My children (16, 14, 12 & 9 yrs)
4. Annette, Pam's friend from her church in Darwin.

When I arrived back in Darwin Marg was at a training workshop on Elcho Island in Arnhem Land. I could not try out my thoughts on her first, which was my custom for unusual ideas. My unsuspecting children provided the first test. I casually said over the evening meal, 'I might need to go to England in a couple of days to see John and Pam. How do you feel about that?'

Not a word of complaint came. The fact we were living on a property where they had friends to play with and other homes to visit and live with was a factor I'm sure. It was good to have Dad around, but he wasn't essential to everyday life. They had no idea they were God's voice. One down, three to go.

I rang Marg on Elcho. Her response was one that I came to recognise over the years. For Marg the only question that needed to be answered was whether I was hearing from God. If that was the case, she was happy for me to go. She was also coming back a day early because she had been unwell, so she would be back in Darwin before I left. Two down and two to go.

I rang Pam in England. Her response was the lynchpin to the whole idea. I enquired how John was doing? He was in a coma but still alive. I then asked as casually as I could, 'How would you feel Pam if I decided to come and see John?' Pam simply responded, 'That would be really nice.' There were no objections or questions for clarity. Pam's response was personal. It cut to my heart.

At our weekly staff meeting I told all my colleagues what I was thinking. I said I welcomed any input. Early next morning I went to my office well before opening hours. I was on edge. I was still weighing up the fact that this was very much my decision, made between God and myself. It was not something the organisation or my colleagues were asking for, or expecting of me. I opened the door to my office and checked the correspondence in the Director's in-tray. There was an envelope marked with my name on it. I opened it and unfolded a single handwritten page from a colleague. The letter specifically addressed my proposed trip to England. It went straight to the point giving clear reasons why it was inappropriate. Each reason was numbered down the page. One, there was no precedent to justify it. Two, it was a misuse of money. Three, it was selfish. Four, I was failing in my duties to those on the Centre. Five, six, seven and eight followed, all of them essentially questioning my motivation and integrity. As I read the letter, the phone on my desk rang. It was early for a call. I picked up the phone laying the letter to one side. It was Pam's friend from her church. The day before I had simply asked her to pray and ask God if I should be going to England to see John. I posed the question as neutral as possible so she could weigh it up free of any expectation on my part. Annette had her answer and filled me in on the process. She told her story:

'When you asked me yesterday to pray about whether you should fly to England to see John I immediately thought the answer was *no* for all sorts of reasons. However, I committed to praying about it. At first nothing changed as I prayed. However, towards the early morning I experienced a growing conviction that you must go. It has become stronger and stronger. I am ringing to say I think this is what God wants. I did not expect to be ringing this morning to say this, but now I am.'

I put the phone down with the letter from my colleague open in front of me. The timing was perfect. I thanked Jesus wholeheartedly for the letter and the person who wrote it. I now knew how I might be misunderstood. I welcomed the misunderstanding. It was, according to the soil, fair criticism. I would not defend myself.

I waited until the clock face nudged past 8:30am and rang my travel agent. I had asked him to tentatively book flights and await my final go ahead. He informed me, 'Mr Borneman I booked a flight to London as you requested. You depart tomorrow morning arriving London on Saturday 9 November. To get a cheaper fare I booked you to stay for twelve days. Do you want me to confirm the booking?'

It was just another booking for the amiable travel agent and a question he would ask many times in the course of the day. For me it was much more than that. I took a deep breath and said to my unseen companion, 'Well God here goes.'

'Yes, please confirm the booking. Thank you.'

I put the phone down and sat silently in my chair. Part of me was in shock. I was leaving behind a full agenda to be with a dying friend. Perhaps Bruce's example and the open starlit sky had found an opening in my heart. The other part of me warmed to the unknown. I mumbled to myself, 'Jesus, I guess I am now going to find out if this was your idea!'

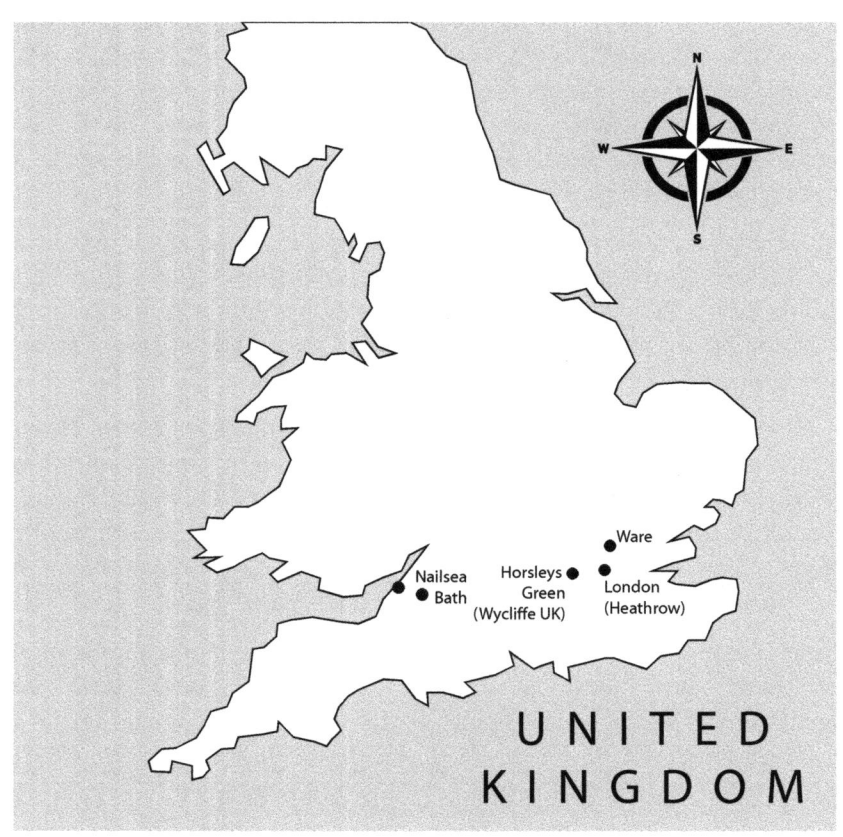

50

Twelve Remarkable Days

Location: Nailsea, England
Date: 1997
Event: Death of a friend

Three hours out of London and flying at 30,000 feet the cabin was slowly coming back to life. The warm face flannel placed over my face and then the back of my neck tipped the balance from slumber to alertness. The stiffness that accompanied flying still lingered. There was not a lot someone with my long frame could do about that. Still the first smell of morning coffee, even airline coffee, promised better things. The last 48 hours had been a whirlwind. I was not a seasoned international traveller and the short preparation time left me hoping I had with me all that I needed. I felt my shirt pocket for the umpteenth time. My passport was still there where I had put it after clearing customs in Darwin. I checked my wallet. The small piece of paper with Pam's address and telephone number was still where I had put it when I packed my bags. The information with the bus schedule from Heathrow Airport to Bristol was in my carry-on bag. I would again check to see it was there when I disembarked. The plan was straight forward. Pam's daughter would pick me up from the Bristol bus depot when I arrived in the afternoon. As a precaution, I also had the telephone number of Wycliffe Bible Translators UK. They did not know I was coming, but they were my emergency backup. I had all bases covered.

'Relax Barry, God has orchestrated the trip,' I told myself. 'Leave it with him to take care of it.'

A middle seat separated me from a gentleman in his mid-30s. He was casually dressed, relaxed and ready for an introductory conversation. I preferred a book to a conversation when flying. I hoped it would be short. His accent immediately gave him away. He was Irish and wanted to talk. He didn't need to ask where I was from. My accent gave me away. The Irish and the Australians have a shared cultural history. Even strangers presume a connection. The conversation was light and jovial. He worked in London, though Ireland was home.

'Freedom of movement was one of the advantages of belonging to the European Union,' he said.

We chatted amiably as the cabin crew walked down the aisle, calling out, 'Anyone not from the European Union needs to fill in a UK customs form. Please take one.'

I took the form. My Irish friend looked on with interest as I began to fill out my name and flight details. 'You have got a visa haven't you?' he asked.

'No,' I replied. 'I'll get a visitor's visa when I arrive.'

A concerned expression crossed his face. 'I don't think you can. Australia is not part of the European Union. You should have got your visa permit before you left Australia. I don't think they will let you in.'

I was stunned. In all the rush I had not asked about visas. I assumed my travel agent would have told me.

The airline breakfast arrived but I couldn't take a bite, not because of my culinary snobbery, but because the knot in my stomach was tightening by the minute. I closed my eyes and listened to the drum of the airplane. My mind wandered off on a series of scenarios vivid in their reckoning.

The immigration officer looked at my passport and said, 'Come with me, sir.' I followed him to an office with a desk and a leather chair on one side and two plain wooden chairs on the other. The interrogation was about to begin.

I prayed, 'Holy Spirit you promised to give me the words I needed. If ever there was a time, I needed your words and not mine, this was it.' Nothing came. The officer opened my passport and simply said, 'I'm sorry, with no entry permit we can't let you in. It happens from time to time. We will simply put you on the next plane back to Australia.'

I resigned myself to my fate and sought deeper spiritual meaning. Just maybe this was the only way God could deal with my pride. If God made me look like an idiot would I still follow him? My reputation for sound judgement in a crisis would be severely damaged. In my mind I tried to embrace this scenario. I said to myself, 'Yes, I would follow you Jesus no matter what. My reputation is not important. Was this the lesson I was about to learn?' I asked myself.

The moment of truth arrived. My Irish friend took the EU line and moved unhindered through Immigration. With a wave he disappeared into the crowd. I waited my turn in the Non-EU line. I tried to look casual as if I had not a concern in the world. It didn't matter. No-one was interested in me anyway. They had enough worries of their own. The immigration officer beckoned me to her cubicle. I passed her my passport. She opened it, glanced at the passport photo.

'What is your reason for coming to England?'

'I have come to see my friend before he dies. He has cancer.'

She stamped the passport with a thump, handed it back to me and said, 'I hope it goes well for you.'

She turned and beckoned the next person in line. It took less than thirty seconds. The three-hour knot in my stomach dissipated immediately. I opened my passport. I had a three-month visitor's visa.

It was late morning when I boarded the bus to Bristol. It was overcast with the temperature edging towards double digits. I was happy to trade the 32 degrees centigrade heat and humidity of Darwin for the freshness of a looming English winter. I also was happy to trade the stress of the last few days and particularly the last few hours, for the solitude of a two-hour bus ride to Bristol. Against the backdrop of the English countryside, I reflected. I had not been stretched like this for a long, long time. It paralleled the small voice that I heard a decade before at Barunga. That time it sent me to Jimmy and the offer to take him and his family to see his seriously ill son in Darwin Hospital. Jesus' story of the Good Samaritan was distinctive because of the generosity and lavishness of a totally unexpected response to a human need. It was a response not governed by the law, by expectations of others or by existing protocols. It was as if the Dreamer was given permission one more time to break the rules because of compassion.

Pam's mother met me at her apartment door. She was an engaging, spritely character *full of endeavour*. She gave an immediate impression of a life well lived, not encumbered with self-doubt. Protocols however, were clearly in place. First I would eat and then Pam would invite me across the hallway to see John. I had entered into the world of English decorum, formality and privacy. After tea Pam rang. I crossed the hall and knocked. Pam opened the door.

'I am so glad you could come. John has been waiting for you,' she said. Pam led me to the bedroom where John lay as a shell of a man, unresponsive to the world around him. It was as if all life had been drained out of him: no colour, and just a hint of life. The death shadows that engulfed John communicated the futility of conversation. But I had come to bring him greetings. I began as if John understood every word.

'Hello John. It is Barry here. I bring you greetings from Darwin.'

I had barely finished my first sentence when John moved his head slightly up from his pillow and let out a loud grunting sound. The sound pierced my soul. Just as quickly his head fell back on the pillow. He immediately returned to his unresponsive state. Silence reigned but the loud grunting noise still reverberated in my head. 'It must be the shocking sound of my Aussie accent,' I thought. 'That would bring anyone to life.'

'John I bring you greetings from your Aboriginal friends and the church on Groote Eylandt. They asked me to pass on their greetings when they heard I was coming. I also bring you greetings and love from your friends at St Peter's in Darwin. They have been praying for you. And I bring greetings from your colleagues and friends at SIL. We will soon have our first graduates of the Certificate in Translating for Aboriginal Translation teams. The course is going well.'

The one-way conversation continued for ten minutes or so. I talked as if he fully understood me. I was also sure God and John were having their own conversation: a conversation that took in more of heaven than it did of earth. Perhaps for those ten minutes the three of us had come together for a final rendezvous.

A few hours after midnight, John quietly passed on from this earth. Pam invited me across the hall to their apartment to see John one last time. All life had gone out of his cancer-ridden body. John, a husband and a father had died at the age of 56. I thanked the Lord that he invited me into this sacred moment and for the journey that got me there.

Over the next couple of days plans were made for John's memorial service. It was set for the day before my flight back to Australia. I was stunned by the timing. Perhaps I should not have been. The sense of following God's leading was a thin line for me. I felt compelled to follow, to find out what it was about, but I rarely saw clearly what the future looked like. It was only in the going that clarity came. I recognised there were often times when God was beckoning me to pursue unexpected possibilities but I preferred to ignore them, but not this time. I now sensed in a tangible way that the Giver of Dreams was pulling the strings and he was enjoying himself. I not only came to see John before he died, but I also came to honour his missionary life in the same way the Australian Diplomatic Corps had honoured David's brother.

Pam asked me to speak at John's service. I consented. It was my honour to do so. Pam then gently added, 'You do have something formal to wear, don't you?'

'It is all fine Pam,' I assured her.

Pam had reason to ask. The Northern Territory culture was the epitome of casual and I fitted the stereotype well. In Darwin a pair of sandals lay under my desk near my bare feet ready for action should we have a visitor. I had not worn a tie in years and did not own a suit. My selection of long trousers and dress shirts were minimal. Added to this I travelled light. I instinctively knew that what would pass in Darwin would not pass in England. John's family were distinguished. John himself was a Cambridge graduate. Suits and jackets were not a public statement, they were everyday wear. I sent a prayer up to God and suggested he arrange something. I did not want to worry Pam, nor embarrass her.

The extra days between John's death and the memorial service gave me time to personally pass on my thanks to those who had supported John and Pam. First, I headed to the Wycliffe Bible Translators Centre at Horsleys Green in High Wycombe. When I arrived I passed on my greetings and thanks to the staff. They could not hide the shock when they heard that I had come all the way from Australia to see John before he died. I wondered what they were thinking. I didn't ask.

I made a discrete enquiry about whether they had a room with secondhand clothes. One of the volunteers happily took me there, unlocked the door, and told me to bring back the key when I had finished looking. I opened the door, stepped inside and just two metres in front of me hung a fine grey woollen pin-striped suit. I took it off the hangar and tried on the coat. Perfect fit. I looked at the waist size. Another perfect fit. A selection of ties caught my eye. Perfect. Five minutes later I returned the key. God had provided.

At the same time fellow Australian Wycliffe friends, Warren and Jessie were also staying at the Wycliffe UK headquarters. On Sunday, we drove to Christ Church at Ware for their service. I blended in perfectly. Perhaps the suit gave them the confidence to ask me to speak in their chapel service. I thanked them for their support for the Fletchers and the Bible translation work on Groote Eylandt. The Glovers then dropped me back to Oxford where I took the train to Bristol, and the bus on to Nailsea.

The memorial service at the Anglican Church was a time to recall John's achievements. Family told of John's brilliant mind and his student years at Cambridge. We heard of his work to build a computer with a small group of his sixth form class mates. Stephen Hawking was one of this group. What was missing was any news of their Aboriginal work and John's overseeing the publishing of Aboriginal New Testaments. I felt privileged to fill in that part of his life. I knew where John's heart was. His ashes would return to Australia and the Aboriginal community where he worked. After the memorial service the family gathered for lunch nearby at The Little Harp. I was seated with John's brother, Roger. I could not help but notice that he wore the same fine wool grey suit as I did. I blended in unnoticed apart from my Australian accent.

Next day I boarded my flight back to Darwin. The last two weeks had been an experience like none I had had before. Jesus had not commanded me to walk on water like Peter, but he had done the next best thing. He had orchestrated time and provision in a way that no human effort could.

As jet lag disrupted my nightly sleep back in Darwin my mind was left rehearsing over and over again the pivotal moments of walking with Jesus.

I recalled:

- It was Jesus who took me into the outback so I could hear HIS voice.
- It was Jesus who gave me the courage to act through David Strickland's story about his brother's death and memorial.
- It was Jesus who selected the people to confirm my trip: my children, my wife, Pam and her praying friend.
- It was Jesus who arranged my ticket to England with a 12-day stay.
- It was Jesus who put the Irishman next to me to test my commitment to follow him and not worry about reputation.

- It was Jesus who kept John alive to hear final greetings from colleagues and Aboriginal and church community.
- It was Jesus who provided me with a perfectly fitting suit suitable for English culture.
- It was Jesus who gave me the privilege of honouring John's years of service
- And Jesus did all this because John was a friend of his and Jesus wanted me there.

A week later Marg and I sat around our kitchen table. The monthly finance statement sat in front of us. I added up my costs for the trip. It came to just under $2,600.

While I was adding up the costs Marg noted additional income in our financial statement. 'There are a lot of extra funds into our account marked for the trip. I see a couple of $200 gifts here.'

We had not asked for financial help but people's hearts towards John and Pam were being demonstrated through these gifts to us.

Marg passed me her list of financial gifts. I quickly added it up. 'I can't believe this. How much did we say we would contribute towards someone else going instead of me?' I asked.

'We said we would give three hundred dollars,' Marg replied.

'Well look at these figures.' I passed the sheet of paper to her and pointed to the final figure. I exclaimed,

'The difference between what it has cost us and what we have received is $300.'

We looked at each other in amazement. It was a holy moment found not in worship, or some ecstatic experience, but in simple accounting!

51

I Don't Need God!

Location:	Darwin
Date:	1999
Event:	Leaving Darwin

'I don't need God anymore,' I told Marg. The look on her face suggested a further explanation was in order.

'This is not about faith. This is about my job. I can do this job with my hands tied behind my back.' That was an overstatement to which I was prone, but it reflected the fact that I was comfortable in my job and comfortable living in Darwin. 'It is almost as if I don't need God anymore. This is what worries me.'

I had verbalised something that had been gnawing away at me for the previous 12 months. Now that it was out in the open we could look at the problem from all sides. I lived out my faith in Jesus by my commitment to my marriage and through the job I did. My job was not an escape. It was a tangible expression of who I was. It was a platform that allowed me to follow my dreams. Now I was saying, 'I can do this without God.'

I knew it was not true but it was how I felt. I feared more the negative effects of long-term complacency, routine, and success than the consequences of short-term upheaval. The gift of *faith* given by God was my most prized possession. I needed to take steps to guard it. The Dreamer needed to pull his feet out of the soil once more and find somewhere else to place them. This is how it was with the Dreamer. He was always a sojourner.

For Marg everyday was an opportunity to connect with people. This is what most defined her faith. The more settled we became the more God could use her with neighbours, friends and strangers. Marg did not invite upheaval. Every move in our married life was a cause of some degree of pain for her. While I looked forward to the open road and what's next, Marg looked back in the mirror at the friends she left behind. My dilemma was not her dilemma. If Marg had her choice alone, we probably would not be moving.

There was no obvious solution to my outcry. But another principle began to emerge that we both recognised. When a significant change was coming we noticed that often the tap roots that held us in that place would begin to dry up. Slowly God began to loosen the soil in small ways.

The Darwin weather was one of them. The amazing *dry season* was followed by the gradual *build-up* towards the monsoon season. I struggled with Darwin's humidity at the best of times and as each build-up season rolled around it seemed to become more difficult. Even Marg, who loved the heat, recognised the physical toll almost fifteen years in the tropics was having on us. Added to this was a very full workload for both of us. At some stage in our lives we would move South to a less taxing climate and a less taxing work environment. The question became, 'When was the right time?'

The natural rhythm of life also suggested it was the time to move. In twelve months' time, our eldest daughter Rachel would complete her tertiary studies and our second daughter Heidi would graduate from secondary school. Both planned to move from Darwin to Brisbane and Sydney for further studies. Our family unit would reduce from six to four. If we moved at the start of 2000 Andrew would complete his final two years of secondary education in the same school and Naomi would move directly from primary to secondary school. Moving at the end of 1999 seemed like the least disruptive time.

For the first time in fifteen years we began to imagine a future outside the Northern Territory. The outburst of being able to do my job without God was the precursor to a bigger discussion. Perhaps it was a necessary precursor, even one instigated by God himself. I could not be sure about that.

I am unsure which came first. The invitation or the personal conviction that it was time to move. Either way the invitation from Neville Southwell, who was the Wycliffe and SIL Pacific Area Director, and hence *my boss*, landed in fertile soil. The role of Pacific Training Coordinator attracted me. It was to support training initiatives in Wycliffe and SIL operations in the region. This included the Australian Aboriginal work as well as Papua New Guinea, Solomon Islands, Vanuatu, and Micronesia. The move offered a broader context to do what motivated me most - providing opportunities for colleagues from the local communities and organisations to develop and grow. There would also be a place for Marg in the team but also have time to connect with our neighbourhood. The one tap root that would not budge were friendships formed amongst colleagues, Aboriginal translators, the church and community. They would all be missed. Marg was right. There was no such thing as a painless move.

The single decision to move required a hundred and one other decisions. The number of personal decisions went off the chart each day. There were decisions about what goods and chattels to give away, sell, or take with us and the bigger decision about selling or keeping our house in Palmerston. Once we decided to keep it, it needed painting before we left. There were decisions about potential schools in Brisbane. Decisions about where we might live and so on. Each day our physical stamina was more depleted than the day before. At the same time work demands increased rather than decreased. And yes we were in the monsoon build up season. The goal was to drive out of Darwin and spend New Year's Eve in Alice Springs with friends just ahead of the Y2K hysteria that filled the newspapers. It was a recipe for exhaustion and a less than satisfactory way to say goodbye to friends and colleagues who had been part of our lives for the last 15 years.

Three weeks prior to our departure our 15-year-old son Andrew became increasingly listless. Marg took him to the doctor. When he said he had a dry mouth the doctor suspected diabetes. She did a finger prick, noted his massively high sugar levels and sent him straight to hospital. The 'smart doctor,' as the hospital intern called her, had made the correct diagnosis and he was admitted just in time before he might have gone into a coma. Teenage onset Type 1 Diabetes meant insulin injections four times a day to stay alive. There was little time for us to process this change. He went into hospital a teenager and came out a man. He told us that it was his situation to manage, not ours.

We finished packing the van after midnight, ready to leave early next morning. We slumped into bed hoping for six hours sleep. Half an hour before our departure a friend and colleague complained to me about something that I had left undone. It was a small thing but one too much for me. I returned his request with a cold stare, and barked back at him, 'Go do it yourself.' I walked off. It was the school boy I remembered who when cornered came out fighting ready to inflict pain on his adversary. I told Marg that I had blown up at our colleague. Marg suggested I apologise. I was in no mood to give either an apology or repentance. He could stew in his own juice. In ten years of leadership, I could not remember a time when I lost my temper, or went off sulking, no matter what the circumstances. I waited to the very last moment to fail miserably.

As we headed south down the Stuart Highway, leaving behind a significant chapter in our lives, I was fully aware that I still needed God big time. I needed him not only to dream again, I needed him to inhabit the soil and refresh the tired vessel that I had become.

Three months later I returned to Darwin for meetings in my new role. My colleague, whom I seethed at on my departure, drove by as I walked out of the house where I was staying. We caught each other's eye. He pulled his vehicle to a stop. I walked toward the truck and without introduction said, 'Sorry mate.' He replied, 'Me too.' We both shook our heads and laughed. Matter resolved. That was repentance Aussie style. I could dream again.

52

The Just Shall Live by Faith

Location:	Brisbane
Date:	2000
Event:	Bank account empty

The move to Brisbane re-ignited the childlike faith that had been dormant for some time. Circumstances simply required it. Schools for Andrew and Naomi were first on the list. With that ticked off we asked Jesus for an affordable house close to the school bus runs and he miraculously provided one. A local church was easily identified when an invitation was delivered to our mailbox. We settled well into our new workplace and enjoyed our colleagues. Responsibilities were less and workload much more manageable. I had more time to take long walks and Marg began connecting with our new neighbours. We adopted a Bible text for the year as an experiment. It was *the just shall live by faith* (Galatians 3:12).

'I am thinking we will get a new computer,' I announced at the dinner table. With computers becoming the norm for both our work and school, it was no longer a luxury but a necessity. Marg spoke to me quietly after dinner.

'You shouldn't get their hopes up. We don't have the money to buy a new computer.' Our approach reflected our different personalities. Marg's primary concern was for others and how an adverse situation might affect them negatively. My primary interest was in creating new possibilities without any thought of disappointment.

But Marg was right about the money. In the previous five months since we moved from Darwin our savings had eroded away. The cost of relocation, rental bonds, weekly rent, and school fees added up. The $5,000 buffer that we kept in a separate account for emergencies was now empty. We had less than $100 in the bank.

It was new territory for us. In more than two decades without a regular income we had not been in a situation of being down to our last dollar. It was the perfect scenario to experiment. We knew the *just shall live by faith* referred to the assurance God had given us that the death, resurrection and ascension of Jesus was sufficient for freedom from sin and the promise of eternal life. If we trust Jesus for that then we surely could trust him to be our provider in our hour of need. This is the year of experimenting with *living by faith*.

During my walks with God I imagined two ways God could respond. God could restore our bank account, or he could give us an extra portion of contentment with an empty bank account. Either solution was welcomed. A couple of days after I made the new computer announcement a letter arrived in our mailbox. It was from our longtime friends Rev Ron and Jan Wood. I did not open the letter with any sense of expectation. Two years earlier in Darwin, I had cheekily declared to Marg and the children that an unopened letter in my hand had a cheque in it for us. When I opened that particular letter a large cheque *was* inside. Wow! How did I know? I read through the letter which included all their family news. At the bottom was a post-script asking us to cash the cheque and pass the money on to another family as they didn't have their address. I laughed at my presumption. It was hilarious. Presumption is never a good thing when it comes to God.

So without any presumption, I opened the letter from Ron and Jan. Inside was a single page folded over. I unfolded the letter and in it was a cheque for $5,000. It represented 20% of our annual income! The letter itself spoke of some of their more recent family events and concluded with the instruction that the cheque was for our personal use only. It is *not* for ministry.

We knew it was for a new computer. Later that night I phoned Ron. I thanked him for their generosity. I also told him how remarkable the timing was. Ron laughed. He said he had been meaning to send the cheque for a long while. He reiterated that it was for personal use only.

The following week we received our monthly financial statement from Wycliffe Australia. To our amazement there was another gift of $5,000 from Ron and Jan designated for our work. $10,000 came in the week when we had an annual income of not much over $20,000 and when our bank account for the first time in our married life was near empty.

Over the following weeks I reflected on what had happened. The Dreamer in me saw things differently to the man of the soil. For the latter God was meeting our need. For the Dreamer it was an expression of something far bigger. The story unfolded in my imagination.

When God saw our need even before we knew about it, he viewed a re-run of our lives. Jesus remembered a gift of a few dollars that I left on the kitchen table at Malmsbury 25 years before. It was not so much the money that Jesus remembered, nor the milk it provided for breakfast the next morning, but the brotherly affection and spiritual bond that had been formed. God doesn't forget such things. 'Let me work with that,' the Holy Spirit had said. So Holy Spirit began to weave his own story long before our time of need had come. When Ron and Jan sold *The Mansions* property they had in mind to bless others who had been part of the community. We were on their list. Each time Ron went to write the cheque the Holy Spirit distracted him. *Then* was not the time. But just at the right time the Holy Spirit whispered in Jan's ear, 'Remind Ron to write that cheque.' Jan passed on the message and Ron wrote the cheque, sent the letter and we received it exactly when God wanted it to be opened. The Holy Spirit was pleased by the scene he had directed. The angels assigned to the Bornemans were applauding, the evil spirits were repelled by the joy, and a new iMac computer was on the way. So ended scene 883 of our ongoing story!

God never grows tired of writing and directing scenes like this. All he needs is a cast. I was glad that Marg and I had volunteered for this. Living by faith in Jesus was not a solo performance. It was a community play under the watch of a Master Director.

53

Being Yourself

Location: Port Moresby, Darwin
Date: 2002-2007
Event: Connecting

The customs officer gave me a friendly nod and beckoned me through. I felt a sense of relief. Inevitably I was bringing in a second-hand computer and a few hard-to-find items from Australia for our PNG colleagues. I may have carried the title of SIL Training Coordinator for the Pacific but a more apt title for any of our Area office staff when we travelled was *pack horse of the Pacific*. I passed through the door leading away from customs and into the Jackson International Airport. The welcoming smile of Stephen Thomas, the Director of the Bible Translation Association of Papua New Guinea (BTA) greeted me.

A few months earlier, Stephen and I were at meetings in Brisbane, when we both found ourselves drawn away from important matters to watch a rugby league game on the television. As we sat together, I commented my uncertainty of adapting from an Australian Aboriginal setting to a Melanesian one. Stephen laughed, 'There's nothing to worry about. We already know you.'

'How do you know me?' I asked.

'When you were teaching at Ukarumpa, I was working in the Printshop. We played tennis together. You always played with the PNG boys.' I was dumbfounded, not just because Stephen remembered this from 20 years before, but equally because I didn't. For the Dreamer it was something to reflect on. If something seemingly insignificant happens by just being yourself but later becomes significant, who made that happen? Was it you or was it God? The Dreamer decided that it was always God. A God who allowed you to just be yourself and used your normal self for his purposes, was a great God to keep company with.

As Stephen drove out of the airport he casually said, 'I have booked a room for you at the MAPANG Guesthouse. I'll take you there first.'

I was familiar with the guesthouse from when we first arrived in PNG on New Year's Eve, 31 December 1980. It was a fine establishment and the normal place for overseas guests to stay. I suddenly sensed it was not the place for me at that time. I battled for a few seconds with the thought.

'Stephen I'm not staying there. I've come to see you and I'd like to stay at BTA.' I added, 'If you don't have room available, I'll sleep on your lounge room floor.'

Stephen's broad smile conveyed everything I needed to know. He swung the car in the direction of the BTA Centre.

This request was not planned. It was not as a result of anthropological or missionary training. It was simply a thought spoken out. It started a very special friendship with Stephen and his wife Elizabeth and family, and a special relationship with BTA.

Two days later I flew to Alotau for the BTA Translator Training Course in my position as SIL Area Training Coordinator. This time I had no choice about my accommodation. Duncan, an experienced PNG translator and trainer, directed me to the accommodation that he and I were sharing. I stooped low into the dimly lit single room with mattresses on two basic wooden framed single beds. I threw my bag on the unused bed. Duncan and I had only met an hour before. He was a warm jovial character whom I immediately felt at ease with. As I stepped outside a car with expatriate staff passed by.

'Where are they going?' I asked Duncan.

'They're going away for the weekend. They'll be back Monday morning.'

I suddenly felt sorry for my new PNG colleagues. Just when they were looking to enjoy a relaxing weekend amongst themselves after a week of study, they suddenly inherited this white stranger. As I was thinking of this, Duncan moved towards the nearby volleyball court where a couple of men had gathered. It was a well-used grass court with sections worn down to the dirt. The net was set high with a few patched-up holes.

Duncan asked, 'Do you want to join us for a game?'

'Yeah, I'd love to,' I said.

I was nearing 50 years of age but was still drawn to any ball game. I could feel the adrenalin start to flow and the competitive edge surface. What was to follow was not what my PNG colleagues expected, but anyone who knew me would not have given it a second thought. I definitely didn't! As we set, spiked, and blocked, we laughed and celebrated every winning point. The first drops of the late afternoon rain were hardly noticed but as each minute passed it came with increasing intensity. 'Do you want to stop?' Duncan asked.

'No way,' came my reply. 'If you're playing, I'm playing.' The rain turned into a short downpour and the ground into mud. Slipping and sliding became the norm. We were brothers in arms. With the rain conquered, one game led to another. We played till it was dark.

With a plate filled with rice, tin fish and bush greens we settled around the campfire talking late into the night. Duncan shared his apprehension.

'When we heard you were coming we were nervous about meeting you. We thought you would be academic and just want to evaluate our course. But once you started playing volleyball in the rain we knew you were one of us.' The truth was I did what was perfectly natural for me. I wondered if God had brought the rain.

The weekend was filled with storytelling and laughter as I heard the aspirations of my PNG colleagues. They loved the training that they received but they were also definitely interested in accredited training that could be recognised by the government and broader community. I asked if BTA trainers like Duncan, would like to gain an *Australian Certificate IV in Assessment and Workplace Training*? Over time I heard a clear 'Yes'. I set my mind towards this end.

It took another two years to put everything in place for the course to start in Port Moresby. An Australian education institution and trainer with whom I had built a friendship was ready to deliver it. The former Director of BTA, David Gela completed the course in Australia and was on staff as a qualified trainer. Marg was the qualified assessor. Wycliffe Australia provided the funds for the course fees. The hard work was about to begin and a dream about to be fulfilled.

Two days before I was to fly to Port Moresby, a longtime friend and colleague dropped into the office. She was aghast at what I was doing. She was adamant it was not appropriate. What would happen if people's motives to study was just because of the accreditation? Wasn't I setting up some of our PNG colleagues for failure. I was shocked to hear that what I considered to be God's initiative she considered a stumbling block. It was not time for turning back. My answer was unequivocal,

'Personal motivation is not for me to judge and failure does not worry me. What worries me is not giving our PNG colleagues the opportunity to aspire and to succeed.'

The Catholic Retreat house on the outskirts of Port Moresby was an ideal location. The participants worked into the night enthused by the opportunity they had. Jason Potter, our trainer from Australia, commented that he had never experienced such a dedicated group of students. A second intensive at the PNG Bible Translation Association centre in Port Moresby saw 12 of the 13 participants successfully complete the *Certificate IV in Assessment and Workplace Training*. If BTA wanted to offer an accredited course they now had trainers accredited to do so. The only thing that could have prevented its stunning success was a lack of opportunity and a fear of failure, not by the students themselves but by their mentors. It was one of the highlights of my time working in the Pacific which was soon followed by another.

The Certificate IV in Translation garnered much enthusiasm from Solomon Islander translators. It was introduced at their request but faced similar opposition from some expatriates who questioned the value of an accredited course from Australia that they did not control. However with support from Wycliffe Australia trainers, the local translators persevered through three years of intensive workshops. They joyfully celebrated their success at their graduation ceremony in Honiara along with family representatives, colleagues and government dignitaries.

The Dreamer adopted a new motto. *Don't be afraid to give someone the right to fail. It is how a new future is forged.* For the Dreamer, Jesus was our greatest example. When signs were leading to his crucifixion on the cross his disciples begged him to not take that path. All they could see was failure. It would destroy him and his mission. They did it out of love but also out of fear. If the disciples' *gatekeeping* had prevailed then the resurrection would not have happened. Life is like that. Some things have to die and those in control need to let go for new opportunities to emerge. For me creating opportunities like this was my happy place. One had to dream to believe it was possible, then work every day with others to bring it to pass.

54

The Bond Of Friendship

Location:	Brisbane and Bendigo
Date:	May 2003
Event:	The second stroke

Jeff was my first mentor in the faith when I was at Teachers College and in my early years of knowing Jesus.

Though he was only three years older he was a colossus who opened me up to the work of the Spirit. But more than that, he was the truest of friends in spite of only keeping in sporadic contact with him. Jeff was a born and bred Bendigo man. He and Lauris had no intentions of living anywhere else. I was a sojourner which took Marg and me to Melbourne, PNG, Darwin, Brisbane and visiting multiple countries in the Pacific and Asia. Our paths only occasionally crossed, often years apart. When we did catch up our first question might unashamedly be, 'How are things with Jesus? Fill me in.' It was as if there was no time between visits. It was how it was.

The Saturday morning ABC radio sports roundup recounted a stirring win by the Collingwood Magpies the night before. Jeff had always been an ardent Collingwood Football Club supporter following in his father's footsteps. Hearing of the win reminded me of Jeff. In thinking of him I heard a still small voice suggest, 'Give Jeff a ring'. The thought would not leave me. It was late afternoon. I picked up the phone and dialled his home number. Jeff promptly answered. 'Barry here, Jeff. How are you going?'

Jeff replied with some urgency. 'Lauris has had a second stroke. She is in a coma. The doctors said she is not expected to live.' Then he added, 'I just arrived back home from the Austin Hospital and I needed someone to talk to. I rang a friend here but he didn't answer. I put the phone down and you rang.'

Unbeknown to me, Lauris, Jeff's beautiful wife, had suffered her second serious stroke and been transferred from Bendigo by air ambulance to Melbourne. Lauris was 49 years old. Jeff was 53. They had been married 27 years.

Lauris' seizure lasted 24 minutes. She fell into a coma giving no external response. The neurologist could not give any certainty that she would live.

I was amazed by the timing. We were friends and brothers in Christ like no other in my life. By me hearing the scores of a football match while in Brisbane, God ensured I was at the end of the phone when Jeff needed to talk. The Holy Spirit was invested in Jeff and my friendship in a way more profound than what I understood. He knew how our life stories connected in the past, and in the present, and would connect into the future.

Jeff talked about the challenges ahead. No answers were needed, just an awareness that Jeff's wife, and mother of their two adult children, was in the fight of her life. The pain for everyone was immense.

Lauris remained in a coma, unresponsive for a number of weeks. The Specialist had done all he could. He sadly told Jeff it was time to remove all life support and let Lauris go. As Jeff sat with Lauris waiting for his children to arrive to meet with the Specialist the most unexpected thing happened. Lauris opened her eyes. She directed the most beautiful smile towards Jeff. Her eyes were alive again. Lauris was completely paralysed, except for facial expressions and movement of one index finger. However, she could remember and understand everything. It was with that little index finger that she would physically connect with her future grandson.

A couple of months later I had reason to visit Melbourne, so I made the 150 km trip to Bendigo to see Jeff. He took me in to see Lauris. While we were there he told me a story that the Dreamer completely identified with. Jeff said, 'Every day I write a devotion for Lauris that talks about who she is, not about doing. The other day I told her she was the light of the world and that everyone sees the light of Christ in her. I told her the light of Christ in her cannot be switched off and that darkness disappears when the light is turned on. When others come into her world, she lights up their day.'

Jeff went on, 'Immediately after I told this devotion to Lauris, a nurse came in, closed the door, and sat by her bed. The nurse said, "I'm having a terrible day Lauris, but I love being with you. Your smile lights up my day."'

Jeff continued, 'Lauris immediately looked directly at me with a stare of delightful surprise. Her eyes told me she knew she was still the light of Christ to those around her. It was amazing.'

Tears welled up in my eyes. It was a story the Dreamer would wish for and now he experienced it. The intimacy of the Spirit and his presence defines who we are. The Jesus revolution lies not in what we do but who we are, and it changes everything.

In Lauris' last months Jeff said they fell more in love than ever before. With the only forms of communication being a blink of the eye and moving her index finger, love was concentrated in a way that made it burn brighter. Lauris left for a realm filled with light, a new body and life eternal on the afternoon of Sunday 19 June, 2005. Jeff recalled their journey together in a booklet he titled *So Beautiful*.

Almost twenty years later on 29 January 2025 I woke in the middle of the night with a burning desire to re-read *So Beautiful*. My reading was interspersed with tears as I read Lauris' daughter's letters to her.

When I finished reading, I sensed that Jesus wanted me to include this story in the *Unfolding Story of a Dreamer*. The next morning I wrote and added this chapter which I previously thought was finished. I sent it to Jeff for his approval. The next day he wrote that he had no words to describe it. Yes, I could put the story in my book.

A day later a stroke paralysed my right side. While I lay immobilised on our lounge floor unable to speak or move, I could hear and understand every word spoken by the paramedics and my family in the room. I felt very alive. I wondered if this was how Lauris had felt inside. As I recovered in hospital, I texted Jeff that I had had a stroke. He quickly got his friends together to pray for me. The timing seemed to be no coincidence. Somehow Jeff and I were connected by Jesus in a mysterious way.

The Dreamer then suddenly saw it. Jesus said to his disciples he no longer calls them slaves but friends. God made us to be friends with him and each other. He removed every barrier to make this possible. When there is connection and love between his people, the Holy Spirit is able to communicate and connect them in a supernatural way to care for and understand each other. It was what the Holy Spirit did for Jeff and Lauris, and Lauris and her daughter, and somehow for Jeff and me.

Love comes as a thought, a prayer, a reminiscence of friends from our past and present that can be easily dismissed in our busy-ness. But when heard and acted on, it is powerful in its doing. Every person who follows Jesus knows this experience and is invited to join in the game of love. We just need to listen. The Holy Spirit is ready to connect!

55

Living With Imagination

Location: Brisbane
Date: 2002-2007
Event: Embracing the Dreamer

The incoming Director of Wycliffe New Zealand, Wayne Freeman, could not believe his ears. He was not expecting elements from his international corporate world to be so prominent at his first Wycliffe meeting. Wayne approached me at the morning tea break.

'I can't believe you are using Belbin Team Roles,' he said. 'We used it with the international leadership team at Bayer Pharmaceuticals.'

I was delighted to meet someone else who shared my passion for Belbin. I explained, 'I was introduced to it eight years ago when I did a *Team Building* unit as part of my Masters of Development. It gave me a framework to understand how I best worked in a team. It also gave me permission to leave the detail to others and get on with developing new initiatives.'

Wayne asked, 'But where did you get the questionnaire to do the analysis?'

'That was easy,' I replied, 'It was in the appendix of one of Meredith Belbin's books. I copied it and have been using it ever since.'

'But don't you know it is copyrighted?'

That caught me by surprise, 'No, I had no idea.'

'Well things have changed,' Wayne said. 'You need to be an approved Belbin consultant to use it.' After a pause he added, 'But I have a solution.

We can do the accredited training in Auckland together. Wycliffe New Zealand will help with the funding.' Wayne's generous offer saw me join him and eight other consultants for the Belbin training in Auckland.

The lead trainer greeted me warmly, adding, 'I have always wanted to meet someone with a profile like yours.' Nothing more was said but it left me intrigued.

It was in the afternoon session that our own Belbin team role reports were handed to us. I already knew my profile so I was not expecting any great illumination. There were two things that differed however in this official Belbin report. First, it was a 360 report including observations from colleagues I worked with. Second, it ranked each person's responses against thousands of other people's scores.

Our trainer explained, 'The average score for each role is measured at 50%. If you score 80% in any team role, then in a room of 100 you are among the top 20 who enjoy that team role. A score of 80% suggests, "This is what I love to do." But if you score over 90% then you exhibit *rampant* behaviour. You can't change how you behave.'

My ranking score stood out in neon lights. I was beyond rampant. For the role of Plant, Belbin's classification for a person who generates new ideas, I was ranked 99%. As a Resource Investigator, or networker, I was ranked 98%. I not only came up with original ideas, I borrowed everyone else's. As a Completer Finisher concerned with every detail, I simply didn't care. I was below 5%.

I remembered Marg asking me one day, 'What will you do when the ideas run out?' I was perplexed. 'Ideas don't run out,' I replied.

There was a reason why I was a Dreamer. It was my natural state. I didn't dwell in the past, I dwelt in the future and all things were possible. Marg may have been right, 'I was not as *normal* as I thought I was.'

This new self-awareness did not frighten me. It was better to embrace it as God's unique gifting. It explained my love of long walks, connecting in silence with the Giver of Dreams. It explained my love of a new idea that created new opportunities for others. It explained why I preferred to start with a blank sheet, rather than someone else's set of procedures.

It explained why I warmed to complex challenges and was bored by projects requiring single solutions. I joined dots that others did not, and for reasons I could not always explain. The life of the Dreamer was full of such occasions. It was his normal, and it touched every aspect of this life. It was why images came easily to mind when praying for people, why intuition and *the vibe* had equal weight to logic, why parables spoke more profoundly to me than concrete theological statements.

I started to give more credence to my imagination as God's means of communicating with others. My preference had always been to share Scripture with people. To that I added a willingness to share a story or picture that came to my mind. The two went hand-in-hand. Jesus knew that the right parable for the right person in the right situation was life-changing when the Holy Spirit gave understanding.

As I prepared to teach the *Program Planning and Evaluation* subject in the final week of the year-long SIL course in Melbourne God specifically pointed out Colossians Chapter 3 as relevant for the class. It included the injunction to,

> *Make allowances for each other's faults, and forgive anyone who offends you. Remember, the Lord forgave you, so you must forgive others. Above all, clothe yourself with love, which binds us all together in perfect harmony.*
>
> NLT Colossians 3:13-14

It was a great text for people who had studied and rubbed shoulders together for a year. While the course material itself was secular I planned to meld these thoughts into my lectures. I felt safe with Scripture. After I introduced myself to the class an unexpected picture came into my mind. I hesitated with what to do with it. Previously I would have dismissed it as my wandering mind. This time I wondered if it was the Holy Spirit. I took the plunge.

'Before we get started I have something I need to share with you. Just now I got a picture of a heart that has been hardened like a rock-solid black ball. It has been with someone here for a long time. Something caused your heart to harden. The only way it can be softened is to allow the Holy

Spirit to continually wash over it until it softens and heals. If that is you, please come and talk to me this week. God will begin to heal it.'

I then went on with my first lesson on program management. Two students came to me that night to share how they struggled spiritually during the year-long course. They wondered if it was meant for them. I knew it was not them. I explained, 'The reason you came tonight was because you both have a soft heart toward God. People who are sensitive to the Holy Spirit often think it is them when such a challenge like this is given. It is the disposition you carry – always wanting to be closer to Jesus.'

After we praised God together, I asked, 'Could you intercede for the rest of the class during the week.' They became my spiritual sisters on a mission.

Each day the class became more spiritually alive. It was on the third day that a reserved young man approached me in the dining room just before the lunch break. He told me, 'When you described that picture on the first morning I knew straight away it was for me.'

He shared a heart-wrenching story from several years before that he had not told anyone. As a result of what happened he said, 'I made the decision not to get close to God because I am not sure I can trust him. On the inside, my heart has become rock hard towards God.'

I asked, 'May I pray for you?' He nodded in agreement.

I prayed in a flat non-emotive voice, 'Holy Spirit wash over my brother's black heart of stone and remove the pain that has come from the story he just told me. Soften his heart as he worships you. Amen.'

He nodded when I finished, and walked away to join the other students at their table. We did not speak again that day. Next morning at devotions something was different about him. He entered into the songs with a joy and abandonment I had not seen before. He gave a big smile in my direction. He was being set free of the pain that had held him back from God. Worship was a great remedy, it was soothing his soul.

So began a journey of listening to the imagination not only for myself but also for others. But the tension remained. When a picture or Scriptures came, the internal debate remained as to what I would do with it. They needed to be spoken out and shared to do their work, yet that knowledge did not make it automatic that I would do so. Perhaps I was resistant to people looking for a word from me when they should first and foremost be seeking Jesus in secret. Perhaps I was fearful of the distraction. I loved serving communities who didn't have the Scriptures in their everyday language. This was my passion. I had no desire to be public property, or a priest, or a pastor, or a person known to have special gifts in the church. Up front ministry in the church, and for the church, held little attraction for me. For all these reasons this gift of the imagination for others remained secret except amongst a few friends who really knew me.

Amongst them were our close friends Ken and Ruth in Darwin. I told them about the picture of the rock hard heart and the Holy Spirit washing over it and tenderising it through worship. Ken immediately said, 'Well you can pray for everyone at our home group tonight.'

I pushed back, 'No, I don't want to do that. I was just telling you about it, that's all.'

Ken smiled and said, 'I am asking you to. I don't think it is your choice.' Ken was a gentle man and not one to demand his way, which gave extra weight to his request.

'Okay,' I replied, 'but this means you are responsible for anything that happens.'

'Yep,' he said. 'You just go for it.'

The lounge-room filled with friends I knew from when we lived in Darwin as well as some unknown to me. Ken called everyone to attention and welcomed me to the group. He simply said, 'Tonight we are just going to have Barry pray for each one of you. That is the program for the night.'

I was sitting in a comfortable lounge chair as he said it. A sudden thought came to me. *Let's make this as casual as possible without any of the normal customs associated with prayer.* I said, 'I'm going to sit in my chair here with a coffee in my hand and say what comes to my mind. Someone else can lay hands on you and pray in Jesus' Name if they want. I won't be doing that.'

The first person came and stood in the middle of the room. Ken and a few others gathered around the person, praying quietly. I said to God, 'Well it is up to you. Here we go.' A picture immediately came to my mind. I described it as plainly as I could, sipping my coffee as I did. It was up to the Holy Spirit and those praying to take it further.

For the next hour this pattern was repeated for each person. A thought entered my mind almost immediately as each person came forward for prayer. I then spoke it out. There was little time between what I saw and what I described. Some people teared up, some cried, some smiled broadly, their faces full of joy. No reaction was the same and each picture was different.

One picture particularly stayed with me because of the impact it had on the lady. I had not met her before. I described a wire bird cage. There was a swing in it with a bird sitting on it. What particularly caught my attention was a gate to the side that was wide open. I described the open gate. The bird could be free at any time but it remained sitting on the swing.

I assumed the picture was about Jesus' offer of *freedom* that had not yet been realised. I did not ask what it meant. My job was simply to describe the picture as clearly as I could. It was Ken and the Holy Spirit's job to take it further, which He did. There was clearly much happening between the person and God.

When finished, Ken and I reflected on the evening. It was one thing to get an occasional picture for someone as against getting one for one person after another. I concluded it happened because Ken asked me to do it. We were mates, and for tonight we combined to do God's work. It did not mean I would make this a practice.

When I returned to Brisbane I told another friend about my experience in Darwin and particularly the vivid picture of the bird cage. He interrupted, 'I know who that person is!'

'I'm not mentioning any names,' I replied.

He then went on, 'When I was in Darwin I had the same picture for a lady, except the cage door was closed. We prayed that the door would be opened and she would be set free from what was holding her back. It was so and so, wasn't it?'

I was shocked. This was going to take some time to get my head around. At one level it was about the lady and God's desire to speak intimately to her in a form she understood. It was a message she could not miss. Jesus had opened the way for her to be set free and she was invited to step into a hope with a new future. I prayed she would be able to do that. I also now understood why this lady's husband welled up with tears as she received this picture. The Holy Spirit was speaking hope to him for his wife as well.

At another level, I wondered why God confirmed the picture to me in the way he did. This conversation with my friend could easily not have happened. Why did God want me to know? Was he trying to tell me something?

Perhaps he was wanting to confirm to me it was him planting the picture in my mind, not me creating it. My imagination belonged to him as much as it belonged to me. Perhaps he was letting me know that the supernatural is really normal. I did not go to a third heaven, or saturate myself in worship and adoration of the Father, or lift my hands in prayer. The pictures came as I relaxed and drank coffee fully in the here and now. This was obviously not a deterrent to the Holy Spirit. I observed that spirituality and ministry are often measured by the form in which they come. Perhaps God doesn't take much notice of the form.

It also suggested that the man of the soil and the Dreamer were more integrated than I had given them credit. They were both redeemed by God's love, and both were his instruments when they had the courage to let him in. The Dreamer was no more a child of God than the man of the soil. One could occasionally be invited to ascend to another realm for an intimate time with Jesus free of the distractions around him. The other could be firmly in the here and now with a coffee in his hand and equally hear from God. They were just a different expression of being human, and the Holy Spirit was intimately involved in both.

56

Nominations Closing

Location:	Chiang Mai, Thailand
Date:	October 2006
Event:	Another fork in the road

Neil and I knew each other well. For more than 10 years we were colleagues and friends sharing our passion for Bible translation. At the 2006 SIL Conference in Chiang Mai, Thailand we shared a room. Neil preferred understatement to overstatement. He said matter-of-factly, 'A few of us have been talking, and we want to nominate you for the position of Wycliffe Australia Director.'

It was totally unexpected, particularly coming from Neil. He knew how much I enjoyed the work I was doing. He was asking a lot. I dug a little deeper, 'Neil you know me better than most. Why would you ask me?'

Neil's response was pragmatic. 'We think someone with your field leadership experience would be good for the job.'

It was true that I had field leadership experience and learnt plenty from further study. However, I saw all this as preparation for my current position working alongside national organisations and colleagues. This was where I fitted best.

The conversation may have finished there but another Australian member working in PNG approached me. Tim said, 'A few of us have got together and we would like to nominate you for Director of Wycliffe Australia.'

I suddenly realised my name was part of a wider conversation. The reason for the sudden urgency was that nominations were to close in four days. An immediate decision was being asked of me. If the request came while I was in Brisbane going about my daily work then it would be lost among a myriad of other thoughts and daily routines. But I was not in Brisbane. I was in Chiang Mai and vulnerable. I carefully crafted an email to Marg informing her of the situation without giving any prejudicial comments either way. My question was simple. 'What do you think Marg?'

It was an unfair question. Marg did not make decisions quickly. Her practice was to first weigh up how a major change might affect our family and those closest to her. It would include how it might affect our two youngest who were now at university. We were living in a rented house with them and they were the lead tenants. We were looking forward to moving into Kim and Ashley's share house in a few month's time and be part of the Christian community offering hospitality to young overseas travellers. This was a dream come true for us, and especially Marg, taking us back to the quirky alternatives we considered when we were first married. It was in this context that Marg would receive my email. She would be expecting some news of who I had met in the first few days of the conference. Instead of that I would be asking her to consider an option that might see us leave our Brisbane family and friends who we had no desire to leave.

Marg's long thought-out response arrived in my in-box. It was not a response stating what we would be leaving behind. Rather it was a response starting and ending with the question, *What does God want?* She quoted from the Bible and suggested I should not be closed to the possibility. Her argument was that if this was what God wanted, then I needed to be obedient to him. I expected some counter argument as to why it was not a good idea but I didn't get one. If she had given me a clear 'no' then it would have been the end of the discussion. Instead Marg basically left it as a decision between me and God.

■ **Marg recalls**

I recall being surprised at Barry's email but thankfully had a day before I needed to respond. I had notes I had taken at the previous Sunday service on the poor widow giving the little she had to God. These

Scriptures jumped out at me. Was I willing to give to God the things that I was enjoying or looking forward to: The free community classes, the teacher training, community hospitality and using the Masters in TESOL I was close to finishing. Should they get in the road of Barry responding to God? It was the Scriptures that helped me respond.

After reading Marg's email I made my way into the conference room. Tim came alongside me and asked with enthusiasm, 'Can we nominate you for the position? I have enough people ready to sign but we need to email it in by tomorrow.'

I weighed up the question. There was no burning excitement to say *Yes*. But equally there was a discomfort about replying *No*. 'Okay Tim, I will accept the nomination if there are enough people recommending me for the job.' Tim left with a smile on his face and a confident step as someone who had successfully brokered a deal.

Marg met me at the pickup zone at Brisbane Airport. I put my bag in the boot and got in the front passenger seat. We were not out of the airport before she asked, 'So what did you decide?'

'I said they could nominate me if they wanted to.'

She blurted back, 'Well I don't want to go.'

I was silent. Outbursts of emotion often paralysed me. I was also slightly bewildered. After an extended pause I asked the question, 'So what was your email response about?'

Marg replied more coolly, 'That was my God answer. It isn't how I feel about it.'

I offered a possible way out. I said hopefully, 'Well it doesn't mean the Board will accept the nomination or even if they do, choose me for the job.'

Marg's response was direct, 'Of course they will choose you. You are the best person for the job.'

More silence. It was time to change the topic. We would wait to hear from the Wycliffe Board before jumping this hurdle.

The Wycliffe Board had done their homework. Tim the interviewer, knew the questions that he wanted to ask and he was not going to be diverted. Perhaps the Dreamer's reputation for repartee had preceded him. *Give him an inch and he will take a mile* he could have been warned. Tim prepared to keep a tight leash on me. There were no general questions on philosophy of leadership or training local translators. Those questions would have given me free-rein. He was not interested in the Dreamer. He was interested in the man of the soil and how he behaved.

'Tell us your response step-by-step to a specific conflict situation you have had to settle,' he asked.

I described one situation and then he asked for another example. At the core of my response were behaviours I was still learning from a question I asked the Giver of Dreams, 'How do I stay free in spirit when my colleagues act badly towards each other?'

The answer I was given was to welcome the fact that the fruit of the Spirit are for hard times, not the easy times. Embrace love, joy, peace ... when it is hard. The next was to remember people's anger and frustrations shows they desperately need Jesus. Nudge them in my direction. And finally there is no situation that should stop you from worshipping Jesus. Don't delay, even after two colleagues disparage each other. Jesus is waiting.

This meant I sometimes found myself worshipping Jesus with my arms held out wide at the seemingly most inappropriate times. It proved my strongest shield. It kept the Dreamer in me alive.

Marg's retort some months earlier, 'Of course they will choose you,' proved correct. Marg and I were both summonsed to meet with the Board. The chair announced, 'We are delighted to offer you the position of Director of Wycliffe Bible Translators Australia.'

It was difficult to know how to respond. I struggled when someone gave me affirmation. The board members gathered around Marg and I, not to interrogate, but to bless us. One prayer in particular spoke directly into Marg's heart. She felt an assurance that it was going to be okay. She was a co-traveller with her Dreamer husband.

There were huge risks and unknowns for us. I had little experience working for a *home office* and in church relations. I was a person more inclined to the big picture than the detail, more attracted to taking a risk than relying on a safety net. I was unsure how I might fit in this new environment and its policy restrictions.

That could equally be said of the Board. They were not oblivious to my penchant for new initiatives, or my unorthodox spiritual journey yet they knowingly appointed the Dreamer as the head of a conservative evangelical Christian organisation. They were taking a bigger risk than I was.

In the week that followed I wondered what impact it might have on the Dreamer. A substantial part of my Christian life was lived solo in my head. It was a life that I shared with God and invited few people into. From time to time my spirit crossed over to his side and left the world of the here and now behind. Other times the Holy Spirit came to me when I was rooted in the soil, interrupting my thoughts with his thoughts, and renewing my passion for Jesus.

The public *me* that showed myself as a father and husband, and as a co-worker and leader supporting Bible translation for the hidden languages of the world, was what people saw. The public life mattered and gave me satisfaction and meaning but it did not describe the total me. It was the Dreamer and his connection with his Creator and the Giver of Dreams that I cherished as much, or even more if I compared them. I wondered how things would change for the Dreamer now that I would be representing Wycliffe Bible Translators. I assumed I would be subject to others' expectations and my daily agenda would be increasingly orchestrated by institutional responsibilities and practices. However, the one thing that enthused me was that once again I was moving outside my comfort zone. Protecting the gift of faith required this movement from time to time. I couldn't and wouldn't take on this new responsibility without Jesus, and that was the best place to be.

57

Dream On

Location:	A church in Queensland
Date:	February 2007
Event:	Be who I have made you!

I looked out over the church auditorium as I placed the outline of my message on the lectern. It was a good-sized crowd. Maybe 300. My message was full of stories of faith and transformation that comes when ordinary people hear the good news of Jesus in their heart language and believe it to be true. It was a message that aligned with Wycliffe's values. But my delivery was more akin to a storyteller at the local pub than a biblical exegete. For a brief moment I paused and wondered what the congregation might be expecting from the soon to be appointed CEO of Wycliffe Bible Translators Australia.

I may have studied New Testament Greek for three years but had long decided that the interpretation of the Greek text was for the experts. If there was a choice between Greek, theological language, or an everyday Australian phrase to describe the mystery of God, I inevitably went for the everyday phrase. I followed my script, lingering a little longer on the Scripture reading before illustrating its meaning with a story. It was then that a picture began to form in my mind. It was for the pastor of the church.

'Give me a break God,' I heard myself thinking in the recess of my mind as I continued on with my message. 'I am now representing Wycliffe. There is a lot more at stake than my reputation.'

When the first image was fully formed, two more pictures followed. The second for a middle-aged lady to my right, and the other for a young man out to my left and towards the back.

I concluded my message. People had warmed to the stories I had told. There was a buzz around the room as I stepped from the platform and down to meet our friends who had arranged the invitation for me to speak.

The three pictures remained in my head. I was unsure what to do with them. Our friends followed protocol and introduced me to the pastor. We shook hands and by way of explanation he said, 'I was out in the crying room with our toddler, but I can tell from the little I heard, and what I see, that your message was well received.'

I was relieved that I had not let Wycliffe down. I then heard another prompt in my head. 'I have given you the opportunity, now take it.'

I was left with a choice: to obey or rationalise it all away.

I stumbled out my request to the pastor. 'While I was preaching I got a picture for you. Do you want to hear it?' I added an escape clause, 'I'm okay with whatever you decide.'

The pastor's response was immediate. 'Yes I would like to hear it.'

I took a deep breath and explained, 'I saw a healthy tree growing beside a fast-running stream. Its roots however, did not draw its sustenance from the stream but went deeper to the subsoil below the stream.'

As I described the picture, understanding what it represented came to me. I continued, 'I would not normally do this but I have an interpretation. Do you want to hear it?'

'Yes,' he replied.

'The tree is you. The stream is all the activities of the church which are many and impressive. But God does not want your energy, or sense of well-being to be drawn from the river. He wants you to draw it from him. He is your source. Let your roots go deep in him.'

With hardly a pause I went on, 'Based on what I shared can I go and talk to two other people in your congregation that I have a picture for?'

'Please do. Go ahead,' he replied.

The pictures for the other two proved very specific to the situation they were currently in. They were deeply moved and the pictures confirmed God's love for them. Getting a picture for individuals in the congregation was not on my *to do* list. I did not seek it, ask for it, or expect it. It felt like the Holy Spirit was both testing me and having some fun. The very first time I speak in a church knowing I am the next CEO of Wycliffe Bible Translators, God seeks out the Dreamer in me, creates pictures in my mind and asks me to take a risk with Wycliffe's reputation.

Three weeks later our friends from the church, sent us a copy of the church newsletter. In the newsletter the pastor wrote that God recently spoke to him about drawing strength from God and not all the activities he was involved in. It was a word he needed and was heeding.

I was also heeding a word from Jesus. He wanted all of me for his mission. He wanted the energy and enthusiasm of the man of the soil, and he wanted the unpredictability and mind of the Dreamer. I was to comply with his expectations not the expectations of those around me.

58

Giving What I Have In Jesus' Name

Location:	Banks of the Katherine River
Date:	Saturday 5 May 2007
Event:	Kriol Bible dedication

A community band was tuning up and the ceremony was not long from starting. I went back over my message and adjusted my English into a Kriol turn of phrase. I was grateful that I was more a storyteller than a preacher, and that Kriol was a great language for telling stories.

The walk to the microphone was surreal, not for its grandeur but its simplicity. The microphone was at ground level not high on a podium. It was placed on dirt not a marble floor. The crowd was relaxed sitting on blankets and chairs spread out across the paddock, not in an air-conditioned auditorium. Black and white mingled as one. This was unique. It was sacred ground: a place of sacred memories.

Twenty years earlier I was present when the second edition of the *Holi Baibul* was dedicated on the same ground. I had then acted out to much laughter Acts 3:1-6 and the lame man being healed by Peter to the song '*Silver and Gold have I None*' in Kriol. Tonight that same story would be the theme of my message.

I held my new beautifully bound gold-edged Kriol Baibul in my hands, looked over the crowd and read from Act 3:6.

Mi nomo garram eni mani. Bat ai garra gibit yu wanim mi garram. Langa neim blanga Jisas Krais brom Nesareth, ai dalim yu blanga gidap en wok!

Silver or gold I do not have, but what I do have I give you.
In the name of Jesus Christ of Nazareth, walk!

The Kriol translators did not let what they did not have, stop them. They gave what they had with passion, determination and perseverance. They completed training in Bible translation, they worked diligently despite family tragedies and occasional community crises. They volunteered their services asking for no monetary payment. Their motivation was personal and spiritual. The Kriol translation team were testament to the fact that God takes the ordinary, and by faith, he does more with his children than they could ever imagine.

Our eldest daughter sat in the crowd reflecting. The Holy Spirit was stirring her to give what she had. In the days following she decided to leave her paid work and help Kriol young people engage with their own Scriptures. She too was a Dreamer.

The Kriol *Holi Baibul* dedication was my first public event as the newly appointed CEO of Wycliffe Bible Translators Australia. The message was also for me. As I stepped into my new role, I was not to be concerned by what I lacked. I had grown to appreciate the complexity of the relationship between the practical man of the soil in me and the audaciousness of the Spirit. The dance between the two would not end even within the constraints of a more corporate world, and the expectations within a large Christian organisation. It was *by faith* that I said yes to the job and it would be *by faith* that I would need to embrace it. At fifty-three years of age a new adventure awaited. The Dreamer's story would never be static or complete. It would always be unfolding.

www.ingramcontent.com/pod-product-compliance
Lightning Source LLC
Chambersburg PA
CBHW061206070526
44583CB00025B/3126